Praise for *The Woman Who Fell*

"Offers the voices of Muslim women torn betw[...] individual freedoms."

—*Newsweek*

"A completely winning account of [Steil's] adventures as a feminist mentor and boss . . . A riveting tale of a life's journey that reads as if it will need a sequel."

—*New York Times*

"A delightful and straight-talking story of one American woman living, working, and finding friendship and love in a Muslim country. Highly recommended for interested memoir readers as well as journalism, Middle Eastern, and women's studies students."

—*Library Journal*

"Anybody who has taken on an unfamiliar task, moved to a new place, or taken on a new role at work or at home without being at all sure about having the necessary skills should find a kindred spirit here."

—*Post and Courier*

"The image of Yemen that Steil paints is one of love, family, honor, and surprisingly, of women who are both powerful and liberated but, because of custom, unwilling to flaunt their beauty in public. . . . An antidote to stereotypes and blind prejudice."

—*Sydney Morning Herald,* A Pick of the Week

"From the first page of *The Woman Who Fell from the Sky,* Jennifer Steil comes across as a person blessed with sensibility and sensitivity in equal measure. She is the kind of woman who's not fearful of culture shock, danger, or the trials and tribulations of life in what is the Arab World's rawest land. Her writing is an absolute delight—no nonsense, clear, funny, and sometimes alarming, as she threads her way through the ins and outs of Yemeni life. Steil has achieved far more than a simple description of a stint working at a newspaper in Sana'a. Rather, her book shines a vibrant light on the region, showing it how it is, with astonishing clarity from the inside out."

—Tahir Shah, author of *The Caliph's House* and *In Arabian Nights*

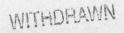

"A fascinating read." —*The Age* (Australia)

"Steil puts humanity and color into her description of a country most Americans know only as a desert haven for terrorists. Her affection for Yemen and its people will make readers want to see it for themselves. A lovely book that offers a large measure of cultural understanding in a region that is too easily misunderstood and caricatured."
—Nina Burleigh, author of *Unholy Business*

"*The Woman Who Fell from the Sky* is that rare animal: a memoir which reads like a novel. From the exquisite detail to the passionate, poignant, and often hilarious story of one powerful woman immersed in centuries of patriarchal tradition, Steil takes us on a journey that left me exhausted and exhilarated. Hugely entertaining and vitally important to our times, the book tucks us under a veil and allows us a unique glimpse into a culture as old as Noah. Not only did I remember what it feels and smells like to live imbedded in the Arab world, I also relearned my craft of journalism along with Steil's students in her dusty classroom halfway around the world. Veils and hats off to this winner!"
—Jennifer Jordan, author of *Savage Summit: The Life and Death of the First Five Women of K2*

"With intelligence, humor, and courage, Jennifer Steil's book helps us see beyond stereotypes of male and female, East and West, conservative and liberal to appreciate the beauty and wonder of deeply rooted cultures— and the authentic relationships that can transcend them all."
—Susan Piver, author of *How Not to Be Afraid of Your Own Life* and *The Wisdom of a Broken Heart*

"Jennifer Steil's voice recalls that of Isak Dinesen and Freya Stark: generous and observant, unabashed in her love for her home in exile, yet unafraid to speak her mind about injustice, and everything laced with wit and rich detail. This is an important book about a corner of the world we cannot afford to misunderstand, and Jennifer Steil is the perfect person to guide us." —Tom Zoellner, author of *The Heartless Stone* and *Uranium*

the woman who fell from the sky

AN AMERICAN

WOMAN'S ADVENTURES

IN THE OLDEST

CITY ON EARTH

the woman who fell from the sky

JENNIFER STEIL

BROADWAY PAPERBACKS · NEW YORK

Published in the United States by Broadway Paperbacks, an imprint of the Crown Publishing Group, a division of Random House, Inc., New York.
www.crownpublishing.com

BROADWAY PAPERBACKS and its logo, a letter *B* bisected on the diagonal, are trademarks of Random House, Inc.

Originally published in hardcover in slightly different form in the United States by Broadway Books, an imprint of the Crown Publishing Group, a division of Random House, Inc., New York, in 2010.

Grateful acknowledgment is made to the following for permission to reprint previously published and unpublished material:

American Institute for Yemeni Studies for permission to reprint a poem from *The Book of Sana'a: Poetry of Abd al-Aziz al-Maqali,* translated by Bob Holman and Sam Liebhaber (2004). Reprinted by permission of the American Institute for Yemeni Studies.

Food and Agriculture Organization of the United Nations for permission to reprint excerpts of the locust recipes taken from their website. Reprinted by permission of the Food and Agriculture Organization of the United Nations, Viale delle Terme di Caracalla, 00153 Rome, Italy.

The *Yemen Observer* for permission to reprint excerpts of articles from the *Yemen Observer.* Reprinted by permission of Faris al-Sanabani and the *Yemen Observer.*

Zaid al-Alaya'a for permission to reprint an excerpt of his note and poem to Jennifer Steil. Reprinted by permission of Zaid al-Alaya'a.

Library of Congress Cataloging-in-Publication Data
Steil, Jennifer F.
The woman who fell from the sky / Jennifer Steil.—1st ed.
    p.   cm.
1. Steil, Jennifer—Travel—Yemen—San'a'. 2. San'a' (Yemen)—Description and travel.
3. Journalists—Yemen—San'a'—Biography. I. Title.
DS248.S26S74 2010
953.32—dc22   2009037172

ISBN 978-0-7679-3051-2
eISBN 978-0-307-71587-6

Printed in the United States of America

Design by ELINA D. NUDELMAN
Cover design by LAURA DUFFY
Cover photography by JESSICA BOONE/GETTY IMAGES (*pomegranate*); JENNIFER F. STEIL (*city*)

10 9 8 7 6 5 4 3 2

First Paperback Edition

For Kawkab,
and all the other feisty Yemeni women
who give me hope for the country

she was a woman
who fell from the sky in robes
of dew
and became
a city

CONTENTS

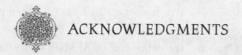 ACKNOWLEDGMENTS

Nothing in this book or my life would be remotely possible without the entire staff, past and present, of the *Yemen Observer*. Thank you for working so very hard for me, despite my mercurial management style. I owe you all an infinite debt of gratitude.

I also owe bottomless thanks to:

Theo Padnos, for getting me here.

My friend Tom Zoellner, whose invaluable assistance and encouragement from the very beginning helped this book to get off the ground.

My agent, Brettne Bloom, for believing in this book, for her unflagging enthusiasm and support, and for her inspirational thoughts on my original proposal.

My editor Kris Puopolo and her assistant editor, Stephanie Bowen, for their wise counsel in shaping this book, their meticulous editing, and their patience with my frequent long-distance phone calls.

My editor Christine Pride, for guiding this book through its final stages of labor and birth and for so indefatigably championing it.

Faris al-Sanabani, for trusting me. Sometimes.

Sabri Saleem, for his warm friendship and for providing me with my first Yemeni home.

Sami al-Siyani, for being the best friend, neighbor, and guide to Old Sana'a I can imagine.

ACKNOWLEDGMENTS

My neighbors in the al-Wushali district of Old Sana'a for their infinite hospitality.

Muhoro Ndungu, for his tolerance of my moods during the darkest times, for his witch doctor skills, and for taking me in when I was homeless.

Bushra Nasr, for her generosity and friendship.

All of my Arabic teachers, but especially Fouad, for their patience with my erratic progress.

Mr. Jamal Hindi and the entire staff of Al Mankal restaurant, who always know exactly what I want for lunch.

The well-behaved taxi drivers who kept their hands on the wheel.

Harris Collingwood, for emotional and material support during difficult times.

Anne-Christine, Angelica, Carolyn, Koosje, and Jilles, housemates who turned my gingerbread house into a home.

Aida, without whom we would all have been wading through several feet of dust.

Rasheed, for showing me his Soqotra.

Anne Leewis, for helping me find a life outside work.

Phil Boyle, for making me laugh, feeding me curry, and granting me a pivotal interview with a British MP.

Don Lipinski, for the wine, movies, and loyal support, despite our political differences.

Marvin and Pearl, for the bootleg gin and Soqotra.

Tobias Lechtenfeld, for the lovely times in Sana'a, and for remaining a friend.

Peter Toth, for his phenomenal generosity, for his devoted friendship, and for Paris.

Chris and Peta Shute, for housing me as I wrote the first chapters of this book.

Lloyd, Dave, Colin, and the entire CP team, for keeping us all safe during the writing of this book and beyond.

Negesti, Alem, and Emebet, for taking such good care of us at home.

Cole and Ali, for keeping their senses of humor when I lost mine.

Manel Fall, for keeping me from bursting into flames.

Nick Janik, for saving me the horror of shopping.

Saleh and Didier, for their friendship and for Taiz.

Abdullah, for never failing to make me feel welcome.

My classmates and professors from the Columbia University Graduate School of Journalism, for their assistance in creating my original training course.

My friends in New York and elsewhere in the world—too numerous to list here—whose love and e-mails help keep me sane.

My parents, who are always supportive, even when they doubt the wisdom of my career choices.

Timothy Achille Torlot, for reading this book more times than anyone should, and for loving me more than I thought anyone could.

ONE

fantasia in gingerbread

I didn't immediately see Zuhra when I walked into the bridal chamber. The room was dim, and she was curled over in prayer on the floor to my left, a mass of white satin with a black scarf over her head. Few people were allowed in the room with her—only sisters and dearest friends—and everyone was quiet. I stood still against a wall, watching her, waiting for her to finish. I hadn't thought I would see Zuhra until she began her slow, deliberate march down the catwalk that ran the length of the wedding hall. But her sisters had summoned me, pulling me by the hand into this back room. Zuhra looked tiny and vulnerable, solemnly whispering her prayers.

But all hint of gravity vanished as she finished and pulled the veil from her face to beam up at me. She stood, the silky scarf slithering from her bare shoulders, and came to let me kiss her. Above the white of her Brooklyn-bought dress, her arms, back, and clavicle were painted with curling flowery vines, rendered in *naqsh,* a black ink favored by Yemeni brides. We didn't speak at first but just stood smiling at each other.

"*Antee jameela,*" I said, touching her tiny waist. "Beautiful. Like a little doll bride."

"Really?" She turned this way and that, so I could admire all of her. Her thick black hair was piled on top of her head in fanciful hair-sprayed loops.

Her dark eyes were outlined in kohl, her face thickly powdered, and her lips colored a pale pomegranate.

"Really. I wish I could take a photo!" We had all been patted down at the door, to ensure none of us smuggled in a camera.

Zuhra pulled me down beside her on cushions at the end of the room, where we stayed for another hour waiting for her guests to finish their sunset prayers and work themselves into a frenzy of anticipation. Zuhra passed the time chatting with me and making calls on her mobile phone, mostly to her groom, who was (contrary to tradition) picking her up at the end of the night. "You are sure you haven't argued with anyone today?" she said into the receiver. "You sound like maybe you argued." She was worried that her husband had squabbled with her brother but was evidently reassured.

"Are you nervous?" I said. All the Yemeni brides I'd seen before had looked stricken with terror on their walks down the aisle. But unlike those brides, Zuhra knew her groom.

"No," she said, smiling placidly. "I am just happy."

Her two older sisters, clad in long, shiny ball gowns, popped in to tell us it was almost time.

I stood next to Zuhra, feeling tall and awkward in heels, which I rarely suffer for anyone. Outside the door, we heard the increasingly boisterous ululations of women, meant as encouragement for the bride. As this Arabic yodeling threatened to reach a crescendo, Zuhra suddenly looked panicked.

"My pill!" She grabbed her purse from a friend standing nearby and rummaged through the pockets of her wallet. She pulled out a blister pack of birth control pills, with all but four missing. We'd spent an entire afternoon picking out these pills, making sure they were the right combination of hormones and made by a legitimate pharmaceutical company.

Zuhra struggled with the package, unable to get the pill out with her fake nails. "Here," I said. "Let me." I popped one out and handed it to her. She washed it down with a swallow of water from someone's bottle and picked up her skirts.

"Jeez, Zuhra, just in time," I whispered as we started out the door.

I entered the room just ahead of her. The hundreds of black-cocooned women I had seen hurrying into the hall earlier that evening had transformed into gaudy miniskirted butterflies, coated with glitter and lipstick, tottering on three-inch heels. There were no men.

Zuhra's youngest sister thrust a basket of jasmine petals into my hand. "Here," she said. "Throw."

Zuhra stepped forward. The lights had been dimmed, and all of the younger women and girls were on the stage at the end of the catwalk, their hands over their heads, swaying like so many colored streamers. Music swelled from behind the screen, where the band was hidden. At first I couldn't quite believe the evidence of my ears. At a Yemeni wedding I expected Arabic music. But no, Zuhra was starting down the aisle toward her married life to Celine Dion's "My Heart Will Go On," from the soundtrack of *Titanic*.

☪

THERE IS AN OLD JOKE about Yemen, told to any traveler who sticks around long enough: "Noah came back to Earth recently, curious to see how it had evolved since his time. In a private jet on loan from God, he first flew over France and said, 'My! Look at France! How it has changed! What exciting new architecture! What amazing innovation!' He then flew over Germany. 'Incredible! I would hardly recognize it! So much new technology! Such thrilling industry!' And then he headed to southern Arabia. 'Ah, Yemen,' he said fondly. 'I'd know it anywhere. Hasn't changed a bit.'"

In many ways, it hasn't. Of course, I wasn't in Yemen back in the first millennium BC, when Noah's son Shem is said to have founded the capital city of Sana'a. But in many parts of the country, people are living exactly as their ancestors did thousands of years ago. They herd goats and cows; they grow wheat, pomegranates, and grapes; they travel long distances to fetch water. They live in simple square mud-brick homes. They paint themselves with *naqsh* for weddings. They pray.

The ancient landscape reveals little evidence of the passage of time. On a flyover today, Noah would find that erosion has run light fingers over the jagged mountains of the central highlands. Long stretches of empty beaches in the south are touched by the same tides that have washed them since the Flood. In the east, desert sands shift in barely perceptible ways. The green terraces carved into the Haraz mountains in the west or the hills around Ibb and Ta'iz to the south may have been there since the dawn of agriculture, cultivated by generation after generation of Yemeni farmers. The dense vegetation of the valleys suggests the whim of a playful god who, weary of the relentless beige of Arabian rock and sand, tossed a thick emerald quilt over Yemen's countryside, creating a fertile layer that has fed the Yemeni people for generations.

Noah would find the most familiar territory in the country's remotest places, such as the island of Soqotra, located 220 miles off Yemen's eastern coast. On Soqotra, there are few roads and fewer electric lights. The dominant structures are not the crumbling stone buildings (which blend so completely into the hillsides that you don't see them until you trip over a small child running out of one) but its fanciful dragon's blood trees, their tall, thousand-year-old trunks erupting into such a wild tangle of branches that they resemble a forest of umbrellas blown upward by the wind.

Many Soqotri people still live in caves, where they boil tea over fires in a corner to serve with goat milk still warm from their animals. Their dining rooms are thin woven mats spread outside their doors, where they eat fish stew with chewy flatbread under salty night skies. There are people on Soqotra who have no idea what happened on September 11, 2001, in America. There are no radio stations, and almost no one can read. Everything they know they have heard from neighbors, imams, or the occasional foreign aid worker. Britney Spears does not exist here. Hollywood is meaningless. Ice cream would not survive—there is almost no refrigeration.

Many of Yemen's mainland villages feel just as remote, tucked along a mountain ridge or at the edge of a stretch of desert. These villages get their news from state-controlled television or from the mosque. Only the elite would pick up a newspaper or read a book. But what use is news of the outside world to these people? Will it help their crops to grow? Will it keep their goats free from disease? Will it bring them closer to God? No? Well, then.

Yemen has not only kept herself looking much the same as she did in Noah's time, but she also wears the same perfume she did when she was young. Cruising at a lower altitude, Noah would smell frankincense, the fragrant resin that put Yemen on the map for traders four thousand years ago and is still burned as incense; the acrid sweat of laboring men and rayon-wrapped women; the purple-and-white jasmine flowers that proliferate in its lush lowlands; and the smoke of wood fires warming bread ovens. In her cities, these odors mingle with the smell of frying beans and jalapeños, fenugreek-flavored meat stews, tobacco smoke, and roasted lamb, while the countryside is fragrant with overtones of manure and ripening bananas, dates, and mangoes.

Following those scents earthward, Noah would soon glimpse clusters of boxy brown houses, their roofs strewn with airing carpets and drying laundry. Through the maze of streets hurry men on their way to mosque, women selling flat disks of bread, and children chasing a ball.

Sana'a is one of the oldest cities in the Arabian Peninsula—and in the world. Built at least 2,500 years ago, it was once home to Sabean kings and Himyarite rulers.

Islam arrived in the seventh century AD, rearranging the face of the city. Many of the buildings erected during the time of the Prophet Mohammed are still standing, though crumbling a bit around the edges. The Great Mosque of Sana'a was built under the instructions of the Prophet himself, according to local legend. It is not only the biggest but the most famous mosque in the Old City (Sana'a al-Qadeema). It contains a large library and a host of ancient manuscripts.

More than a hundred other mosques now populate the Old City, a fact that is particularly evident during the calls to prayer. No matter where you stand, you feel as if you are directly underneath a mosque loudspeaker. The muezzins drown out conversations and make it impossible to listen to music. Which of course is the point. Prayer is the only appropriate activity at these times. When Allah's messengers talk, you should be listening.

No modern buildings mar the ancient aesthetic of the Old City, which was declared a UNESCO World Heritage Site in 1984; it probably looks much the same as it did thousands of years ago. Noah would definitely recognize it.

This is Yemen yesterday, this is Yemen today.

☾

YET THERE ARE unmistakable signs of change, too. The city roofs are now dotted with satellite dishes. Billboards advertising GIRL brand ghee, the Islamic Bank of Yemen, cardamom and cinnamon toffees, and the fabulousness of President Ali Abdullah Saleh deface the sides of buildings. Women can be seen walking to jobs in government ministries. Men sport pinstriped Western suits or polo shirts. Brides march down the aisle to Celine Dion. A few silver Porsches can be spotted maneuvering down congested, Chinese-built roads. Even remote rural villages are now knee-high in modern detritus—plastic bags, candy wrappers, and soda cans.

And if Noah were zooming by in June 2006 and looked very, very closely, he might have seen me, clinging to the edge of a building in the center of Sana'a, terrified, exhausted, but bursting with wild hopes for changes of my own.

☾

I WAS TEETERING on a ladder, under siege by my outfit. The long black skirt I'd bought back in Manhattan wrapped itself around my legs every time I took a step and the scarf kept slipping off my hair. Altogether too much material was swirling around me. I clung to the ladder with one hand and pulled at my drapery with the other.

I was standing between two roofs of a tall gingerbread house in Sana'a. It was my first morning in the country—my first morning in any Arab country, for that matter—and my first time attempting to dress like a Yemeni. The building I was climbing belonged to Sabri, the amiable director of the Yemen Language Center, and housed his apartment, a dozen or so students of Arabic, and, temporarily, me. I needed a place to stay while teaching a three-week journalism workshop to the staff of the *Yemen Observer,* and Sabri had kindly accommodated me.

Having landed in the middle of the night, I had no idea what Sana'a looked like. All I remembered from the hazy, nausea-inducing car ride from the airport was a series of bright storefronts, wheelbarrows brimming with mangoes, and *men.* Hundreds and hundreds of men. Men in long white robes (called *thobes*) with daggers dangling from ornate belts; men in Western suits; men in patterned *foutahs,* traditional Yemeni man-skirts.

There had been no other women on my flight, and I saw none at the airport. I found this most peculiar and striking. Yemen seemed to be a land without women.

Sabri was leading me up the side of his house to show me one of his favorite views of Sana'a. The bright early-summer sun sailing up the sky made me squint as I climbed, and I resisted looking down until I had managed to haul myself—and several yards of black fabric—up the last rung of the rickety ladder and staggered to Sabri's side. I was out of breath. Sana'a lies at 7,218 feet above sea level, and you can always tell who the foreigners are by who is panting on the stairs.

I stood next to Sabri on the flat, dusty rooftop and gazed around me. Sand-colored mountains rose from the plain in every direction. Having spent my formative years in Vermont, I have always found the sight of mountains enormously reassuring, and this morning was no exception. Below us stood the fantasia in gingerbread that is Sana'a's Old City, a cluster of tall, square, cookie-colored homes trimmed with what looked like white frosting, surrounded by thick, high walls. Sabri pointed out some of the more prominent of the city's hundreds of mosques, liberally sprinkled across the city in every direction, their slender minarets thrust perpetually toward God.

Sabri's house stood just outside of the Old City, on September Twenty-sixth Street, named for the date on which the Yemen Arab Republic was officially formed in 1962 (sparking civil war that lasted until 1970). As I stared silently at the improbable landscape, Sabri carried on, explaining to me which direction was north (toward Mecca) as well as the locations of various neighborhoods, hotels, and major streets. He also pointed out the antennas for his wireless Internet, on a roof below. He was particularly proud of these.

I was overcome with gratitude for Sabri. When I had shown up on his doorstep close to midnight the night before, reeling with disorientation, he had rushed downstairs to welcome me with the sprightliness of a woodland faun. In his early forties, Sabri was slim, dark-eyed, curly-haired, and quick to dissolve into laughter. Even better, he seemed delighted to see me.

June was the busiest time of year for Sabri's school, and most of the rooms were full, so Sabri had given me a room in his personal quarters.

"I took a look at your face and in your eyes, and I decided I could trust you," he said to me. "We make instant judgments, we Yemenis. And then we open ourselves completely. In New York, maybe you do not make such instant hospitality. But I could tell you were a good person, and I like your sense of humor. And also it is good that you are not young."

"Not young?" It's the jet lag, I wanted to say. Usually I look much, *much* younger.

"I mean, not twenty-two."

Well, that was true enough. I was thirty-seven, an age by which many Yemeni women are grandmothers.

Up about fourteen flights of uneven stone stairs, in my plain little white room near the top of the house, I was enormously relieved to find a wooden double bed, a desk, a closet, a chest of drawers—things I recognized. The bathroom, complete with a tub, was just across the hall. It looked like paradise. I don't know what kind of dwelling I had expected, perhaps a straw mat on a floor in a hut with no shower. But I hadn't expected this.

Sabri's quarters were palatial, particularly to a Manhattanite. The kitchen was about the size of my one-bedroom apartment, if not larger, and had all the modern conveniences, including a fancy espresso maker from Italy, a dishwasher, a microwave, and shockingly, even a wine collection. I had none of these things in New York. I didn't even own a toaster or a television. Next to the kitchen was a wide hallway hung with paintings by Sabri's German wife, from whom he was separated. Past that was his office. Between this floor and the floor where I was staying were Sabri's bedroom suite and his personal bathroom, which included a Jacuzzi. When I woke that morning, Sabri made me espresso, which we drank at his king-sized wooden dining table, the sun streaming in through the stained glass windows all around us. He had plants everywhere. Thick, leafy vines climbed around the whitewashed mud walls of the rooms in search of light.

Then he took me to his roof.

(*

THE SKY AROUND US was a clear, cloudless blue. Still wobbly from my twenty-four-hour journey, I inched slowly along the edge of the roof, letting my headscarf slide down and trail in the dust, and peered at the streets seven stories down. Tiny men in white below walked by in pairs, holding hands, as children in bright greens and pinks and yellows careened from side to side in the alleys, calling to each other.

Then I saw a woman. She was the first I had seen since my arrival. Completely shrouded in black, she looked like a dark ghost drifting by on the street below. The sight sent an unexpected shudder of fear and revulsion through me. Her features were utterly erased. She was invisible. I was immediately ashamed of my instinctive horror and relieved that I had seen her from the roof, where she could not sense my reaction. I said nothing to Sabri and took a steadying breath. The furnishings of his well-appointed house had felt so familiar, I had nearly forgotten I was in a place so utterly foreign.

☪

BEFORE I LEFT NEW YORK, several friends and colleagues had asked me if I would wear a *burqa* in Yemen. This is always one of the first things Americans ask me about Yemen. The various Eastern ways of swaddling women are perhaps the most perplexing and problematic part of Muslim culture for westerners.

"The women in Yemen do not wear *burqas*," I said. This much I had learned. When westerners think of *burqas*, they generally envision the Afghan *burqa*, which is a one-piece garment that covers the entire body and has a grille over the face so the woman can peer out. Here, women instead wear a black *abaya* or *balto*. An *abaya* is a wider, fuller garment that is pulled on over the head, whereas the narrower *balto* has buttons down the front. Both garments are worn over clothing, like raincoats, and do not cover the head. Underneath, almost every Yemeni woman I would meet wore Western-style jeans and T-shirts.

In addition to these robes, almost all women wear a black headscarf called a *hijab* over their hair and a swath of black fabric called a *niqab*, which reveals just the eyes, over their faces. All of these terms—*abaya, niqab, hijab, burqa*—have shifting definitions depending on what country you're in. Some Muslims use the word *abaya* to mean a garment that includes the head covering, so that it is nearly interchangeable with the Iranian *chador*. And a *niqab* is also referred to as a *kheemaar*.

None of these garments is required by law in Yemen, which is one of the more (officially, anyway) liberal Muslim countries when it comes to the covering of women. Nor is the veiling of women mandated by the Holy Qur'an. Yet the social pressures to veil oneself are enormous. A Yemeni woman daring to venture out without cover is often harassed by men, who order her to cover herself, call her a shameful whore, and worse. Like many practices in Yemen, it is a cultural tradition dating back centuries rather than a religious rule. But the roles of culture and religion are often confused, by outsiders and Yemenis alike.

The tradition of veiling can be traced back to the Hadith of Sahih Bukhari. The Hadith is a document that contains the teachings of the prophet Mohammed, and Bukhari's interpretation is often considered the standard, although there are several others.

According to the Hadith, "My Lord agreed with me ('Umar) in three things . . . And as regards the veiling of women, I said 'O Allah's Apostle! I wish you ordered your wives to cover themselves from the men because good and bad ones talk to them.' So the verse of the veiling of the women was revealed" (Hadith, verse 1, book 8, *sunnah* 395).

Like many westerners, before I came to Yemen, I thought of the veil as an oppressive practice that kept women from being who they are. But the women I would meet in Yemen often told me the opposite was true. These women consider their coverings a statement of identity, an important defense against men, and a source of freedom.

The *hijab* is not to keep women from looking too alluring, one woman told me. "It is because I respect myself. And when the beauty is hidden, the more important things rise to the surface."

My initial reason for covering my head was simple: I wanted to fit in. I stood out enough, with my blue eyes and pale skin, and it didn't seem wise to call even more attention to myself by allowing my waist-length hair to fly about unfettered. I also wanted to demonstrate respect for my host culture, and the head scarf was a way of broadcasting that I knew how things were done here and that I was happy to play by the rules.

So I had arrived with a suitcase full of long black skirts, long black Indian blouses, and a black head scarf. My friend Nick coached me through these purchases, as I have a morbid fear of shopping. The head scarf we bought had actually been a dressing-room door in a small boutique, and Nick had talked the owner into selling it to me for $10. "It'll be just perfect," she said, holding up the length of dusty black cotton. "Once it's cleaned."

But while I planned to cover my head when I left the safety of Sabri's house, I had never considered covering my face. To have cloth over my nose and mouth gives me an intense feeling of claustrophobia. The thought of the heat of my breath being pushed back against my skin all day long made me queasy. I was already having enough trouble getting oxygen at this altitude.

And I had to wonder if there wasn't also a bit of vanity involved. I didn't know how to be *me* without my face. I suddenly felt terribly shallow. I wanted people to know what I looked like. It mattered to me. Perhaps these Yemeni women were simply more evolved than I was, not needing to flaunt their features. Imagine, though, going years on end without anyone outside of your nuclear family telling you that you looked pretty!

☾

VIEWING SANA'A from above is a wholly different (and much quieter) experience from living it on the ground. After we climbed down from the roof, Sabri announced that he wanted to prepare a special lunch to welcome me, and we set out on a shopping expedition. We couldn't head for the markets before two P.M., he said, or people would ask him why he wasn't at mosque on a Friday. So, just after two P.M., we went downstairs and stood in front of his black Mercedes as the two skinny boys who guarded the house opened the car doors. Inside, Sabri placed his thumb on the gearshift and the car thrummed to life.

As Sabri maneuvered through the crowded, labyrinthine streets toward the *souqs* (Arabian markets), I clung to my door handle. Yemenis are worse drivers than Bostonians. It doesn't seem to matter what side of the street one drives on, and traffic lights are mere suggestions. No one wears seat belts (except me, on the rare occasions they're available), although Sabri finally put his on when his car wouldn't stop beeping to remind him.

The honking was incessant. Yemenis, I noted, drive with one hand on the horn and the other on the wheel. In New York, drivers honk to warn of danger. In Vermont, they honk as a friendly greeting. In Yemen, people honk simply because they are driving.

The majority of the white-and-yellow taxis and other cars passing us appeared to be held together with duct tape and a prayer, belching clouds of black smoke. The absence of any semblance of emissions testing in Yemen has turned Sana'a's air into a soup of particulate matter.

The streets teemed with people, mostly men in white robes, hurrying home for the afternoon meal. Many carried long bunches of shiny green leaves tucked under their arms, which Sabri told me was *qat,* a plant whose stimulating leaves Yemenis chew for hours every day. I'd read about *qat* and was eager to try it, despite the fact that drugs don't usually interest me. But most of Yemen's social and political life revolves around ritualistic *qat* chews, and so if I were really going to learn about Yemeni culture, a chew was de rigueur.

As we hurtled on, I tried to decipher the Arabic writing scrawled on storefronts and mosques. I had taught myself the alphabet and a few phrases, and it was rather thrilling to see the graceful Arabic letters everywhere. On every sign! On every restaurant! I desperately desired to learn how to decode them. So far, I only recognized the occasional S sound and an article meaning "the."

We drove first to the fish markets in the old Jewish quarter, where rows of one-story buildings crowded around small squares packed with men pushing wheelbarrows of prickly palm fruits or cucumbers. Peddlers swiftly pared the skin away from their wares so that their customers could eat them right on the spot, dripping juice into the wheelbarrow. Men waiting at the fish stalls jostled and pushed each other to get to the front. There was no discernible line. Stepping over pools of water and fish blood, Sabri and I walked up two steps into a tiny, grimy storefront, where heaps of bloodied fish lay on the stone counter. A wall of smells accosted me: brine and decay and *fishiness.* My empty stomach began to seize, and I backed out into the street to wait for Sabri. Passing men turned to stare at me, wide-eyed. "Welcome to Yemen!" some said. How did they know I had just arrived? I wondered. (More than a year later, men would *still* be welcoming me to Yemen. While it was nice to feel wanted, the greeting irritated me. I *live* here, I wanted to say. I've been here *forever*.)

Sabri rejected all the fish in the first shop, and we moved on to the second. A man in a bloodied apron held up a medium-size *hammour* and opened the gills for Sabri's inspection. This fish passed muster and was placed in a plastic bag and handed over.

The next stop was a small, foul-smelling fish restaurant. We stepped through the doorway and Sabri handed our catch through a window to the kitchen, where it was split open, painted with red-orange spices, and shoved down into a deep, cylindrical oven. Men in stained aprons rushed platters back and forth to the small dining room, where tables of scrawny men (obesity was obviously not one of Yemen's problems) were tearing off strips of bread and fish with their hands and stuffing them into their mouths. In the kitchen, other men stirred chunks of fish into orange sauces or kneaded bread into large disks to be roasted. In the back room, Sabri directed a worker in the preparation of a salsa (called *zahawek*) for the fish. Garlic, tomatoes, peppers, and a slab of white cheese were pushed through what looked like a hamburger grinder, and the resulting sauce was poured into a plastic bag. I stood in a corner, watching, trying to stay out of everyone's way.

The white-clad, dagger-sporting men eating lunch stared at me, despite the fact that I was draped in black from head to toe, my hair covered. Their eyes made me feel like I had accidentally left the house in a sequined bikini. I had never felt quite so conspicuous. "Welcome to Yemen," each said when he first caught sight of my pale blue eyes. "Where are you from?"

One bearded man told me he had lived in New York for two years, but he left because there were too many drugs on the street. Another man told me he was a neighbor of Sabri's. A third man asked me if I had children and if I was married. They were so curious and excited to see me that you'd think Julia Roberts had walked in. Only these men probably had no idea who she was.

I said that I was married, and the men insisted that I have children. I promised to try. (Not only was I unmarried, but the thought of it terrified me. And at thirty-seven, I was still ambivalent about children.) Not a man in the place took his eyes off me until I turned to walk away. Maybe not even then.

Our fish at last was cooked, and Sabri collected it, along with bread and sauce. We headed out to a chorus of good-byes. *"Ma'a salaama!"* the men cried. "Welcome to our country!" Their attentions were flattering and sociable, but I was relieved to escape. There are no compunctions about staring in Yemen; none of the men are the least bit self-conscious about it. But for a woman to stare back was (I had read) ill-advised. This would be one of my greatest challenges. I am the kind of person who makes eye contact with strangers on the subway, flirts with men I meet on planes, and gives my phone number to random bus drivers. I can't *help* it. But now I would have to help it. Being too social a butterfly was likely to get my wings singed.

☪

BACK IN THE CAR, Sabri cranked up the air-conditioning although it didn't feel very hot. Sana'a is so high and dry that the heat never really gets unbearable. The car filled with the scents of cumin, roasted fish, and bread. We headed to the fruit market, where we picked out mangoes, skinny Yemeni apples, oranges, and cigar-sized bananas. Sabri split open a fresh fig and offered it to me. It tasted refreshingly like grass.

I was beguiled by the mounds of pomegranates, which didn't look anything like the small, red pomegranates I knew. These were enormous, yellow-green, and grapefruit sized, with just the faintest pink blush. I wanted to ask Sabri to get some but was afraid of looking greedy. Besides, pomegranates are terribly difficult to eat. The thought of peeling off all that tough skin and prying loose each little juicy seed was, at that particular moment, exhausting.

We stopped once more to pick up spiced saffron rice and headed home. I was relieved to return to the security of his First World quarters, where I could catch my breath and let all of the new sights and smells settle. We were setting the table when Theo arrived. Theo, my high school sweetheart and the reason I landed in Yemen, had already been living in Sana'a for nearly two years, doing research for a book and occasional work for the *Yemen Observer*. Frustrated with the chaos and lack of standards at the newspaper, he had summoned me to come instill a few basics in the heads of its reporters. He had no journalism training himself. I still wasn't sure why he had chosen me. Surely he knew other journalists. I couldn't help wondering if it could be, at least partly, a faint hope of rekindling our long-expired romance. It had been probably seventeen years since we'd been together, but I still felt naked in his presence—the kind of vulnerability only a first love can inflict. We still mattered a little too much to each other to be at ease. But I hadn't come here for romance. I came for the adventure of spreading the journalistic gospel in an utterly alien culture.

We had a massive amount of food. Sabri even broke out one of his best bottles of white wine, which we drank warm. Wine was a precious resource in this dry country, where it was illegal to sell alcohol or to drink it in public. Non-Muslims caught drinking in public could be sentenced to up to six months in prison, while Muslims faced a year behind bars, plus (in theory) eighty lashes with a whip. So I was fortunate to be staying with one of the very few Yemenis with a wine cellar. Theo was impressed with Sabri's largesse and told me that I was being spoiled. "Don't get used to this," he said with a hint of warning.

We ate everything with our fingers from communal platters, ripping off pieces of chewy flatbread, using it to pull chunks off the blackened fish, and then dipping the bundles in the *zahawek*. It tasted of garlic and cumin. I loved it. The fish was sweet and tender, falling off the bones. All of the new foods preoccupied me, while Theo and Sabri talked about Faris, the mysterious founder and publisher of the *Yemen Observer*, whom I was to meet the next day.

I had examined several issues of the *Observer* online before my arrival and now listened carefully as Sabri and Theo enumerated the myriad faults of the paper. The biggest problem was management, said Theo. There wasn't any. Nothing seemed to come in on any real deadlines, and there were no procedures for getting story ideas approved. When I wrote for newspapers, things generally worked like this: Reporters ran around town talking to sources and coming up with ideas for stories. They pitched these ideas to their editor. The editor either approved, refined, or killed the ideas. The reporters then reported, wrote, and sent their stories to their editor. That editor checked the reporting and basic structure and sent it along to a copy editor, who checked solely for grammar and style. And then it was published. The *Yemen Observer* did none of this. According to Theo, people wrote what they wanted to write, and it went into the paper as is. Quality checks on either the reporting or the prose were non-existent.

This bit didn't bother me too much. It wasn't my problem. After all, I was there for only three weeks, to help the journalists hone their skills. I certainly wasn't going to muck about in management and I didn't have time for a revolution.

"And no one has any training," Theo said. "The whole staff is made up of English majors who have no background in journalism. They have no idea how to structure a story. Or how to report it. Oh—and you will have to convince them that it is wrong to plagiarize from the Internet."

I paused, a handful of fish midway to my mouth. "They *plagiarize?*"

"All the time."

"What about copyright law?"

"There is no copyright law in Yemen. Intellectual property rights don't really exist." He took a sip of wine.

"Oh."

"And they also write about advertisers all the time. Faris has them write about his friends and such."

"But that's unethical!" I protested. "You can't write stories about advertisers. It destroys credibility."

Theo shrugged. "Explain that to Faris."

Sabri, a friend of Faris's, smiled knowingly. "I've also noticed some mistakes in the reporting," he said.

"*Some* mistakes?" said Theo. "Anyway, that's why Jennifer is here." He turned to me. "And could you teach them how to do Internet research? And how to know which sources are valid? And, you know, they sometimes refuse to put bylines on stories. You should get them to do that."

I tried not to dissolve into a puddle of terror.

I'd been a journalist for more than ten years, but I had never taught a journalism course before, let alone in the Arab world. I was jellied with nerves. "You'll need to show them you are in command right away," said

Theo. "You will have to find some way to make them show up on time every day. Oh—and you will need to tell them you are married. No woman your age here is unmarried, and if they find out that you are single they will assume something is terribly wrong with you. You don't want to give them any reason to look for something wrong with you."

He had said this to me before I left New York, which is why I was wearing my divorced friend Ginger's wedding ring on my left hand. I don't normally wear jewelry, and it felt tight and uncomfortable on my finger.

Sabri was westernized enough to be able to handle the knowledge that I was unmarried. Earlier that morning, when he found out I was vegetarian (except for fish, a recent addition to my diet) he said, "Well! You would make someone a very cheap wife!"

Still, to be careful, I told him I had a boyfriend in the States, as a kind of insurance policy against any possible advances. It wasn't a lie; I did leave behind a romance. But it was complicated, like everything in New York.

C·

AFTER LUNCH, Theo and I left Sabri to his work and walked through Tahrir Square, the large plaza at the heart of Sana'a, to the walled Old City, weaving our way to his apartment.

As we walked, emaciated cats and children darted across our path. The streets were so narrow that if I stretched out my arms I could touch rough stone on either side. An earthy, damp smell wafted up from the ground. We passed men asleep in wheelbarrows, their legs dangling over the sides.

I was overwhelmed by the city's architectural beauty. I never could have dreamed up the edible-looking buildings. I wanted to take a bite out of their walls. It is almost impossible to see into the boxy tower houses; they have few windows on the lower floors, to keep men from spying the women within. The upper floors are adorned with elaborate stained glass windows often referred to as *qamaria* (although I was later informed that the word *qamaria* originally referred only to alabaster windows, which were used to soften the sun's rays and keep the interiors cool). I had never seen a lovelier city.

I quickly realized that a map would be utterly useless. Even as I followed Theo to his house, I knew I would not be able to find my way back easily. He had told me that there were no addresses in Yemen, and he was serious. The Old City is a labyrinth of seemingly unnamed streets and addressless buildings. While each neighborhood does have a name, I would eventually learn that even Sana'anis could rarely locate streets outside of their own neighborhood.

Tiny boys wearing tiny daggers in their belts ran after us as we passed, calling out, "Hello! I love you!" Theo spoke to a few of them in Arabic, and they laughed and scattered. A man in a white robe passed us carrying an enormous television on his shoulder.

Little girls were running around in pink satin princess dresses with puffy short sleeves. When I asked Theo if they were dressed this way for the holy day, he said, "They are dressed that way because they are princesses of the dust."

Theo's apartment, located at the top of a gingerbread building, was magnificent. We walked up a dozen flights of uneven stone steps—there is not a uniform set of stairs in the entire country—to a large metal door with three locks. Inside was a warren of rooms, including a large, airy *mafraj* filled with cushions and illuminated by a half dozen *qamaria*. The word *mafraj* literally means "a room with a view" and is usually the top floor of a Yemeni house. I was interested to learn that the word comes from the same root as an Arabic word for "vagina." In this room nearly all social activity takes place, from meals to *qat* chews. Theo had the top floor of his building and thus the only apartment with a true *mafraj*.

We settled there, on deep blue cushions, to talk about my class and finalize the plan for my first day. This had the effect of making me feel simultaneously more at ease and more apprehensive. "They will love you," he'd say. "Don't worry." And then a moment later he would add, "But you cannot show them any weakness. You cannot show them a flaw, or they will become completely disillusioned and lose faith in you."

After a few cups of tea, we climbed to his roof so I could take photographs before dark. The roofs around us were draped with carpets airing in the sun. I leaned over the walls, trying fruitlessly to see in the windows of other buildings. I was hoping to spot that elusive species, womankind. Already I missed them so much.

As evening fell, the stained glass windows in these buildings lighted up like gems, glowing from lamplight within and splashing color into the night. I couldn't take my eyes off of them. I felt as though I had caught sight of an extraordinary woman and was spellbound by the details of her face.

"Allaaaaaaahu Akbar!" a male voice suddenly blared through the speakers, which sounded as if they were set in Theo's windowsills. The sound jolted me, although I'd heard the call to prayer at least once before, that afternoon. And then Theo tossed me out of the nest.

"You haven't truly arrived until you've gotten lost in the Old City," Theo said. "So go, get lost."

Now, as independent a traveler as I am—I have nearly always traveled alone, usually without any concrete plans—I came very close to begging him to come with me. I had no idea how to find my way around this medieval city. It was getting dark. I was tired. I didn't speak Arabic. I was a little frightened. But hadn't I battled scorpions in the wilds of Costa Rica and prevailed? Hadn't I survived fainting in a San José brothel? Hadn't I driven a van full of theater sets over mountain passes in Montana during a blizzard? Hadn't I once arrived in Ireland with only $10 in my pocket and made it last two weeks? Surely I could handle a walk through an unfamiliar town. So I took a breath, tightened the black scarf around my hair, and headed out to take my first solitary steps through Sana'a.

I remained apprehensive as I headed up the alley toward the *souq,* having no idea where I was going. A clutch of black ghosts drifted by, their curious eyes following me. I imagined I could hear them whispering, "Who is *that?*"

"I don't know, but she obviously doesn't belong here. Her *hijab* is tied all wrong!"

As they brushed past me, I caught a whiff of musky incense rising off of their clothing. A man hurried by carrying a plastic bag of tomatoes and dragging a boy by the hand. Though I kept my eyes cast toward the ground, everyone I passed stared at me as though I were an escaped zoo animal. A Western, bare-faced, blue-eyed ocelot.

As soon as I had turned a corner, a small girl called out to me in English, "Hello, Bostonian!" and I laughed, feeling a little insulted. I may have been born in Boston, but I am a New Yorker to my bones. The laughter loosened the knot of fear in my chest. Another little girl in a tattered green taffeta dress followed me, saying, "What's yer name, what's yer name?" But when I finally answered her, she turned mute and ran away.

I quickened my pace, wanting to find the markets before it got too dark. But I was distracted by a flash of green on my right. I stopped and retraced my steps. A window was cut into the stone wall on the right side of the street. I stood on tiptoe to look through, into—a secret garden! Behind the wall was a lush oasis of palm trees and unidentifiable green crops that filled an area the size of several city blocks. Green! Bright, shiny green! Elated by the sight of something photosynthesizing in the midst of all of the urban brown, I carried on.

Emerging from a series of twisting alleys, I found myself in a wide plaza in front of a mosque. To the left was a tiny storefront restaurant with outside tables, where several men sat drinking tea from glass cups. Across from the mosque was a pharmacy, busy with both male and female customers. To the right were more gingerbread houses. A herd of mangy-looking goats trotted by me, followed by a boy with a stick and the faint scent of garbage. Children pushed wheelbarrows piled so high with produce they could not see where they were going.

I wasn't sure which way to turn, but a steady stream of people seemed to be heading down a street to the right, so I joined the flow.

Several men called out to me, "*Sadeeqa! Sadeeqa!* I love you!" But the women did not speak. They just followed me with their dark eyes, the only exposed part of their bodies.

At several points in my journey, I attracted a retinue of children, most of whom seemed to be completely unattended by adults. The girls were still in their fancy dresses, although many of them were smeared with dirt, while the boys wore suit jackets over their *thobes* and curved Yemeni daggers called *jambiyas*. They trotted after me, asking my name and where I came from, crying, "*Soura! Soura!*" I didn't learn until days later that *soura* was Arabic for "photograph." They wanted me to take their picture.

At last, I entered the maze of shops that made up the *souqs*. There are several different kinds of *souq*, arranged by type of merchandise. Handmade jewelry is sold in the streets of the Silver Souq; cloves, cardamom, and cumin are found in the Spice Souq; and *jambiyas* are found in the— you guessed it—Jambiya Souq. There are also sections devoted entirely to woven shawls (mostly from Kashmir), livestock, *qat,* and coffee.

The shops were mostly tiny storefronts, with shelves behind the counters where men reclined on cushions with cheekfuls of *qat*. Some called out to me, gesturing to their wares, while others just chewed and stared. I didn't stop. This was reconnaissance work, not shopping.

The scents of cardamom and coriander overwhelmed the spice market. Piles of orange and yellow powder were teased into perfect pyramids that sat on tarps spread on the ground. How is it that they could make these perfectly uniform towers of spices, yet not create an even set of stairs? Another Yemeni mystery.

Raisins in an astonishing array of sizes and colors—green, yellow, black, blue, chartreuse—were also arranged in careful pyramids, next to bins of red pistachios, almonds, and cashews. Entire stalls were devoted to dates. Big, gluey, warm globs of dates under heating lamps. I'd never seen so many dates, or such *sticky* ones.

I walked on, past rows and rows of *jambiyas*. There were tiny *jambiyas* the length of my hand and giant ones as long as my thigh. They were made from silver, steel, wood, and rhinoceros horn. (It is officially illegal to sell rhinoceros-horn *jambiyas*, but that doesn't stop the traders in Old Sana'a.) The *jambiya* sellers were particularly keen to get my attention, waving me over to their stalls. I smiled but kept walking.

From a distance, even in the urban areas, it appeared as though everyone was dressed alike. The women were draped in black from head to toe, and the men in white. This was a world before color, before fashion, before the rise of the individual. Before God was declared deceased. The homogeneity of dress obscured the devastating poverty of most of Yemen's people. You could not tell a person's class or income bracket until you got close enough to see the embroidery along the wrists and collar of a woman's black *abaya* or the engraving on the *jambiya* dangling from a man's embroidered belt. Yemenis, of course, can size each other up in an instant, discerning by a few telling details a person's tribe, class, and level of devoutness. There are ways to tie a head scarf, for example, that indicate an especially pious nature, and a man demonstrates his wealth and prestige by flaunting a pricey rhinoceros-horn-handled *jambiya*.

The men looked so cool and comfortable—so much more comfortable than the women, swathed in their dark polyester. I wanted to trade outfits with them. I liked the daggers and their pretty sheaths. When I had asked

Sabri, earlier in the afternoon, why he didn't wear a dagger, he said, "You are my dagger." And laughed. I had no idea what he meant. Only weeks later would his comment make sense, when I learned how men appraised each other by the kind of dagger they wore. A cheap wooden-handled *jambiya* suggested a lowly social position, whereas a fancy ivory-handled *jambiya* conveyed the opposite. Strutting about town in the company of a Western woman, Sabri had implied, was another indicator of status. Only the most elite Yemenis spoke English and could therefore conduct business and socialize with foreigners.

☪

ENTIRE STREETS were full of shops flaunting brightly colored polyester prom dresses—lacy red floor-length confections, low-cut green satins, and flouncy pink ball gowns. This piqued my interest. I wondered if it were possible that women wore these scanty, frothy frocks under their black *abayas*. And where did they *go* decked out like that? I had to find out!

As I continued on, having no idea where I was headed, a teenage boy called out, "Hello, heavenly!" Which I have to say is somewhat of a step up from what I get called on the streets of New York.

I left the busiest part of the *souq* for quieter streets. I had no idea where I was or which direction was home. It got darker. Intrigue lurked in the shadows at every corner. The winding, dimly lighted cobblestone streets seemed ideally suited for a first kiss. And yet, this was a temptation to be resisted here, where a simple gesture of affection between a man and a woman could ruin their lives. The most romantic of atmospheres, squandered. Not, I reminded myself, that I was here for romance.

I felt my gait change as I walked farther and farther into the heart of the city. Gone was my confident New York swagger, gone was the flirtatious swing of my hips, gone was the dare in my eyes. Rather than holding my chin up and brazenly meeting the gaze of passersby, as I was accustomed to doing in New York and everywhere else, I kept my face cast downward. I became someone else.

TWO

reading, writing, and robbery

Eight pairs of dark eyes were fixed on me as I scribbled "THE ROLE OF THE PRESS" on the dry-erase board at the front of the classroom in large green letters. There were three women, all but their eyes obscured by black fabric, and five men, most in polo shirts and slacks. They sat around a long, rectangular table that took up most of the room. Across the hall from us was the newsroom, where these reporters had been busy at their computers before Theo and I had rounded them up.

So far I had managed to disguise my stark terror that I would be found out to be a charlatan. I was still waiting for one of these strangers in front of me to raise his or her voice in scorn and say, "And who are *you* to tell us what to do? Do you think you know better than us just because you are a *westerner?*" Who was I indeed? Just a smallish New Yorker dressed up like a poor facsimile of an Arab, who had no idea if she had anything of use to offer these people. I wished I had had more time to see the country, to read the Qur'an, to study Arabic, more time to sink into this baffling culture, before trying to teach something to its people. I was still off balance, dizzy with the thin air and unfamiliar scents.

It helped a little that I did not look like myself. I had braided my hair and pinned it up on my head, had left my face free of makeup, and wore a long loose black blouse over a black skirt, with a black shawl over that. I felt like a spinster schoolteacher, someone sexless and dry. The costume was already altering my behavior; it is impossible to feel flirty with one's form obscured by yards of fabric.

My every affectionate impulse had been carefully handcuffed and tied to a chair. Yet I still fretted that I would accidentally smile flirtatiously at one of the men and instantly lay waste to my reputation. I couldn't, however, refrain from looking men in the eyes. Certainly not here, when I had to see their eyes to know if they had received what I was saying.

The classroom was plain but comfortable, like the building that housed it. While the three-story *Yemen Observer* office building, protected by high walls and a guard, was a less charming, more modern version of the Old City's gingerbread houses (factory-made *qamaria* instead of handcrafted windows, simple stone instead of mud bricks), it still managed to be pretty. Filigrees of white wrought iron shielded the dozen or so arched front windows, and the large, sunny courtyard was draped with a canopy of grapevines. Three marble steps led to a spacious central hallway, where Enass, the newspaper's zaftig secretary, served as gatekeeper. To the right was the newsroom, to the left the conference room I was using for my class. Upstairs was the office of the mysterious Faris al-Sanabani, whom I still hadn't met, as well as the office of *Arabia Felix,* the glossy magazine he owned in addition to the *Observer.*

"So, why do we have a press anyway?" I asked, turning to my class. "What kind of role do you think it should play in society? Why is it important?" The hand holding the marker trembled slightly, and I lowered my arm to hide it.

Silence. I could hear the sound of water running outside in the courtyard, where a tall man was spraying the rows of flowering plants with a hose. Finally, a small pillar of rayon piped up.

"Press is the consciousness of the public."

"Okay," I said, turning to her with relief. "How?"

She leaned forward, releasing a sudden torrent of words that tumbled over each other in their hurry to leave her lips. "It is a judge without a court; its authority comes from people. Therefore, people have to respond to journalists; otherwise they hide the truth. Press people know that they are the mouthpiece of people. People do not understand that we are like messengers; our mission is to deliver the message. If we deliver the message, without any faults, protecting the message from being changed during the way, and hand it over to the right people, in the right manner, we are doing the best favor to people and to those who sent the message."

She went on, without taking a breath, without even looking around her, the words flying out as if she had been waiting for someone to ask her this question for years. Her tiny hands stretched across the table, making rapid, birdlike gestures to give emphasis to her words.

"Life is a cycle. Each one of us has his or her part; if we are able to do that successfully, we will have a successful life. For example, how many nominees for the U.S. election fail because there are some journalists who reveal some truth about them? So, if there are not some good journalists, those people might win these posts and then make a damage to the country. Take the Abu Ghraib scandal as an example: If there were not good journalists to dig up the truth, no one would find out. After the journalists reveal that prison's scandals, the role of the NGOs and others follows. It is like the players at the opening ceremony of the Olympics: Each one gives the other the torch until they light up the biggest torch. If someone fails, there will not be the Olympic torch."

At last she took a breath, her eyes anxiously searching my face. For a moment, I was rendered speechless. Her classmates stared at her. Two of the men, Farouq and Qasim, began laughing.

"Hey," said Theo, who in high school would have been laughing alongside of them, "we have to respect everyone's opinion here if we're going to learn. If you want us to listen to you, you have to listen to everyone else."

"That's right." My mind was slightly eased by this reassurance that Theo was on my side. "Everyone's opinion is equally valuable to me. I want to hear what all of you have to say."

The men quieted down.

I turned to the woman I would quickly come to know as Zuhra and smiled at her. While it was difficult at first to tell the women apart, Zuhra was easy to identify by the silver-rimmed glasses perched between her *hijab* and *niqah* And the fact that she pretty much never stopped talking.

She had been the only person in the newsroom when I arrived, so I had met her first. "This is Zuhra," Theo had said. "She should be running this place."

"That was a lovely definition. You are right in that by reporting something responsibly, by telling readers about the atrocities committed in Abu Ghraib and Guantánamo, we could possibly keep such things from happening again. And yes, the press is, in a way, the conscience of a people. You've obviously been thinking about this!" I copied a few of her comments to the board. "Thank you. What else?"

"It can help expose corruption?" This from a more sober Farouq.

"Yes, certainly! The press exists in a large sense to keep an eye on the government and let the people know what it's doing. So we know what our officials are up to with our money."

More men decided to join in the conversation. "The press can tell people about diseases," said Adel, the thin, solemn man who covered health and science.

"And about car accidents," added Qasim. Qasim wasn't a reporter at all, but was in charge of advertising for the newspaper. He wore a pin-striped suit and tie and reeked of cologne. He looked just like the advertising guys in the New York offices of *The Week* (where I worked), or advertising guys anywhere, really. Qasim never stopped smiling and had a high-pitched giggle that could be heard from any corner of the building. He looked better fed than the other men, who were painfully thin.

"Good. It can also get roads repaired, schools built, and presidents elected. It can help put criminals in jail and facilitate political change," I said. "It is a powerful tool. Which makes *you* powerful people. And when we are given that kind of power, we want to make sure that we use it ethically, to help people make informed decisions about their lives, their votes, and their investments."

The other women stayed silent, but Zuhra leaned forward again. "Sorry I am so talkative but there is so much I have to ask you! Could you please tell us, what is it that makes a journalist professional?"

I didn't have an immediate answer for her. Or rather, I had several. Professional journalists get paid? Professional journalists are accurate? "Professional journalists," I finally said, "are objective. This means that they keep their emotions out of their stories, that they keep their opinions to themselves, and that they report every side to a story."

"Why is that important?" Zuhra again.

"Well, because . . ." This was something we had taken for granted in graduate school as the crucial pillar of journalism. Wasn't it obvious why objectivity was important? "If you just report one side of a story, your reader is not going to trust you. He will think you are pushing some sort of personal agenda. If you accuse a politician of corruption, but then you do not call the politician for his side of the story, then you have failed to report the whole story and are not using your power responsibly. Also, that politician will decide you are a bad journalist and be afraid to talk to you in the future. More importantly, objectivity is the way to get closest to the truth."

"But how do you keep yourself from having feelings about a story?" Zuhra again, her pen poised over her notebook. Had I really worried that none of the women would speak up?

I had just begun to answer her—it's okay to have feelings, as long as they don't influence your work— when Theo leaped up from his chair.

"Give me my fifty dollars back," he said.

I stared at him. "What fifty dollars?"

"You took my money yesterday."

"No—I paid you back, remember? I changed money in the *souq* and gave it to you in *riyals*."

"You're lying!"

"I never lie! I'm a journalist!"

"You lie like a rug! You never gave me any *riyals*!"

"I cannot believe you would accuse me of such a thing! I thought we were friends!"

"Give me my money back or I'll take it."

"I don't owe you anything!" I glared at him, hands on my hips.

"Fine." He reached across the table, grabbed my big ugly black purse (bought especially so as not to attract attention in Yemen) from the table, and ran from the room.

"I'll get you for this!" I called after him, running to the door. "But I am not going to chase you! I refuse to interrupt my class!"

I turned back to my students, who were suddenly very alert, staring at me wide-eyed.

"How could Theo do this to you?" said one of the women. They had known Theo for months before I arrived; they liked and trusted him. They were shocked by his behavior toward a guest of honor—one whom he had invited, no less!

I had opened my mouth to answer her, trying very hard not to laugh, when Theo returned to the classroom, tossing my purse on the table, smiling broadly.

"You better check the contents," said one of the men.

"Yeah," concurred the others, getting excited about the prospect of drama. "You had better check!"

I looked inside. "Theo? Where's my camera?"

I couldn't help smiling a little, and the students caught on to our little performance. "Yes! Where is her camera, Theo?"

"What camera?" asked Theo.

"Okay," I said. "I want you to write me three paragraphs about what you just saw. What just happened here? Can you remember exactly what we said and did? Make sure you have a good lead, and turn it in to me by eight A.M. tomorrow." They scribbled furiously in their notebooks.

At one end of the table the three women—Zuhra, Radia, and Arwa—sat clustered together. At the other end were the men: Qasim, Farouq, Adel, Mohammed al-Matari (who went by al-Matari), and Theo. The women were all in their early twenties, as were Adel and Farouq. Qasim was a bit closer to my age, and al-Matari was at least a decade older. Theo was exactly my age. I had asked Theo not to participate, as his presence made me nervous, but he had insisted, promising to be supportive and to refrain from the kind of class-clown behavior that got him in trouble in high school. I didn't believe him, but if I had locked him out of the classroom, he would have simply climbed in the window. Theo had the obedience skills of your average housecat.

Before class, each of my student reporters had greeted me with passionate reverence. "We have been waiting so long for you," they told me, clutching my hand until my bones hurt. "We are so grateful you have come. We are so honored." Where was all that anti-American sentiment I had read so much about? Where were the bitter tirades against Western tyranny? The only times American newspapers ever wrote about Yemen were to report violence against Western interests. Yet so far, not one person in this country had been anything short of hospitable. My reporters fell upon me as though I were bestowing on them the greatest favor imaginable. I felt like Princess Diana. I felt like Seymour Hersh. I felt like a tribal sheikh. (Later, I would in fact be given the nickname Sheikah Jenny by the current editor of the paper, Mohammed al-Asaadi, who was curiously absent from my first class.)

There is quite a difference, however, between being an honored guest and being a boss. In these early days, it was impossible to imagine that one of these sweet, docile journalists, who treated me with such courtesy, would some months later try to tear up one of my editorials or storm out of my office. Just as it was impossible to imagine that I would ever raise my voice to them or threaten to dock their pay.

☪

I HAD BEGUN the class by introducing myself and telling them a few highlights of my ten-year journalism career so as to reassure them they were dealing with a professional. Not that anyone had questioned me. On Theo's advice, I had explained to them that this was a training course designed for professionals, to alleviate their fears of being patronized with a beginners' course (though Theo told me this was what they desperately needed).

I had planned to start by saying, "I am not here to teach you the American way of journalism. I am here to teach you the reporting and writing techniques that have served me over the past ten years." But Theo had vetoed this. "They *want* to learn the American way," he said. "They *dream* of going to America!"

We began by discussing the role of newspapers, the definition of news, kinds of stories, and how to cover a beat, but I ended up talking about a much wider variety of subjects than I had planned, because they had so many questions. Shyness and modesty are prized in Yemeni women, so Theo had warned me the girls might not be as vocal. Yet Zuhra was one of my most avid interrogators. "What do you think of anonymous sources?

Do we have to put a byline on a story if we worry it could get us killed? What's the difference between news and features?" She was relentless. She was, in short, a true journalist.

But I didn't want my class to be all talk, theory without practice. "I want to get all of you out of this office and onto the streets," I told them. "News doesn't happen in this building."

"How do you find stories on the streets?" they asked. They told me they left the office mainly to go to press conferences. It didn't occur to them that their corner grocer or a taxi driver or the local midwife might give them an idea for a story. Only press spokesmen and politicians were deemed worthy of quoting. Yet I knew from long experience that PR people and those in power were the least likely to have a good story. I would have to explain to my reporters how to wire a beat, how to cultivate sources, and how to convince people to trust them. I added these to my list of essential things to teach them, which was growing longer by the minute. I was starting to sweat.

And then the women told me that they weren't really allowed to approach men on the streets. And that they couldn't ride in cars with men. This meant that if a woman went out to report a story, she had to take a separate taxi from the photographer (all of whom were male).

"What are your other major barriers to getting stories?" I asked, curious.

"Well, no one wants to talk to reporters," said Farouq. "Or give us their name."

"That *is* a problem." It seemed it wasn't just this group of reporters who needed to know the various ways the press could serve society, it was the entire society itself. Almost all of Yemen's newspapers were blatantly partisan, and so anyone interviewed would of course assume a reporter had an agenda other than the truth.

I planned to assign them stories that they could publish in the paper, coaching them along the way. I wanted everything I taught them to contribute to the betterment of the *Yemen Observer*. There was much that needed bettering, starting with the English. For example: "The security source denied any dead incidents happened during the riots." Or, from another reporter, "Nemah Yahia, an elderly lady, said that they went to a mill in Raid, have an hour takes them, to crash the cereal." I suppose that "crash the cereal" isn't all that inappropriate a phrase to describe what occurs at a mill. But still.

Then there was the utter lack of structure to the stories, the dearth of legitimate sources, the three-paragraph-long sentences, and the nonsensical headlines. One notorious headline in the *Observer*, before my time, accidentally referred to the Ministry of Tourism as the Ministry of Terrorism. The folks at the U.S. embassy were so entertained by this that they pinned the story to their bulletin board. It was hard to know where to begin, but I figured I couldn't go wrong by starting with the country's biggest news story.

"There's a presidential election coming up in September," I said. "What role do you think a newspaper can play in the months before the elections? What are its obligations to its readers? In other words, how does the press contribute to the creation of a true democracy?"

The mention of democracy immediately perked them all up. The Yemeni government is officially quite keen on democracy and forever issuing statements about the glorious progress of its march toward such a political system. Yet at the moment, true democracy is but a speck on the horizon. Yemen has existed as a unified country only since 1990. After the end of Turkish occupation in 1918, the North was ruled as a quasi-monarchy by a series of politico-religious leaders called imams. In 1962, a civil war in the North resulted in the overthrow of the imamate and the establishment of the Yemen Arab Republic.

South Yemen was under British rule from 1839 to 1967, when the last British forces withdrew from Aden and the country became the People's Republic of South Yemen (renamed the People's Democratic Republic of Yemen in 1970), the only Arab Marxist state in history. After the Soviet Union began to dissolve in 1989, North and South Yemen began talking seriously about unification. They unified formally on May 22, 1990, though a bloody civil war erupted in 1994 between the (still unmerged) northern and southern armed forces.

Yemen has had the same president for more than thirty years. Well, technically President Ali Abdullah Saleh has only been president of all of Yemen since unification. But before that he ruled North Yemen for twelve years. While grumbling about President Saleh's leadership is a popular national pastime, the Yemeni people have not experienced a peaceful transfer of power in their lifetime and thus struggle to imagine such a thing.

Still, this year, for the first time, Yemen has a real opposition candidate. In 1999, when the country held its first direct presidential election, Saleh handily defeated a candidate from his own party with a majority of 96 percent. Now, opposition candidate Faisal bin Shamlan is providing the press with the thrilling opportunity to write about someone other than Saleh and about a political party other than the ruling party, the General People's Congress. My reporters were bursting with pride about their country's democratic efforts. They seemed to feel that this transition could finally earn Yemen the respect it deserved. Even so, no one really doubted that Saleh would win reelection.

"But the press has an obligation to report impartially about *both* candidates," I told my class. "And to give voters as much information as they can, so that they can make informed choices." No easy task when it's against the law to directly criticize the president in the paper. And when the owner of the paper actually works for that president. Theo had explained to me that the *Yemen Observer* was just one of Faris's many enterprises. His main job was working as the president's media adviser. He also owned a security franchise, campaigned against corruption, helped organize investment conferences, and had his industrious fingers in many other ventures. While I found it clearly unethical for the owner of a newspaper to work for the president, it seemed best to keep my thoughts to myself. I was there for only three weeks. I would just have to try to get my reporters to report as fairly as possible and hope Faris wouldn't meddle too much.

The *concept* of even-handed reporting seemed to be going over remarkably well with my students, who said they wanted their stories to read like those in the *New York Times*. It remained to be seen how well they could execute this. They gave me several different ideas for kinds of election stories they could write: candidate profiles, issue-specific stories (on the eradication of weapons, say, or fighting corruption), and news stories about the direction of the candidates' campaigns. Farouq, the paper's main political reporter, was already working on a story about the opposition party's threatened boycott of the election.

I ended class by giving them each an assignment related to their beat, due at six P.M. This would help me learn more about Yemen as well as more about what my reporters considered news.

Arwa, for example, wanted to do a story about an all-women sports club, but I had trouble getting her to tell me what was *new* about it.

"We need a reason that we are writing about it *today*," I told her. "Tell me what is *new*. Did it just open? Is it the first club for women?"

"No . . ."

"Did it just introduce some new kind of sport? Or is it part of a growing trend? Are more women than ever before doing sports?"

"Yes!" she said to the last one. "More women are doing it."

"Good," I said. "So that is the information we lead with."

I kept referring to it as a health club, and she kept correcting me. "Not health! Sports!"

Adel went off to report on the recent Guantánamo suicide, Radia to write about street children, and little Zuhra to write about the new respect hairstylists were getting in Yemen.

After class, a tall, chubby man with greenish eyes and a shiny round face lingered in the classroom with visible anxiety. He had arrived halfway through class, just before my staged fight with Theo. "I am so sorry for being late," he said. "I had to take my wife to the hospital. She had surgery on her eye, and now there is something wrong with her—" He glanced at Theo, who was standing with us.

"Cornea," Theo supplied.

"Yes. Cornea. And she will need another surgery."

This was Zaid. I expressed my sympathy and sat down with him to go over everything he had missed. I liked him immediately. He was obviously bright, joked with me, and told me he had just won a scholarship to study next year in Britain. He was frothing with excitement.

I was beginning to sag with the relief that the first class had finished without catastrophe when Theo reminded me that I still had a hurdle ahead (other than the 1,001 new challenges I had just uncovered): I had to impress the Boss. He gave me a minute to take a breath and collect my papers, and led me upstairs to meet Faris.

☪

FARIS AL-SANABANI was tall, dark, and handsome, with just about the worst case of attention deficit disorder I've ever seen. He did nothing in real time. He moved in fast-forward, spoke in fast-forward, and demanded an equally speedy response. A conference with Faris was an aerobic workout.

Faris was educated in the United States at Eastern Michigan University. Michigan is home to the largest population of expatriate Yemenis. Because Faris was elected the university's homecoming king—the first minority ever to win that honor—he was invited to many events held by campus organizations. One of these was a talk at a black fraternity on the theme of giving back to the ghetto. The speaker, Faris told me, said something like this: "You are at a good university. You have good lives, good educations. I want you to reach out to where you came from. I want you to let them see you. Not just as a basketball player or a singer. But as a successful educated person in another field."

And Faris sat there, thinking. He had been planning to accept a lucrative job in the United States as soon as he finished school. He had no intention of returning to Yemen. He was married to an American woman.

"But I realized that Yemen is my ghetto," he told me. "If everybody leaves the ghetto, dresses nice, and marries a nice white lady, then they in the ghetto will have nothing. They will have no hope. So I said, 'I am going back to Yemen. I have to go to my people.'"

He gave up the job offer and moved back to Yemen, where he took work as a translator, development worker, and government employee before deciding to launch the *Yemen Observer*.

Until then, there was just one English-language newspaper, the *Yemen Times*. But Faris felt that this paper was too relentlessly critical of his country. How was Yemen ever going to attract tourists if all they ever read about the country was negative? He decided that starting his own newspaper would be the best way to contribute to Yemen's development. An English-language paper would be most effective, he thought, because he wanted foreigners—especially Americans, because he had lived there—to be able to read about Yemen.

His American wife helped him write and edit the paper on their one computer. One thousand copies were printed of his first issue, which he delivered himself on foot, by bicycle, and through friends. That was more than a decade ago, in 1996. Faris had since divorced his American wife, who hadn't taken to life in Yemen, and married a Yemeni woman.

By the time Theo summoned me, the paper was printing about five thousand copies of each issue. It still lost money, but it was important enough to Faris that he continued to personally fund it. Besides, Faris was a wealthy man. Profits from his business ventures—not government money—funded the *Yemen Observer,* Faris was quick to tell me. This was his way of claiming the paper was independent, despite his lofty connections. After all, serving as the president's media adviser (and later his secretary) was not an ideal position for someone who owned a newspaper struggling to be seen as objective. But it was a perfect position for a driven, passionate man with infinite ambitions for his country.

When I arrived in Faris's office, he was seated behind an enormous desk, fiddling with his computer. He stood up to shake my hand. Only briefly did his eyes meet mine before darting around the room, as if making sure I hadn't arrived with a retinue of spies. Faris's eyes were always moving. I introduced myself and explained what I hoped to do with my class. He seemed properly impressed and expressed deep gratitude for my presence. I expressed deep gratitude for the opportunity to assist him. I gave him a copy of *The Week,* the magazine for which I write science, health, theatre, travel, and art pages, which he flipped through so quickly the pages blurred. I suddenly panicked as I realized I'd given him the copy with a cover story on gay marriage. The minimum punishment for homosexuality in Yemen is death. I stammered an explanation, but Faris didn't seem concerned.

"Of course we understand," he said. "Things are different there."

Before I left, he handed me a stack of thirty issues of the *Yemen Observer.* "Read these and tell me how to make it better," he said. "What sections are good, what sections to get rid of, and also, please read this interview I wrote and tell me what you think of it and how I can do better interviews in the future."

Staggering under the tower of newsprint, I took the papers to an empty office downstairs and read until my eyes dried out. I had managed only about an hour of sleep the night before. I can't remember ever having had such terrible insomnia, a combination of jet lag, nervousness about teaching, and the wild euphoria of travel. I was in rough shape.

Despite this, the excitement I felt about my class carried me along, and I managed to take about thirty pages of notes on the back issues of the *Yemen Observer.*

Reporters kept popping in to see me. "About that argument with Theo," said Adel. "Has he ever lied to you about money before?"

I was impressed—I had thought that none of them would think to interview either Theo or myself. Bravo, Adel! Then al-Matari popped in to ask me several questions about his story and journalism in general. Several small boys visited me periodically to bring me silver cups of water. I had no idea where they came from. Several men stopped in my doorway simply to stare at me.

During our meeting, Faris had asked me if I had any special needs during my stay, and I had told him that I would like to go for a swim if at all possible. I am hopelessly addicted to exercise. So after I had a quick falafel lunch with Theo, Faris sent one of his drivers to fetch me and drive me to the Sheraton, which has one of the only lap pools women can use. (All sports clubs in Yemen are sex-segregated, but the biggest hotels—the Sheraton and the Mövenpick—have coed pools.)

Water is my second home, and the emotional relief submersion brought was instantaneous. Stripped of my Yemeni drapery, I was exhilarated to feel the water and sun on my skin. I was Jennifer again. I recognized myself. As my elbows began their rhythmic rise and fall, the anxieties of the morning dispersed, rising through my body and out my fingertips, dissolving in the chlorine.

I swam for an hour, despite the best efforts of the small boys playing at the end of the pool to thwart me. At first, they just liked to get in my way and dodge me at the last minute, but then they began to imitate my stroke, splashing clumsily after me. I outlasted them, and finally they pulled their shivering grayish-brown bodies out of the pool and wrapped themselves in blanket-size towels, staring reproachfully at me as I serenely continued my laps.

When I arrived back at the *Observer,* revivified and still damp (it wasn't until nearly a year later that a Yemeni friend informed me that going about with wet hair was frowned upon, as it suggested one had just emerged from a bedroom romp—Yemenis shower after sex), I met with Faris and a new reporter named Hakim, a Detroit-born Yemeni. Hakim had joined us from the rival *Yemen Times*, where he and the editor had mutually decided to part ways. Faris had great hopes for him, as his English was better than that of most of our reporters and he had a modicum of journalism training. They peppered me with questions about the paper's format, and I told them exactly what I thought should be on every single page. After slaving away for other people for ten years, I was filled with the heady satisfaction of being treated like an authority. I was surprised by the things I knew and by how certain I felt that my suggestions were right.

By eight P.M., I thought I might swoon from exhaustion. But just when I feared I would be there all night, Faris invited me to dinner with him and three Tunisian models for *Arabia Felix*. So, at nearly eight thirty, after more than twelve hours of work, we headed out of the office.

Faris escorted us to a Chinese restaurant, where he ordered for all of us. Thirty dishes must have arrived, heaped with vegetables and fish and meats and rice and spring rolls. As soon as we were seated, the three stunning Tunisian women leaned back in their chairs and lighted their cigarettes in unison. They smoked through most of the meal. The chubbiest girl (still devastatingly beautiful) ate nothing but a few grains of rice, smoking cigarette after cigarette. Refusing an offer of food from a Yemeni is a major slight, so I ate twice as much to make up for her rudeness. But Faris was rude right back to her.

"You are not eating much but you are a big girl," he said. "Will you go eat when we are not watching?"

The girls spent most of the meal complaining about Yemen in various tongues. They had so much *fun* in Tunisia. In Tunisia, women don't have to cover their bodies. In Tunisia, the food is much better than Chinese food. Yet their contracts as flight attendants with Yemenia Airways would keep them in Yemen for the next three years. God help the Yemenis.

"Tunisia is a dictatorship," Faris told me. "But the dictator is liberal— he had all of the women remove their *hijabs,* and now they are free. But if Tunisia were to become a democracy, the Islamists would win an election in a landslide, and women would be sent back centuries." This fascinated me. "In Algeria, this happened," said Faris. "It used to be fairly liberal until it became a democracy, and the Islamists swept elections. They are still fighting there."

I wondered if the same could happen here. Yemen was moving toward democracy. Would that result in an even more conservative and restrictive culture? Faris didn't seem to think so. Saleh was almost guaranteed re-election, and Yemen was already an Islamic country.

When we left the restaurant at around ten P.M., Faris invited me to watch the World Cup with him and his friend Jalal, who had joined us, but I begged off. "If I don't get to bed I will be useless to you tomorrow!"

So Faris had Salem drive me home. I was asleep three seconds after I crawled into bed, although I woke briefly at three thirty to hear *"Al-laaaaahhhu Akbar!"* wail through loudspeakers across the city. A sound that would become as familiar to me as the rumble and blare of Manhattan traffic.

☾

IF I HAD THOUGHT that things would slow down after that marathon first day, I was seriously mistaken. Every day I accumulated new students, every day more of my reporters dragged me off after class to edit their stories, every day Faris would think up some new thing he wanted from me. In addition, I began studying Arabic for an hour a day with a tutor. I almost never slept.

But while I had never worked so hard in my life, I had never felt so useful or so motivated to get to the office. Letting down this group of reporters who had so willingly handed me their trust was unthinkable. They really thought I could turn them into professional journalists. I had to live up to their hopes. Besides, I kept telling myself, it's only three weeks. I can go flat out for three weeks. There will be time for sleep when I get home.

Still, there were moments when the size of the task overwhelmed me. I was expected to achieve something lasting during my short stay, but when I saw the stories my reporters wrote about my staged fight with Theo, that suddenly seemed impossible. Almost all lacked a coherent first sentence. Most got the facts wrong. And not one of them used anything approaching proper English. This last problem was not something I could fix. No matter how dedicated I was, I could not perfect the English of fifteen reporters in a few weeks. So I focused on what I could change: structure, reporting, and accuracy.

We began our second class by reading these pieces aloud. Here is Zaid's, in its exuberant entirety.

It was very surprising for everybody to see Theo acting that way. The exchange that people heard between the two, Theo and Jennifer is anything but understood. Theo talking to Jennifer or let's say quarreling with her over a fifty dollars that she owed him or he give it to her, we don't exactly know. The quarrel heated a little and we all saw Theo snatching Jennifer's purse and rushed outside after asking for her camera. What did he do with her purse outside we all didn't know if really did something from her purse.

I myself was perplexed as I have never seen Theo in this manner especially with a nice woman like Jennifer. We all knew Theo very well. To him money is no object and will never quarrel over it with anybody specially those who are very close to him. Probably Jennifer is the last person who would quarrel with over it. She is the one who responded to his call and came to Yemen in order to train us. She left a dying grandfather and rushed to middle of a place she never knew about. She can never ever be treated this way. It was more of a joke I reckoned in second thought.

But when I looked deeply inside the eyes of the two I saw chemistry. I learned that they both were together in grade 11 and 12 and very competitive. So the whole thing happened between the two is Theo recollection of the memories that he terribly missed back in his school days that were brought back to his mind with the presence of Jennifer. Jennifer brought back all the sweet memories and things that Theo was craving. One could see that from the way he talks and the active attitude he took since the arrival of Jennifer.

Theo and I were laughing too hard to talk at first. "So," I finally managed. "I see you've written an opinion piece. Or was that news analysis?"

After all, I had not told them what *kind* of news story to write. I wasn't quite sure where to start.

"Um, Zaid, I guess I wasn't looking for quite so much *interpretation*. I want to see all of you write a straightforward news lead, with that who, what, where, when, and how that we talked about. Tell us what happened without your personal views interfering with the action."

Zaid nodded and wrote something down in his flowered notebook. (Yemeni men were quite comfortable carrying around notebooks festooned with flowers, hearts, or cartoon characters, something that charmed and amused me, given how macho their culture seemed from the outside.) I noticed a tape recorder on the table in front of him, its red light flashing.

"Zaid? Are you tape-recording me?"

"Yes!" He smiled. "I am going to memorize everything you tell us. I need to have it to refer to."

"I see." I was flattered, but now I'd have to watch what I said.

"Okay then, who is next? Let's look at Arwa's story."

Arwa had written a newsier piece. "In her first class as a trainer in *Yemen Observer,* Jennifer's camera is taken by Theo Panderos who work also as an editor of *Arabia Felix* magazine," her story began.

This illustrated a few more of my challenges. Where did I start with prose like this? Grammar? The importance of spelling names correctly? (Theo's surname is Padnos.) The use of the passive voice?

Arwa continued: "The accident happened after a cute an argument between them . . . Eyewitnesses said that Theo burst in anger shut the windows close, picked up her bag from meeting table before he pushed out of the room, neglecting all her attempts to explain. 'Don't attend my class again, Theo,' Jennifer said."

Most of this was patently untrue. So we had a little chat about factual reporting and the unreliability of eyewitnesses. "Many people who witness the exact same event will remember it in different ways," I said. "As you have seen. Even people who believe they are telling you the truth may not be telling you what actually happened. Each person is telling you her *version* of what happened. You need to be aware of this.

"I am unclear, however, whether this is what Arwa believes she actually *saw* or if she was merely trying to heighten the drama of the whole incident. Which is something we should try to avoid if possible. Let the facts be enough. Okay, next?"

Arwa bowed her head and I couldn't see her eyes. I hoped I had not embarrassed her. I couldn't bear the thought of hurting any of the women or giving the men something to tease them about. I was still a little afraid of the women, afraid to intrude on their carefully drawn boundaries.

While my reporters would often laugh at each other and openly criticize their colleagues' work, they never questioned my authority. My status as a westerner who had written for national magazines and newspapers in the United States granted me their automatic respect and immunity from criticism. I was surprised that the men were so deferential right from the start. I had expected them to challenge me, or to refuse to take me seriously, because I was female. But this was far from the case. The men were almost obsequious, falling over each other to try to please me. My education, career, and foreignness, it seemed, trumped my sex.

This passive attitude in the classroom wasn't unusual. The Yemeni education system does not encourage critical thinking. Children learn almost entirely by rote, and corporal punishment is common. Teachers are never, ever questioned, and school is largely a grim, daunting place. I have never heard Yemenis speak with fond nostalgia about their early school days.

After all the stories had been read, I took a marker out and walked to the board. "I notice a few things missing from all of these stories," I said. "First, no one, except Adel, interviewed me, and no one interviewed Theo. Yet the story was about *us*. Didn't you want to know if Theo had a history of stealing things from me, or if maybe we had had another fight before, if there might be other reasons we are angry at each other?"

We went over what else they should have done to get this story right—interview their fellow classmates and witnesses, ask to inspect my purse, and spell our names correctly.

For homework, I passed out a *Wall Street Journal* story with a textbook-perfect anecdotal lead and a BBC news story with a direct lead, so we could spend the entire next class on leads. My reporters were unclear on the concept. Every single story in the *Yemen Observer* began with a lengthy attribution. For example: "The Ministry of Arabian Absurdity spokesperson said in all his glorious wisdom today June 11 that . . ." Or "The Minister of Myopia announced in a beautiful way today that on June 17 they will plan a meeting to deal with the issues of the opposition party signing a contract about the election with the dignitaries of the Party of the

Usual Insanity, affirmed Ali al-Mallinguality . . ." That isn't much of an exaggeration.

So, in our next class, I taught them what I call the "Hey, Jolyon!" rule, which I developed at *The Week*. Jolyon used to write the art pages at *The Week* and sat next to me. Whenever I saw a really interesting story, I'd swing away from my computer and say, "Hey, Jolyon! Listen to this!"

I told them to write the leads of their stories as if they were telling their story to their own Jolyons. "Look away from your notes, your sources, your lists of names, and simply tell me what the story is about. In one sentence. So that when a Yemeni man, for example, reads the paper, he will turn to his wife and say, 'Hey, Arwa! Listen to this!'"

☾

AS THE DAYS PASSED, my relationships with my students grew warmer. When I arrived at work on my third day, Zaid met me at the door, wearing a long white *thobe* and *jambiya*, with a flash drive dangling from his neck. "Look, Jennifer!" he said, pointing to the *jambiya* and the flash drive. "I am both old-world and new-world!" He then followed me into the newsroom and bombarded me with questions about word definitions and how things were done in the West until my lesson began.

Now that we had all grown at ease with each other, I had no trouble getting anyone to speak up in class. They were so eager to tell me what they knew that they were continually interrupting each other.

The men often behaved like schoolboys, hiding each other's shoes in wastebaskets, stealing each other's chairs, and trying to one-up each other. They asked me things like "My lead was better than Zaid's though, right? Mine was the best? Jennifer! Tell us who is the *best!*"

One morning, Qasim and Farouq would not stop taunting each other. Qasim dialed Farouq on his cell phone while holding it under the table, just to get Farouq in trouble for having his phone on in class—which I had strictly forbidden.

"That's it," I said, extending my open palm. "Hand them over." Both men sheepishly handed me their phones, which I tucked into my purse. The women gazed at me in awe.

Qasim also handed me a television remote control that was lying on the table. "Great idea," I said. "Now you can only talk if I am pointing this at you!"

This helped enormously.

Theo, to my surprise, turned out to be one of my most enthusiastic cheerleaders. Not only did he help me to steer classroom discussions in constructive directions, he also cooked me dinner most evenings and helped me to plan out my days. Life outside the *Yemen Observer* offices (what little there was) was rarely more relaxing than life inside them, given how unfamiliar everything remained. I had to negotiate fares with taxi drivers in Arabic several times a day, for one thing. Grocery shopping was still beyond me and I never saw women eating alone in restaurants, so I ate only when either Sabri or Theo fed me. There was no time for me to meet people outside of work. I wondered how single foreigners survived the seeming dearth of romantic possibilities.

☾

AFTER CLASS ONE DAY, Zuhra, who was showing herself to be the most passionate of my reporters, asked me to sit and go through yet another story line by line. There were many corrections to be made, but she was learning quickly. Her questions had no end. She was a starving little plant and she thought I was the rain.

The office was empty; everyone else had gone home for lunch and a couple hours of *qat*-chewing. When we were finally finished, at close to three P.M. (too late for me to get to the pool before the evening class), she grasped my arm with both of her tiny hands and fixed me with fierce brown eyes. "Jennifer. You have to tell me. Please. Do you think I can do it? Can I be a journalist? A *real* journalist? I want to know, because this is the career I have chosen for myself and I want you to tell me if you think I can do it. So I am not wasting my time. I do not want to delude myself."

"Zuhra. I have no question that you can do it. But——"

"But?" Her eyes grew anxious.

"I don't know," I said truthfully. "I don't understand yet enough about you, enough about Yemen, to know your particular challenges. As a woman, I mean. Aren't there things you are not allowed to do? Like, could you interview a man?"

"Not alone. My family would be upset. Maybe in a group?"

"Okay." I thought. "Could you interview a man on the phone and over e-mail?"

"Yes." There was no hesitation. "But I cannot go out at night."

"So you can work a day shift. This is something that can be worked around. Men can cover things going on at night. Can you run around town interviewing women?"

"Yes!"

"Well, that's half the population, after all," I said. "That gives you something to work with. You could certainly find plenty to write about women and children." My brain was already at work, churning out story ideas for her. She could write about what was being done to combat the illiteracy of 70 percent of Yemen's women. Or the astronomical maternal mortality rate. Or the polio epidemic that continued to cripple children. Or . . .

She nodded. "So?"

"We can find a way for you to do this."

"But you think *I* can do it? Jennifer, I want this so much; I have chosen this. I need you to help me." *Tell me you believe in me.*

"Zuhra. If this is really what you want, you absolutely can do this. And I will help you every way I can."

She squeezed my hands even more tightly. "I won't let you down," she said. "I want to make you proud of me. Just as long as I have your help."

"You do, you do!" But my stomach twisted. I had no idea how much I could really help her. How, I wondered, was I ever going to be able to tell her everything she needed to know in three inadequate weeks?

I should have known then. I couldn't.

☾

THE NEXT DAY, I ducked into my classroom for a minute to fetch something and discovered the women having their lunch. Somehow I had failed to notice that the women were never with us when I ate with the men outside in the courtyard. Faris had always invited me to eat with the men as an honorary member of the sex. We ate standing up, dipping Yemeni baguettes called *roti* into a communal pot of stewed beans called *ful*. How could I have forgotten the women? Of course they couldn't lift their veils to eat among the men!

44

Now the women were laughing at the surprise on my face. Wait a minute, I could *see them laughing*. They had mouths and noses and white teeth! They had lifted their veils. It had taken me a moment to realize this.

"You have never seen us before!" they cried out gleefully. It took me a minute to figure out who they were. I didn't recognize them without their *niqabs*! I had to start with the eyes, the only part of them I knew. The long lashes belonged to Arwa, the large round eyes to Enass, and the smiling, almond-shaped eyes were Radia's.

"Come, eat with us," said Arwa.

"I'd love to!" I said. I was trying not to stare too hard at them, for fear of making them shy. I had not yet been alone with the women, not yet been privy to this secret society. I wanted to memorize their faces before they disappeared again.

They were so much easier with me away from the men. They laughed more often, spoke more freely, and teased each other. Every time a knock came on the door, they hastily flipped down their veils.

Enass, the paper's secretary, said that all the men tell her how smart I am. That I am the smartest woman they have ever met.

"Really?" I said, elated.

"They say this," she replied.

One of the other girls said something to her in Arabic and they argued for a minute. "Oh!" Enass said, turning back to me. "I didn't mean smart. I meant pretty! I got confused."

"Oh." My face fell. "I think I'd rather they thought I was smart."

I was disappointed that Zuhra wasn't with us. I didn't know if she had gone home for lunch or already eaten. But then, just as I opened the door to leave, she flew toward it from outside. Clutching my arm, she dragged me back into the conference room.

"You haven't seen me!" she said. She pulled me past the door and closed it tightly behind us. Then, as we stood facing each other just inside the doorway, she drew back her *niqab*. Unlike the other women, she yanked off her *hijab* as well, loosing thick ink-black hair that tumbled to her waist.

"Why, you're *adorable*!" I couldn't help myself. She really was, with chubby brown cheeks, dimples, and flashing black eyes. She glowed with pride, laughing, as she turned this way and that to let me admire her.

I can't express how thrilling this was. They had let me into their world; they had trusted me with their faces.

"People have the wrong idea about the *hijab*," said Zuhra with a toss of her glossy hair. "I wear it because I respect myself. And when the beauty is hidden the more important things rise to the surface."

"So people can appreciate you for your brains and not your beauty?" I said.

She laughed. "Yes. But there is more. I can talk to you for hours about the *hijab* if you would like."

"I would!"

"Careful!" said Arwa. "She can talk to you *forever* about the *hijab*!"

"She can talk to you forever about *anything*," said Enass.

"That's okay," I said. "There's an awful lot I need to know."

THREE

an invitation

Faris summoned me to his office a few days later. He had given me a copy of a
long, dull, and confusing interview he did with a man from USAID and
wanted me to critique it. I hardly knew where to begin; there was so little clarity or interest in the piece, I would never have let it run.

I dragged my feet up the stairs. Sleep deprivation and information
overload were sapping my strength. Little pieces of cultural knowledge
and news and Arabic were continually escaping from my head and scattering about me on the ground. I was exhausted from constantly trying to
pick them all up and stuff them back in. It's only three weeks, I told myself. It's not forever.

I staggered into Faris's office, where he welcomed me with a broad
smile, waving me to a chair. "Tell me," he said without preamble. "Tell me
what you think of this interview."

I perched on the edge of my chair and pressed my palms against his
desktop. "Now, it's okay for me to be totally honest with you?" Exhaustion
tends to vaporize my ability to speak anything but the naked truth. I didn't
have the energy to coddle him.

He spread out his arms again. "Totally honest. This is what I want."

I took a breath. Why was I scared? It wasn't like he was really my boss
or anything. He wasn't even paying me! "Your lead . . ." I pointed it out on

the paper spread between us. "It says *nothing*." And we went on from there. I had nearly twenty pages of notes and took his story apart piece by piece and told him how to make it better. To his credit, he never got defensive and expressed deep gratitude for my help, so I relaxed as we carried on.

The interview really contained several stories, so we talked about how the information could be better reported and organized. He nodded and said he understood. But every time I explained anything to my students, they would say the same thing, regardless of whether they truly got it. But I was grateful for the chance to spend time with Faris so that he could get an idea of the kinds of things I was telling his staff and perhaps help to carry on my ideas after I left.

Looking back, it's incredible that I was ever that naïve.

☪

THEO RESCUED ME from work that night and took me to the British Club, a bar next door to the British ambassador's residence in the upscale Hadda neighborhood, where most diplomats live. I'd hardly been anywhere outside of the *Yemen Observer* offices, and the mere prospect of encountering a pint glass and perhaps a native English speaker filled me with wild euphoria. We caught a cab down a long dusty road past neon-lighted supermarkets, travel agencies, furniture stores, spice markets, and bright windows displaying pyramids of honey jars.

The taxi turned left at an anomalous Baskin-Robbins creamery and dropped us off at a black-and-yellow-striped concrete barrier. Men in blue army fatigues clutching AK-47s stood around on street corners and at the gates of walled mansions along the street. Just beyond the British Club, I could see the Union Jack flying over a massive green building. As we approached the large black gates on our left, a small window flew open and a Yemeni man peered out. Theo flashed his membership card and the gate swung open to admit us to—a miracle!—a bar.

The warm scent of stale beer and fried food greeted me as we walked in, and I inhaled deeply. I love bars, everything about them. Though I am not a big drinker, I love the community, the chance for unexpected encounters, the eclectic mix of people. In New York, I spent nearly every

Sunday night at my local Irish pub, doing the *New York Times* Sunday cross-word puzzle and talking with Tommy, my favorite bartender in the world. For the first time since I arrived in this ancient city, I was completely at ease, in a place I recognized.

Operated by the British Embassy, the British Club draws an assortment of expats—diplomats, oil workers, development workers, teachers, and the odd journalist—desirous of escaping Yemeni prohibitions. It was relatively empty when we arrived. The World Cup was playing on television screens at either end of the room, and a scattering of Brits sat at the small tables with pints of forbidden beer. Beyond a long porch out back was a tennis court and a pool hidden by a row of shrubs.

Theo introduced me to the bartender, a slim, smiling Yemeni-Vietnamese man named Abdullah. My first—and likely only—Yemeni bartender! Theo ordered us a couple of Carlsbergs, which we had only just tasted when his French friends Sebastian and Alain arrived. Theo promptly abandoned me to go play tennis with them.

I didn't care. I was just happy to sip my beer and amuse myself with strangers. The beer made me tipsy nearly immediately—a combination of the altitude and the fact that I hadn't had time to eat. There were two men next to me at the bar, so I turned and asked them what they were doing in Yemen—thrilled to be able to talk to strange men without the risk of being thought a shameless harlot. Well, with slightly *less* of a risk of being thought a shameless harlot.

"Construction," the man next to me said. "Embassy specialists."

The two of them told me about the British embassies they'd built all over the world. We traded stories about our travels and love affairs. One man wore a wedding ring but was not married. The other was married but not wearing a ring. The ring wearer explained to me that a long time ago his Norwegian girlfriend gave him a wedding ring as a gift. When he left her and moved to Amsterdam, his jealous Dutch girlfriend bought him a second ring. And when he moved back to Britain, his British girlfriend bought him a third. He lost that one, so she bought a replacement ring, the one he still wore although he'd just broken up with her and sent her back to England. This is why I love bars. Maybe living here wouldn't be so difficult after all, if there were oases like this one.

After a second beer, I joined Theo and his friends. The night was delicious, cool and breezy. Stars flickered on over the tennis courts. We ordered another round of beers and some fish curry. As we talked, it occurred to me that the last time Theo and I had spoken French together was in 1986, in a small classroom on the top of a hill in Vermont. And that if I had not been on that Vermont hilltop in 1986, I would not have been in Yemen some twenty years later. Interesting where one teenage romance can lead. Eventually the Frenchmen left, and I sat talking with Theo until long after dark.

I was surprised by Theo's unabashed enthusiasm for my class. "They love you, you know," he said. "Zaid told me, 'Jennifer is the best American in the world.'"

"Really?"

"I was interviewing him for the article I wrote about you, and I wanted to move on to another subject, but he said, 'No! I want to talk more about Jennifer!' He asked me if he could marry you."

"Isn't Zaid already married?"

"Yes, but he wants to marry you too."

"I don't think I could get around the teeth." Zaid's teeth, like those of most Yemeni men I met, are stained dark brown with *qat* and tea and tobacco. Many Yemenis do not brush their teeth at all, though some chew on a stick called *miswaak* to clean their teeth. As a dental hygiene fetishist, I was horrified by the crumbling, putrid teeth and rotting mouths.

"Well, he loves you. They all love you. And it's funny how the girls have taken you in. You're like their leader now."

"I love them, too."

"I can't tell you how happy they are with your work, how happy I am with what you are doing. I don't know what I am going to do when you leave."

This was a historic first. Theo had never, to my recollection, praised anything I had done, and certainly never with this kind of passion. I glowed with a sense of accomplishment that dimmed anything I had ever felt writing my science pages at *The Week*. Maybe I really could make a difference here after all.

☾

THE NEXT MORNING I met yet another new student. Shaima worked for the World Bank and had called Faris looking for a place to improve her writing. Faris recommended my class.

Shaima smiled. She was very pretty, with a narrow face, long doe-like eyelashes, and full lips. She wore a *balto* and *hijab* but left her face bare. It was a terrific relief to speak face to face with a Yemeni woman for more than a few fleeting seconds. We sat down in the conference room, and I ran through everything we had covered so far. She asked what else she could do to improve her writing, and I told her to read something in English every day. "It doesn't matter what—read something you enjoy. But make sure it's written by a native English speaker." I wrote her a list of newspapers and websites.

Shaima had had an unusually privileged life for a Yemeni. She received a full scholarship to the American University in Cairo, although her mother forced her to turn it down because she was too worried that Shaima would come into contact with drugs and alcohol. But Shaima did manage to go to university and then graduate school—in Jordan. Though she was thirty, she still lived with her parents, in the upscale neighborhood of Hadda. "We are stuck to our families until we are married," she told me.

I enjoyed talking with her and sensed that she could become a real friend. Worldlier and more independent than my reporters, she could move about with greater freedom. She also was the only Yemeni woman I knew who owned a car—a Mercedes.

When I was through with Shaima, the women took me to one of the back offices, where they had spread out newspapers on the floor. They locked the door and lifted their veils, smiling at me.

"You don't think it's wrong?" Enass asked me. "To sit on newspapers, since that is your work?"

"Oh no," I said. "We line gerbil cages with them."

Three of the four girls hiked their black *abayas* up to their waists in order to sit comfortably. All were wearing blue jeans.

They handed me a rolled Jordanian sandwich of pickles and falafel and watched closely as I took a bite. "Do you find it delicious?" Arwa asked anxiously. I assured her that I did.

Zuhra then launched into one of her high-speed monologues, telling

51

me about her seven brothers and sisters, her hopes for her future, and her criteria for a husband.

"I expect never to marry," she told me. "I expect that. Because I will never compromise my career. And I will only marry a man who will support my career. But he must also be religious. There are very few Yemeni men like this."

Zuhra and I were the last to finish our sandwiches. "Because you never stop talking!" said one of the other girls.

☪

A PILE OF WORK awaited me the next morning. Faris had asked me to go over the most recent issue in detail and critique it for the whole staff. I spread out the paper on Sabri's dining room table and, for three solid hours, read and took notes on every page, every story, every line. I was becoming obsessed with my students' stories. I thought about them when I was lying in bed. I mentally corrected them while riding in cabs. I found myself thinking of a crucial prepositional phrase that would make Zuhra's beauty parlor story perfect as I swam laps at the Sheraton.

By the time I finished writing my critique and covering the paper with circles, cross-outs, and blue ballpoint scrawl, I was zinging with energy. It was Thursday, which most Yemenis have off, as Thursday and Friday are the weekend. The *Yemen Observer* staff, however, worked every day except Friday.

I arrived at the office early, anxious to speak with Hakim before class. Faris seemed to have special hopes for him, thinking he could help revolutionize the paper. But so far he had done little to distinguish himself, other than to argue with me in class, rarely in constructive ways. He claimed that we didn't need to use the word "said" in attributions, because *Time* magazine doesn't. This was not only untrue but considerably unhelpful when I was trying to teach my reporters plain, straightforward language. They were hopelessly dependent on the words "affirmed" and "confirmed," which they generally used when quoting someone who didn't have the authority to affirm or confirm anything. They *needed* the word "said." I wanted to explain to Hakim, as diplomatically as possible, how helpful it would be to everyone if he supported my authority and followed the same rules as everyone else.

Hakim was late, however, so I had no chance to speak to him. Instead, I cornered editor in chief Mohammed al-Asaadi, who had only made it to one previous class, and asked him sweetly if he wouldn't mind joining us for an hour. He was the person I most needed to reach, but Theo had told me he felt threatened by my presence. Apparently he didn't believe his journalism skills needed improving, which was disappointing. I wanted him to be able to reinforce what I was teaching and carry on some of this work after I left.

Once Hakim and al-Asaadi were both settled amidst my other reporters, I launched into my critique. To my delight, both al-Asaadi and Hakim (and the rest of the class) were quite receptive. I got through everything I wanted to say with minimal disruption. I began with praise, saying how much I liked the layout of the front page, some of the front headlines, and most of the story ideas. Baiting the hook.

I especially praised Adel, the paper's health reporter, because his was one of the better pages. "Poor Adel," Theo often said. "He is the lowest-caste person on staff, and the rest of them treat him like an animal, even though he is one of the best journalists they have." Yemen is divided into several social strata, including *bedouin* (desert nomads), *fellahin* (villagers), *hadarrin* (townspeople), and *akhdam* (literally "servants"), which include Adel's family. So I told everyone what wonderful stories Adel had picked for his page, in the probably vain hope of boosting his status.

Then I reviewed some things that needed to be done more consistently. Every story should have a byline, I told them. (Often, the stories just said "Observer staff.")

"You all work hard on these stories," I said. "You deserve credit for them. I want you to be proud of your work. Putting your name on your story tells your readers that you stand behind your reporting. It enhances your credibility. And it keeps you accountable. If you are ashamed to put your name on a piece of work, it does not belong in the paper."

Theo raised his hand. "What if you are writing a story that could get you killed? So if you put your name on it, someone will come after you?"

"Well, in that case, we can make an exception. I don't want to get any of you killed. If you are quite sure that someone will come after you with a gun or any other weapon for a story you are writing, you have my permission to withhold your byline. However, every single one of the stories in this issue should be able to safely have a byline without getting anyone killed."

Next, we talked about the importance of spelling. "The word 'conference' is misspelled in a front-page headline," I said. "As a reader, I see this and say, 'If they make mistakes about things as small as spelling, what other kinds of mistakes are they making?' You increase your credibility when your grammar and spelling are perfect. And you erode it when they are not."

They nodded and scribbled.

A new fellow joined us for the critique, a blond, blue-eyed Californian named Luke, who had been hired to help with the copyediting. He radiated goodwill, and I was happy to have someone else there to reinforce the proper use of the English language.

When everyone had finally dispersed, Theo looked at me. I was crumpled against the blackboard. "Worn out?"

"I feel like I've just run a marathon. My diaphragm hurts." I get so enthusiastic when I am talking that I wave my arms a lot and lunge back and forth from the dry-erase board to the table. My calisthenics seemed to worry my students, who kept offering me a chair. But they often had just as much trouble sitting still.

"I've only just realized this since you've come here," said Theo a few days later. "But this entire nation has ADD. This is their central problem; this is why nothing gets done."

☪

THE NEXT DAY'S CLASS focused just on leads. I needed to do something small and focused with them; it was too difficult to fix entire stories. If they could get just that first sentence of the story right, the rest would follow——I hoped. We went over everyone's leads, critiquing and rewriting them until they were perfect. Or at least printable. I gave them the last fifteen minutes of class to interview me and told them their assignment was to write a lead and three paragraphs based on their interview. They'd been very curious about me and were thrilled to have permission to quiz me. They asked me where I lived, whether I was married, where I had worked before Yemen, what I thought of them, what I thought of Yemen, and who was the best student (this from Zaid). I warned them that I might lie and said that they should investigate me on the Internet, to make sure I really am who I say I am and have done the things I say I have done.

They proved a little too good at this. That night, as I was halfway through dinner, Theo texted me. Apparently my students had discovered (via Google's image search) scores of photos of me in cocktail dresses at New York media parties. It had not occurred to me that they might find things I would rather keep concealed. I immediately panicked, worried they would think less of me after having seen me in lipstick and a low-cut cocktail dress, holding a glass of wine. I rang Theo immediately after dinner, and he assured me that they still loved me.

"For my brains?" I asked fretfully.

"Of course for your brains," he said. "What else could they love?"

☪

WHEN I WALKED into the newsroom the next morning, Zaid was sitting there gazing at a photo of me that he had installed as his desktop. In it, I had an arm draped around my photographer friend David, and I was smiling through my hair, which was loose and tumbling down to my waist. I was relieved, however, to see that only David was holding a beer. I immediately apologized for my scanty outfit and the fact that I had an arm around a man, but Zaid said, "Jennifer, I lived with an American family for three years! You don't need to explain these things to me. We understand."

"I just don't want you to get a poor impression of me," I said.

"Never! We love you! We just think you are beautiful, these are beautiful," he said, gesturing to the photos.

The women, Zuhra and Arwa, said the same thing. I relaxed slightly.

☪

LATER THAT AFTERNOON, I was updating Faris on my activities with his staff when he asked if I would be willing to report on a conference on democracy in the Arab world at the Mövenpick Hotel across town. I could write a story about democratic progress in the region for *Arabia Felix,* he said. Before I had time to think about it, or suggest that perhaps democracy in the Arab world was a bit broad for one magazine piece, a van arrived to sweep me off to the hotel, along with Adel, who became my translator.

We spent six hours at the hotel, interviewing professors, writers, and politicians from Egypt, Pakistan, Iraq, the United Arab Emirates, and Saudi Arabia. Exhausted from sprinting after interviewees and translating my questions, Adel begged for a rest. "Not until we have enough for a story," I said. By the end of the day, we had plenty. I was most excited about interviewing Iraqi parliament member Safia al-Souhail, as I was curious to hear her views on the situation in Iraq.

"People think that it's the Americans who are foisting ideas of women's rights and human rights on Iraqis," she told me. "This is not true. Iraqi women have been fighting for these things for a generation. I have always dressed like this." She gestured to her yellow pantsuit.

She was surprisingly optimistic about Iraq's future. The turmoil and bloodshed there were to be expected after so many years of oppression, she said. (Several other attendees had expressed similar views.) "The people don't know how to be free," she said. "Iraq needs help from the U.S. and other countries right now. But as soon as Iraq is independent, it will waste no time throwing them all out of the country. Just not yet."

☾

I BEGAN CLASS the next day by asking Adel to describe our reporting process at the Mövenpick. We talked about how we tracked people down and about how much more efficient it had been to take notes than to use a tape recorder. My students always wanted to record their interviews, which forced them to spend hours transcribing. I loathe tape recorders and believe they should be used only as a backup, when interviewing someone who might sue the paper. I told my class how one Egyptian woman had shied away when Adel produced his tape recorder. "It can intimidate people and keep them from talking to you."

And then I showed them my notebooks. I had filled them front to back and then written on the back side of every page. "Reporters for daily papers go through one to three of these a day," I told them. Their eyes widened. From what I could tell, they'd been using the same notebooks since I got there.

This led to a discussion of interviewing techniques. We talked about how I interviewed people at the conference and went over the interviewing handout I'd given them. Then came the fun part. I asked them to interview each other in pairs in front of the class. Zaid and Adel volunteered to go first. I asked the class to critique them. Which they enthusiastically did. Nothing got them more excited than criticizing each other.

I wanted to involve the women, who had been shyer about speaking up, so I asked Arwa and Zuhra to go next. Arwa was resistant but with a little encouragement agreed to interview Zuhra. She was a much better interviewer than the men—more focused and quicker with her questions. She also had the good fortune to be interviewing someone who answered every question with a torrent of words.

Faris rang me that afternoon as I was leaving my Arabic lesson and invited me out to dinner. At eight thirty P.M., he arrived promptly on my doorstep, beautifully dressed, in a dark pinstriped suit. Clouds of cologne wafted off of him. We climbed into his Mercedes and drove to Hadda, where we ate at an Americanesque Greek restaurant called Zorba's. "It's a five-star restaurant," said Faris. "One of the best in Sana'a!"

This it most certainly wasn't. The food was very basic: burgers and fries, salads, fish, spaghetti. But the place was packed with foreigners and the Yemeni elite and was one of the few places where women and men could be found in somewhat equal numbers. Faris knew the owner, who waved us to one of the front tables overlooking the street.

On the way, Faris had given me a flattering speech about how incredibly grateful he was to me for the work I had done. He asked if I would write up a few of my pithy pieces of advice for my students so he could frame my words and hang them around the newsroom to remind his reporters of what I had taught them.

"You mean, things like 'This is a NEWSpaper, not an OLDSpaper; let's put some news in it'?" I asked.

"Yes! I want that one. And as many others as you have."

He also said he wanted me to see the countryside and promised to arrange a car to take me on a day trip to the villages of Kawkaban and Shibam on Friday. He would pay for me to eat at a restaurant there. Like so many of Faris's promises, these turned out to be as insubstantial as the Sana'ani air.

Faris also said he wanted to have a dinner in my honor on one of my last nights and present me with some gifts. "Don't buy any jewelry," he said. "I have plenty for you." The chances of me buying jewelry were slim to none, and slim just left town. I didn't wear any jewelry, save Ginger's wedding ring.

Then he offered me a job. "I will pay you one thousand dollars a month"—most journalists at the paper made $200 a month—"plane tickets back and forth to New York, and occasional three-day vacations in Beirut," he said, "if you will come to run the *Yemen Observer*."

"To *run* it?" I thought he must have been joking. I had no management experience, almost no Arabic, and Faris had never even seen my résumé. Theo had hinted that Faris might offer me some kind of job, but I hadn't expected to be handed the entire paper. Not one newspaper editor in the whole of the United States would have looked over my résumé and thought, "I want this woman to run my paper."

"You would have total control," Faris continued. I would? I wouldn't have to write flattering pieces about the president? Was this possible?

"I'd be the editor?" I fleetingly imagined my name at the top of a masthead.

"We'd have to make you managing editor or something. The editor in chief must by law be Yemeni. But you would be in charge." Hmmm. I wondered if the Yemeni staff would really let me be in charge if there was a Yemeni name above me on the masthead.

For a moment, I allowed myself to contemplate the heady thrill of being the boss. Then, almost reflexively, I declined. "I am still paying off American debts," I said. "I don't see how I could possibly live on that." I was making $60,000 in New York and could hardly manage to scrape by.

"Think about it," he said.

"I'll think."

"I could make it fifteen hundred dollars."

"Do you know what I make in New York?"

"It will be cheaper to live here."

I looked out the window at the darkness settling over the city's scores of minarets, the slow brightening of the colored glass *qamarias.* I watched the women hurrying to beat the darkness home, laden with sacks of food, and the men, their cheeks fat with *qat,* striding past in long white robes. I thought about the gray New York office where I had spent the last five years.

"I'll think," I said.

FOUR
things to chew on

A few days before my departure, I woke up at six A.M. in a blind panic. Was it possible I had so little time left? There was so much still to do! I hadn't taught my reporters how to do research on the Internet. I hadn't given them enough investigative skills. I hadn't talked with them about follow-up stories. They often wrote a breaking news story about something—a new kind of irrigation being introduced, for example—but then never wrote about the effects of the project. The paper was full of the launchings of brilliant new projects, but my reporters never bothered to find out whether they met their goals. Given that a large percentage of development projects worldwide fail, I felt that it was the press's job to monitor them and hold them accountable.

I also hadn't finished writing my democracy story for *Arabia Felix* or my overall report on the paper. Then, in class that day, something happened that made me forget how much I *hadn't* done.

On the dry-erase board, I wrote a list of facts: A murder was committed. Thabbit al-Saadyi, ninety-four, murdered Qasim al-Washari, forty-nine. (I let the students pick the names.) The murder happened in a casino. It was committed with an AK-47. On Saturday at three A.M. Qasim was found riddled with five bullet holes, with three thousand *riyals* in his pocket. Next to him were a bottle of vodka and two roses. (Again, details courtesy of my students.)

They then had fifteen minutes to write me a really good lead.

And—miracle of miracles—they *did*! Farouq read his lead first, and it was *perfect*. "Thabbit al-Saadyi, 94, killed Qasim al-Washari, 49, with an AK-47 at a casino Saturday at 3 A.M." He included the who, what, where, when, and how. He included a subject, verb, and object. And he used the correct style for the ages of the men! It may sound ridiculous, but I was so moved that my skin tingled and tears came to my eyes.

"That is so perfect," I told Farouq. "That is just what I've been looking for."

☾

THERE WAS ALSO so much of Yemen I had left to see. On Fridays, my days off, I immersed myself in Yemeni life—in what my life might be like if I lived there. Yemenis are quick with hospitable invitations, and a thin, professorial man I met one night at the National Museum, Dr. Mohammed Saleh al-Haj, immediately invited me to lunch with his family. This is how Yemenis are—they will invite you home to lunch five minutes after meeting you. And after you have gone once, they will then want you to have lunch with them *every* Friday.

We met in the morning and took a taxi together to the fish market to pick out lunch. A little nervous to be heading home with a complete stranger, but curious to get a glimpse of Yemeni home life, I wandered around taking photographs of children. I was fascinated by the little girls, the dirty little street princesses, their bright taffeta dresses streaked with grime.

Dr. al-Haj's brother-in-law Khaled, sister Leila, and niece Chulud fetched us from the market in their car, and we drove to Dr. al-Haj's home, a two-room apartment up a flight of stairs and across a rooftop. After we removed our shoes and stepped inside, Leila and Chulud immediately stripped off their *abayas,* emerging looking like two Western women. Chulud wore skintight blue jeans and a loose short-sleeved shirt over a black bra, like any American fifteen-year-old, while Leila wore a checked shirt over loose plaid pants. They took over the kitchen, while Dr. al-Haj settled me in the living room/dining area. The room was carpeted with oriental rugs and lined with sitting cushions. A TV hulked in the corner, blaring a Friday sermon. Khaled came in wearing his long white robe and switched the television to an American channel showing a swimsuit fashion show. *"Amreekee!"* he told me, smiling. I ought to have been grateful for some American television, so I smiled, though the reverse was true. I have never owned a television, I have no interest in fashion, and it made me uneasy to watch women in bathing suits in the company of Yemeni men. In fact, I'd become rather taken with this whole modesty thing. Why should I let a man who is not my lover see any part of me? I was getting used to hiding.

Dr. al-Haj disappeared for a moment and returned with a gift for me: a lovely woven bag stuffed with something soft. I opened it to find a long, silky *abaya* and matching scarf, with glittery flowers along the edges. I was overwhelmed by his generosity.

"So you will be safer," he said, though I was already covered from tip to toe in loose black, so much so that when Dr. al-Haj saw me that morning, he had said, "Ah, so you are Yemeni now!"

"If you don't like it you can throw it away," he said. "And if it's the wrong size I will buy you a new one."

"I would never throw it away! I love it. Thank you. *Shukrahn.*"

The neighbors heard that I was visiting and came by to take a look at me. First came a little girl, dressed up like royalty in a frothy green dress. She was shy at first, and then impish, stealing someone's cell phone and playing with it. Then three boys came in. Each one solemnly took my hand and greeted me, and then the third boy kissed me on each cheek and then once on the top of my head. If I lived here for a year, would I ever cease to be a curiosity? Or would I simply adjust to being an object of study?

When lunch was ready, Chulud carried each of the dishes into the room. "This is *salatah,*" she said. "This is *roz.* This is *chobes.* This is *samak.*" I nodded approvingly and repeated the Arabic words after her.

Dr. al-Haj took me to the kitchen to wash my hands, and then we began to eat. Yemenis are lightning-fast eaters, so it was hard for me to keep up. We started with the yogurt-drenched spongy bread called *shafoot,* pouring chopped salad and chili sauce on our little corners of it and picking up clumps with our hands. Then there were roasted vegetables, potatoes, flaky white fish (the best pieces of which were flung in front of me, the guest of honor), and *bint al-sahn*—"the daughter of the dish." This was my favorite. It resembled an enormous flaky pancake, made with flour and butter and drizzled with honey. I ate until I could eat no more, despite the urging of my hosts. All of this we washed down with tiny glass cups of gingery tea. I could live with eating meals like this one every week.

Now that our stomachs were lined with food—an important prerequisite to chewing bitter *qat*—Leila and Chulud took me to my first *qat* chew, a women-only session at a friend's house, not far from where I was staying. I had been waiting eagerly for this, curious about the drug and the ritual so essential to Yemeni life. We walked through a ground-floor courtyard where children were playing to the *mafraj* in the back. There, I was introduced to the five women already sitting in identical postures on the cushions around the room. When Yemenis lounge in a *mafraj*, they customarily sit with the right knee bent so that it points skyward, the foot pulled close to the body, and the left knee dropped out to the side, with the foot tucked under the right leg. My left leg constantly falls asleep in this position, so I keep adjusting my posture, sometimes pulling both knees up to my chin, always keeping the soles of my feet hidden, as it is impolite in Arab cultures to show anyone the bottoms of your feet.

Women continued to stream into the room, each one circling to kiss the others several times on the cheek. Some of them had a rhythm: two quick kisses, a beat, then three quick kisses. Each seemed to have a signature way of kissing hello.

The women spoke to each other and over each other in rapid-fire Arabic. Without Dr. al-Haj, I had no one to translate for me; no one else in the group spoke English. Communication was accomplished with my few Arabic words and scores of hand gestures. If I were to stay, I thought, I'd learn Arabic quickly, out of sheer necessity. Leila told me they were discussing democracy. I should have liked to hear that, particularly because I'd been told that Yemeni women rarely talked about anything other than babies and other domestic matters. This did not seem to be true in our group.

When everyone had arrived, the group consisted of about twelve or thirteen women in various states of *abaya*. All had their veils pulled back from their faces, and many had taken them off entirely. I sat with Leila on my left and a faux-blond woman on my right. The blonde did most of the talking. She asked me if I were married, pointing to my ring and to hers. I told her (and all the other women, who stared at me the entire time I was there, as if I'd just landed from Pluto) that I was indeed.

"Babies?"

I shook my head. "Not yet." Then, as an afterthought, I added, *"In-sha'allah"* ("if God is willing"). At that, everyone smiled and nodded, and seemed to relax a bit. I wasn't so different then after all. Despite my uncertainty about children, it did occur to me that if I accepted Faris's offer, I would be spending one of my last fertile years in a country where there was little chance I would find romance, let alone a partner with whom to raise a child. Should I decide I wanted one.

A large elderly woman, who I believe was our hostess, passed around a tray of cups of sweet tea before preparing the enormous water pipe standing in the corner by placing glowing-hot lumps of tobacco atop it. A three-inch-thick hose snaked from it across the floor, so that the mouthpiece would reach even the woman sitting farthest away. The mouthpiece was passed from woman to woman, each keeping it for the space of approximately ten inhalations. *"Khamsa wa khamsa,"* Leila said to me. "Five and five." I was grateful that I had learned all of my numbers before I left New York.

When the water pipe came my way, Leila showed me how to smoke it—you don't inhale all of the way, just slightly. I accidentally took in too much and began to cough. My eyes widened and I touched my hand to my heart, which was enough to make the women take it away from me. When I couldn't stop coughing, the blonde whipped out a little vial of oil and rubbed some on the back of my hands. She and Leila both gestured that I should sniff it.

"Oxygen," said Leila in English. I wasn't sure why sniffing rose oil on my hands would increase my oxygen levels, but I wasn't about to debate the issue.

An African-looking woman pulled tinfoil-wrapped pie shapes from her bag and began passing them around. I thought perhaps they were little tarts, but they were cakes of strong homemade incense. Many Yemeni women make these. She sold one to Leila (images of Avon parties flashed through my head), who broke off a piece and burned it in a small ceramic burner. She turned to me and held the incense under each one of my pinned-up braids, until the sweet smoke had suffused my hair. Then she made me stand and held the incense burner underneath my skirts. The smoke was hot on my bare legs. The blond woman picked up my head scarf from the cushion behind me and handed it to Leila, who scented that as well. I now smelled strongly of 1968.

Several women took out their bags of qat and began to place the little green leaves in their mouths. Leila placed a handful of her qat on my lap. The blond woman on my right added a sprig. We began to chew. The goal is to keep the leaves in the left cheek, between the gums and the cheek, while gnawing on them to release the juices. They were bitter, as if I were chewing something slightly poisonous.

My initial impression was that qat was a very mild drug—less of an immediate jolt to the body than coffee. I had been chewing for nearly an hour before I felt anything at all other than nausea. Then the curtains of my mind began to slide open. The fog of exhaustion dissipated, and I felt lucid and sharp. My thoughts rang like crystal. I suddenly felt like running a marathon, writing a novel, or swimming the English Channel. If American journalists were to ever get ahold of qat, I am sure they would promptly deplete the supply.

But this is just the first phase of the drug. During this phase, chewers customarily banter with each other, trading barbs. In the second phase, the conversation becomes more focused, zeroing in on a topic. After that is Solomon's Hour, named for the Prophet Solomon, rumored to be fond of meditation. During this time, everyone slips into thoughtful trances and cannot be bothered to talk.

I didn't stay long enough at this chew to get to that stage.

By the time Dr. al-Haj called to check on me, I was ready to go. I couldn't sit *still* any longer. What I found most mysterious about qat chews is how people were able to sit for so long while ingesting a stimulant.

Dr. al-Haj walked me home, where I was hugely relieved to be alone again. It wasn't until I was standing in my room that I realized the monumental effort it had cost me to be someone other than myself for the hours of lunch and the chew. It was obviously easy to make Yemeni friends, but for how long could I pretend to be a virtuous married woman who had never had a lover? It seemed impossible that I could ever manage this feat on a daily basis for as long as a year. Concealing so much of myself made me lonely. It also felt dishonest. This is what made spending time with Yemeni people so exhausting—all the parts of me I had to hold back. Restraint has never been my strong suit.

Not that I was thinking about staying. Was I?

☪

BACK AT WORK, I finished my piece on Arab democracy for *Arabia Felix,* which I titled "Cultivating the Desert." (Faris subsequently lifted this title for a coffee-table book on the elections he published later that year.) My students claimed the rest of my time as I crammed as much as I could into my final lessons. For a class on Internet research, I herded my reporters to the computers. We began by examining a site that collects tax forms of international nonprofits; a site that gives profiles of every domain; and snopes.com, an urban legend–debunking site, which everyone loved. They wanted to look up all kinds of urban legends. I found it intriguing that the men wanted to look up urban legends about marriage, whereas the women wanted to look up stories about Hurricane Katrina and war. So much for gender stereotypes. I bet if Yemen had a *Cosmo*-like magazine, the men would devour it at least as enthusiastically as the women.

The point of this exercise was to show my students how to figure out which sites were reliable sources of information and which were sources of unfounded rumor. They had a remarkable inability to tell the two apart. They believed *everything* they read on the Web, which made for some interesting assertions in their stories. They did not question what they were told. If I could teach them just one thing, I decided, it would be skepticism.

☪

EVERYTHING I DID during my last few days in Yemen was suffused with curiosity about what would happen if I actually accepted Faris's job offer. What would I be like as an editor in chief? Could I keep up the exhausting pace Faris expected of me? And what if I gave up my life in New York to come here, made myself a home, and then failed? What if I couldn't get my reporters to meet deadlines? What if I couldn't actually get an entire issue organized and out in time twice a week?

☾✶

FORTY-FIVE PEOPLE showed up at the farewell banquet Faris threw for me on my second-to-last night at Shaibani, a fish restaurant. No one had ever thrown me such an extravaganza! Almost everyone I invited showed up: Dr. al-Haj, Shaima, Sabri, the entire staff of the *Yemen Observer*, other friends, and even a jazz band from New York, scheduled to play at the American Embassy the following night. But I didn't realize until we were all assembled that my women were missing. Where were Zuhra and Arwa and Radia and all the people I loved best? I was heartbroken. I had forgotten that they were not allowed out this late.

Faris stood up and gave a speech, saying how much I had changed the newspaper in just a few weeks, that his staff had demanded that I return, and that they all loved me. He showered me with gifts, which were stacked in a pyramid on the table in front of me: a whole set of silver jewelry in an enormous blue velvet box, two *jambiyas* with belts, seven baseball caps (one signed by the entire staff, telling me not to go), and five miniature Yemeni houses to bring home as gifts. He also handed me an envelope containing three crisp $100 bills.

Faris had hired two photographers to capture the event, and they took pictures of me nonstop throughout the dinner. I had paparazzi! I felt like Madonna. We ate Yemeni fish and bread and salsa and bananas with honey. The honey—for which Yemen is renowned—tasted of jasmine and God. It was that good.

I went home alone that night feeling weepy and confused, and lonely in that particular way one gets lonely when one is in between places, belonging nowhere. My heart sank at the prospect of going back to my New York routine. But could I possibly ever belong here?

On my last day in Yemen, I stopped once more at the office. My reporters threw themselves at me and begged me not to go. Zuhra pulled me aside in the hallway and pressed a purple alligator-skin wallet into my hands.

"It's not new," she apologized. "But it's my favorite thing I own and I love it. I wanted to give you something I love."

I was so moved by this I couldn't speak. I just took both her small hands in mine and squeezed them. If I come back, I thought, this will be why.

FIVE
you'll die over there!

The most dispiriting thing about returning to work at **The Week** *after a holiday was that no one wanted to hear about it.* I'd traveled quite a lot in my five years at the magazine, and it never failed to irk me that no one ever asked questions about my journeys beyond a polite "Nice vacation?" Perhaps this was understandable when I had been to well-trodden places such as Paris, Barcelona, and Dublin. But now I had been to Yemen! Few people in the office had even been able to place it on a map before I headed off there, and so I thought perhaps its exoticness would prompt some curiosity. After all, my colleagues were journalists, whose job it was to be professionally curious. They would surely be interested in the lands beyond the shores of Manhattan.

I was wrong. No one wanted to hear about the *Yemen Observer,* my students, or daily life in Arabia. A couple people asked what I wore while I was there, but that was the extent of their interest. This baffled and wounded me. I couldn't help but take their lack of interest personally. I always spent my first few days back from holiday feeling irritated with the world. I wanted to share my experiences with the people with whom I spent eight hours a day. I wanted to be found interesting. Instead, I stared at my gray computer screen and began, with dread, the return to my tired routine.

After less than a week back in New York, I found I was tired of pretty much everything. I was tired of my morning rituals, tired of running in the same parks, tired of swimming in the same pools, tired of spending eight hours of every day in a drab midtown office, tired of the United States and our embarrassment of a president. I was tired of feeling underestimated by my boss and undercrutilized at the magazine. I was tired of the bleak cynicism of my coworkers. I was tired of media cocktail parties. I was even tired of my favorite fruit stand on Fortieth Street and Broadway, where the Afghan fruit seller who measured out my cherries and grapes took more of an interest in my Yemeni adventures than anyone in my office.

In New York I was always maniacally social and spent most of my evenings at art openings, parties, the theater, the opera, book readings, or simply drinking with friends. But now I found myself growing increasingly restless and malcontent. I craved novelty and the chance to spend my energy on something more personally meaningful than *The Week*. I had loved working for *The Week* for many years. I was one of the magazine's first hires and had started there as an associate editor before its launch. It had been thrilling to see it through from conception to adolescence.

Still, five and a half years was longer than I had ever spent at any job, and my work at *The Week* sapped my energy for other projects I wanted to finish—some short stories, a novel, my stalled acting career.

Back in New York, I felt the years dwindling away, with little to show for them other than a few weekly magazine pages. Something had to be done, and before I got a day older. There had never been a better time. I was single, child free, and almost rid of my student loan debts from my two graduate degrees. If it took a year in Yemen to launch me out of the predictable routine of my life, so be it.

It was this combination of panic and thirst for novelty that prompted me finally to take Faris up on his offer. This was my chance to take a place on the front lines of the struggle for democracy in the Arab world! After all, democracy cannot take root without a free press. Perhaps I could help to make Yemen's freer, just a bit, by loosening the tethers restraining my timid reporters.

My life would certainly feel more meaningful if I were helping my

Yemeni journalists learn what they so ached to learn. I imagined revolutionizing the newspaper, breaking stories exposing government corruption, election fraud, and human rights abuses. I imagined writing pieces that would trigger policy changes, reduce terrorism, and alter the role of women in society. I imagined polishing the staff of the *Yemen Observer* into a well-oiled machine that scarcely needed interference or line editing from me. Oppressed peoples all over the world would beg me to come and transform their own press! (It's difficult to write this now, years later, without dissolving into hysterical laughter at my naïveté.) I also imagined Zuhra, waiting for me to return.

☾

THE FIRST PERSON to tell was Bill, my editor at *The Week*. The entire morning of July 13, 2006, I was a nervous wreck, waiting to talk to him. I'd never worked anywhere for as long as I had worked at *The Week,* and I had never walked away from a job for as uncertain a future. I was giving up the highest salary I'd ever earned. I was kissing fantastic health insurance good-bye. I was turning my back on stability.

"So, what's on your mind, Nif?" said Bill, tipping back in his chair. He was the only one in the office who used that particular nickname, which was reserved for my closest friends.

I took a breath. "I've just accepted another job."

The front legs of his chair hit the ground with a bang. For once, I had thrown him. "What are you going to do? Run off and work at a newspaper in Yemen?" he joked.

"Actually . . . yes. I am going to be the editor of the *Yemen Observer*. I've been offered a year's contract."

His response could hardly have been more satisfying. "*Holy fucking shit,* are you *kidding* me? Are you out of your fucking mind? You're *crazy*! You'll die over there! I can't believe you are seriously doing this! Why?"

This was a much more exciting reaction than I had expected. I had never seen Bill lose his cool like this. He ranted for a while about my questionable sanity, but when I finally calmed him down and explained what I was doing, he seemed to understand. He told me that it had been a swell five years and that the magazine would miss me. "We'll hire someone to do your job," he said. "But we'll never replace you."

The rest of the staff of *The Week* and most of my friends were just as surprised, although they expressed this in a slightly less dramatic fashion.
Several people promptly sent me names of companies that provide kidnapping insurance. My parents, who know me fairly well, just said re-
signedly, "We thought something like this might happen." One friend, a
journalist for the *Wall Street Journal*, forwarded me a cautionary note from
a woman who worked for the Foreign Service.

> Yemen's not too bad (beautiful country), as long as one stays in Sanaa. I wouldn't rec-
> ommend traveling outside of town, as people will take pot shots at you (generally just
> small arms fire) in some parts of the country. Also, Yemenis tend to kidnap foreigners
> for ransom—the most recent was only a few months ago, so one has to be incredibly
> vigilant. Lots of unsavory characters have been known to move through there on their
> way to other places.
>
> On the other hand, it is gorgeous, and it has the largest open air arms market in the
> world, which is pretty cool. And the history is absolutely amazing . . . [But] why
> Yemen? There are lots of English language newspapers in the world that need editors.

While this was less than encouraging, around this time I found the following article on the website of the Yemen Observer, which I had failed to
notice before.

Professional Journalist Raises Yemen Observer's Standards
By Zuhra al-Ammari

Jul. 4, 2006

The American journalist who has been teaching at the Yemen Observe, Jennifer Steil,
was presented with Jambia, necklace and various gifts at a farewell dinner on Sunday
night in Al-Shaibani restaurant.

"We are paying farewell to a friend and to a teacher," said Faris Sanabani, the publisher of the *Yemen Observer* as he presented Ms. Steil with the jambia. He thanked
her for making a change in the newspaper in term of technical writing, and ap-
pearence," he said.

Jennifer, "This is my first time in Yemen and the Middle, it has just been remarkable, you are the most open-hearted and friendly people ever, I love you guys and I

hope to come back and can be with you again. Thank for you again" Everyone feel satisfied to the noticeable progress in their performance.

However, they feel sad too to say "farewell" to her and hope that she comes back.
Adel, a journalist, said "I like this teacher for her spirit of volunteerism; she has been a
patient teacher. I benefited a lot from her experience. I learned how to better my writing. She is really a queen." Hassan, a journalist, said "Really, she is a smart journalist.
It is enough for me to listen to her experience in field of journalism. She taught us modern principles of editing news and how one could do his or her news professionally."

Arwa, a journalist, said "It was the first training course for me in English. I benefited
by learning how to write. She is one of the best journalists I have seen. I make sure to
attend all her classes. I benefited tremendously." Radia, a secretary, said "She is a perfect woman. She is like the candle, she burns to give light to the others. I benefited a
lot from her" Jennifer Steil has come from U.S.A to teach the Yemen Observer's journalists some of the press skills.

She was observing the progress of every journalist. She gave them the advices for
which they upgrade heir profession.

The funny thing is, Zuhra was not allowed to attend my farewell dinner. Yet she managed to somehow get an accurate account of the evening
and even a fairly accurate quote from me. Did she hire a stringer to take
notes for her? Naturally, I would have been even happier if the story were
grammatical, but that was one reason for going back, after all.

Knowing I was about to leave, I fell in love with my city all over again.
I fell in love with my book-crammed apartment, with my belly-dancing
neighbor downstairs, with my local pub, the Piper's Kilt. I fell in love with
the A train, the Harlem YMCA, Inwood Hill Park. I fell in love with each
of my friends and went out almost every night that wasn't spent packing
to soak them all up. I went to art galleries and the theater. I went to one
last ecstatic baseball game at Yankee Stadium, where I euphorically inhaled
beer, popcorn, Cracker Jacks, peanuts, and everything else they had for
sale, because I didn't know when I could do it again. The Yankees gra-
ciously made the night perfect by winning.

The last Sunday I was in town, my friends in the neighborhood gathered at the Piper's Kilt, which was holding its first karaoke night. My friend Tommy was bartending and shook his head at me. *"Yemen,"* he said, setting a gin in front of me and moving down the bar. "The next time I see you will be in a kidnap video."

I wore a tiny red dress and red lipstick. Who knew when I could dress like that again? What I remember most from that night (other than standing on the bar barefoot singing "Leaving on a Jet Plane") is that when I told Tommy I was heading home, he told me to wait a moment and came out from behind the bar. Tommy had *never* come out from behind the bar to say good-bye to me before any of my other trips abroad. He hugged me and kissed me on the cheek. "My god," I said, looking at his mournful face as I stepped out of his arms. "You really don't think I'm coming back, do you?"

My last morning, I went for a run through Inwood Hill and Fort Tryon parks in a torrential rainstorm. After five minutes, my shorts and shirt were plastered to my body, and my braids had glued themselves to my arms. I plunged on. A montage of memories of the countless mornings I've spent trotting past these lilies, these dripping trees, this gray river, accosted me. Jennifer Steil, I thought, this is your life. This *was* your life.

SIX

when, exactly, is insha'allah?

*I arrive at the offices of the **Yemen Observer** on September 2, 2006, to find* no one waiting for me. Faris is away, I presume with the president, who is madly campaigning for reelection despite the fact that there is little doubt of his victory; editor Mohammed al-Asaadi has vanished from his corner office; and the rest of the staff is nowhere in evidence. My heart sinks. Surely they haven't forgotten me? I don't have a phone yet, so I have not been able to call anyone to tell them I have arrived.

My footsteps echo on the marble floors as I walk through the empty office. I am amazed to find the entire building festooned with my quotes. It's a bit unnerving to see my own words, *framed,* in both English and Arabic adorning every wall.

"This is a NEWSpaper, not an OLDSpaper! Let's put some news in it!"

"When you think your story is perfect, read it again."

"Never, ever begin a story with an attribution."

"A lead must contain a subject, verb, and object!"

I feel a bit like Chairman Mao. At least I know I haven't been totally forgotten.

I'd overslept my alarm this morning at Sabri's house, where I was temporarily housed in student quarters, and woke in a panic. I couldn't be late on my first day as the boss! I skipped coffee, skipped my planned walk to work, and dashed through a quick shower and into a cab, breathless. To find that I apparently have not been missed.

But wait! There are noises in a back office. The door opens, and a tiny pillar of black rayon launches herself across the front foyer and into my arms. "I cannot believe I have you before me!" Zuhra says, stepping back to look at me, keeping hold of my hands. Her dark eyes sparkle. "I have waited so long for this day. I love you so much! And now, we are for the first time going to have a woman in charge. I am so very happy!"

"I am so happy too!" I say, though perhaps with less confidence. "Where is everybody?"

She tells me that Faris is indeed with the president, that al-Asaadi rarely appears this early, and that Farouq is out because his one-and-a-half-year-old daughter has just died of a mysterious illness. He hasn't been able to work, she says. He is overwhelmed with grief. I cannot imagine. I have no idea how anyone recovers from the death of a child. "And Arwa has quit," Zuhra goes on. "She went to find a different job. And Zaid of course just left for London. Hassan and Adel are both working for the EU observers until the election is over." Theo, who is still in Yemen, has left the paper, apparently burning some bridges behind him. I fell out with him myself after he sent me a series of bizarrely discouraging e-mails about my return. I think he rather resented the invasion of what he saw as his turf.

"Do we have anyone left?" I am beginning to panic. How can I transform a paper with no staff?

"Radia is here! And we have some new ones," she says. "Come, meet them."

Radia, who is officially Faris's receptionist and not a reporter, emerges from the back room, where the women have been breakfasting, to tell me how much she missed me and how pleased she is that I am back.

They take me to the newsroom, where we find two women and two men hunched over computers. Zuhra tugs me over by the hand.

"This is Noor. She is doing the culture page." Noor has thick, long eyelashes and eyes that crinkle when she smiles. Like Zuhra, she wears glasses, but unlike Zuhra, she ties her *hijab* in the back of her head. I make a mental note of this so I can identify her later.

Najma, Zuhra tells me, has been writing the health page. Najma shyly takes my hand and tells me how glad she is to meet me. Her eyes are wider and more frightened than Noor's.

The men, a tall, bespectacled man named Talha and a stouter, boyishly attractive man named Bashir, are equally polite and welcoming.

"How long have you been here?" I ask them. They hadn't been hired when I left Yemen two months ago.

"A month or so."

All four of the new hires are recent graduates of university. None has any journalism experience. I am dismayed. So many of the people I had already begun to train are gone. I will have to start all over again.

(*

ZUHRA SHOWS ME to al-Asaadi's office in the back of the first floor, where I sit and take notes on recent issues of the paper until al-Asaadi arrives, close to noon. I've forgotten how tiny he is; just a bit taller than my shoulders (and I am only 5'6"). He's handsome, with doll-like features and Bambi eyelashes. I would guess he weighs something approaching ninety pounds. He wears a suit jacket and slacks.

"*Ahlan wa sahlan!*" (Welcome!) he says, taking my hand and smiling warmly.

"*Ahlan wa sahlan!* I am sorry for invading your office. I wasn't sure where to go."

"My office is your office."

Theo had warned me, when I was last in Yemen, that al-Asaadi would prove my biggest challenge. He won't want to give up control, he said. He is used to being in charge.

So I am cautious. I don't want to wound his pride and jeopardize our relationship by throwing my weight around and acting like an Ugly, Imperialist American. I tell him how much I look forward to learning from him and how much I hope we can work as partners.

"It is I who will learn from you," he says. "Faris feels—and I feel the same way—that you are to be the captain of this paper. You are to run the entire show."

My knees begin to tremble. "*Shukrahn*," I say. "But perhaps you could help me begin? Can you walk me through how things work now, what your deadlines are?" I have no idea where to start.

"Of course."

He and I sit down with Zuhra in the front conference room to come up with a tentative game plan. Al-Asaadi explains all of the deadlines (which he concedes are generally missed), and Zuhra gives me a printed sheet detailing which reporters write which pages. I tell them I would like to hold editorial meetings at the beginning of each publishing cycle, one at nine A.M. on Sunday, and one at nine A.M. on Wednesday, so that each reporter can tell me what stories they are reporting, who their sources are, and when they will be handing them in. My goal is to somehow streamline the copy flow so that all the pages aren't coming in to edit at the last minute. This will clearly take a miracle.

After our meeting, Zuhra walks me to the grocery store (I forgot that the bathrooms at the *Observer* never have toilet paper; Yemenis use water hoses to clean themselves, which means the bathroom floors are nearly always flooded with what my copy editor Luke often refers to as "poop juice") and then to the Jordanian sandwich shop for one of the rolled-up spicy vegetable sandwiches I love so. I haven't eaten anything all day, although Zuhra has fetched me several cups of sticky-sweet black tea. "You are the only one I would make tea for," she says. "No one else." Like me, Zuhra does not cook. Tea is one of the few things she knows how to make.

After lunch, she hands me a story by Talha. No other copy has yet been filed for the next issue. I spend nearly an hour going through his story, making edits. It has no coherent structure, no clear first sentence, and a dearth of sources. I sigh. I will have to teach him everything.

A second desk has been moved into al-Asaadi's office for me, although I can't use the drawers yet as they are locked. It's a plain office, white walls, gray carpet, with no decoration save for a map of Jerusalem on the wall near the door. Light floods in from the windows along two walls of the office. Outside, stray cats yowl in the yard.

I seem to have gone numb. All the panic and fear and grief of those last few days in New York have fallen away, but nothing has moved in to take their place. I probably should be feeling stark terror about the challenges of this job, but for some reason I feel bizarrely level.

(☪

LATER THAT AFTERNOON, after a swim, I am happy to find Qasim, whose irrepressible high spirits I'd enjoyed in June. He was the rascal always stealing people's shoes and hiding them in the wastebaskets, the one making prank phone calls, the one most likely to be caught singing in the office. But he is in charge of advertising, not a reporter, and thus not really part of my staff.

I also find my copy editor Luke, the blond Californian surfer dude. I've no idea if he actually surfs, but he looks like he should. He's not entirely sure what he's doing in Yemen, he tells me. He and a friend are thinking about launching some sort of business. "Yemen is a great place to be because they have nothing," he says. "Everything is new to them. You can do anything. And it's easy to rise to the top here."

Still, he complains that Yemen is destroying his health. He hasn't exercised since he got here, and he smokes way too much.

"And drinking? Do you drink?"

"Not anymore!"

"Guess you picked the right country."

"Actually, I didn't come here to get away from alcohol," he says. "I came here to get closer to the *qat*."

I find Talha in the newsroom and pull him aside to go over his story on the hazards of buying prescription drugs in Yemen. Drugs sold in Yemen are often either contaminated with toxic substances or completely ineffective sugar pills. Talha is quiet, serious, and eager to hear my suggestions. I explain to him all about leads, and story structure, and why we *never* begin a sentence with an attribution!

Mohammed al-Asaadi gives me the last ten issues of the paper to read after work before handing me off to Salem, who drives me and Radia home after nine P.M. They insist I ride up front, while Radia perches on a stack of *Yemen Observer*s in the back of the van. I offer her my seat, but she refuses.

As we near Radia's house, she leans forward and touches my arm. "Come with me," she says. "Come to my home." I look at her. Does she mean now?

"Come to my house," she says again. "Come sleep with me?"

This is not quite as provocative an invitation as it would be in New York. I learned on my previous trip that girls often invite new friends to sleep at their homes. Still, it catches me off guard.

"Why, I would love to!" I say. "But not tonight. I have things I need to get from home. Books and things. Presents to take to the office tomorrow."

She nods. But when she gets out she asks again. "But you will come, another time?"

"I will."

Salem teaches me several new Arabic words on the way home. I am famished by the time I arrive, close to ten P.M., and polish off a yogurt and a peanut butter and raisin sandwich. Did I mention I don't cook? I read a few issues of the *Observer,* try not to despair, and slip into sleep.

☪

IT IS A HUGE RELIEF finally to begin working. The anticipation and anxiety that have been building up since I accepted this job were harder to bear than the work itself. I don't do well with leisure time or stillness. I had arrived in Sana'a just a day and a half before my first day of work, and that was more than enough downtime. I'm not type A, I'm type A-plus.

On my second day of work, I arrive hours before my staff. (I have a staff! Okay, I am a little excited.) Only Qasim is there, so I give him one of the Jacques Torres chocolate bars I brought as gifts (it is impossible to find good chocolate in Yemen) and three Hershey bars for his three kids (who aren't yet picky about chocolate). When Radia and Zuhra arrive, I give them embroidered silk Chinese purses, stuffed with soap and chocolate and hand-woven change purses. Accessories are important in Yemen, where the basic outfit doesn't alter much from day to day. Radia is shyly pleased, while Zuhra announces her gift to everyone in sight.

I hold my first staff meeting that morning. Everyone tells me which stories they are writing and when they will get them to me. It is difficult to pin down exact deadlines, because when I ask, for example, if Bashir can get me a story by one P.M., the answer is *"Insha'allah." If God is willing.* Never, in my entire year, would I be able to get a reporter to say to me,

"Yes, I will finish the story by one P.M." In Yemen, nothing happens unless Allah wills it. And as it turns out, Allah is no great respecter of newspaper deadlines.

"Insha'allah" is also murmured reflexively after almost anything stated in the future tense. It makes Yemenis nervous when you leave it out. If I were to say to a Yemeni man, for example, "I am traveling to France next week but will return to Yemen Thursday," he would automatically add *"insha'allah."*

Ibrahim, who writes front-page stories for each issue from his home office, joins us, expressing great joy over my arrival. He invites me to a *qat* chew, which surprises me because I didn't know that women could go to *qat* chews with men. But apparently Western women are treated as a third sex in Yemen and thus can wander back and forth from male to female worlds. Western men, on the other hand, do not have this advantage.

This explains why my male staff members offer me immediate deference. To them I am not really a woman; I am a giraffe. Something alien and thus unclassifiable in the familiar male/female cubbyholes. Were a Yemeni woman to take over the paper, most of the men would quit in protest. They do not treat their female colleagues with anything like the respect with which they treat me, and they'd rather die on the spot than ask a Yemeni woman for help or advice on a story. But oddly, they rarely mind deferring to me.

Al-Asaadi is the exception. It doesn't take long for me to figure out that he *does* mind deferring to me, though he makes an initial effort to disguise his resentment. He is always smiling and polite, but he never shows up at the office on time in the mornings, when all of the other reporters arrive. He often ignores my deadlines, filing his stories when he feels like filing them. These things tell me that I may be filling his shoes, but he is still his own boss. Thankfully, though, he does show up to the editorial meeting on my second day and is helpful in suggesting which reporters should work on which articles.

After I send everyone off to pursue their stories, I spend the bulk of the morning editing a health story Najma has written about the psychological impact of eating various foods. There isn't a single source in the entire piece. When I go to the newsroom to ask her to come talk with me about the story, her eyes widen in terror.

"This won't be painful!" I say, trying not to laugh. "I am just going to help you."

Zuhra rushes over to reassure her. "Do not be afraid," she says as I lead Najma toward the conference room. "There is no one more supportive."

I explain to the trembling Najma that we need to know where the information in her story comes from, so that our readers can judge its legitimacy. If we are to contend that Brazil nuts can elevate a person's mood, then we need to be able to quote a specific study from a university or a hospital that proves such a thing.

This is all new to her. It seems she had thought that the mere fact that the words would appear in newsprint would give them authority. This was a common mind-set. One of the greatest challenges I would have working with Yemeni journalists is that they are too trusting, too willing to believe whatever they are told. In a deeply religious society such as this one, children are raised to take everything on faith, unquestioningly. The flip side is that they often do not feel they have to prove their contentions. I have to undo years of conditioning.

I spend the rest of the day editing other health stories and election briefs, and fretting about the dearth of stories we have for the front page. Farouq is still out, and he's our main political reporter. There is no one to replace him. The new guys have none of his political contacts and no idea whom to call for story ideas or quotes, and the women are busy with culture and health.

Only late that evening, after running out through a rainstorm to cover a batik exhibit at the nearby German House, do I finally find Faris for the first time. I am happy, as I have a long list of requests for him, including reimbursement for my plane fare. I give him the dental floss he had requested from the States, and he is happy too. He gives me a warm little speech about how he now considers me family and that if I need anything at all, money or anything else, I am to come to him. He has VIP passes for me to cover election events, as well as hotel rooms, he says, which I hope means I will be traveling to cover the polls. (None of which comes to pass.) He also has a phone for me, but it is still charging, and no one is sure of the number, so I will get it from the office tomorrow. *Insha'allah.*

☾

I GO BACK TO WORK after this meeting to edit an unreadable story of Hassan's. Despite the fact that Hassan was in my original class, every single paragraph of his story begins with an attribution. I call him on Luke's phone to tell him that this is no longer acceptable. "Before you hand in anything else, please make sure you are not starting all of your sentences with 'according to' or 'he said.'" Hassan, being the sweet and deferential man he is, thanks me enormously and says he hopes we can talk more about this problem of his.

My day began at eight A.M., and I don't leave the office until nearly eleven P.M. that night. Salem drives me home, where I finish editing a few more stories in my small suite in Sabri's dormitory over some carrots and hummus, the first real meal I've had all day. I've stumbled upon a foolproof diet plan: Take over a newspaper in a poor, semiliterate Islamic country, and watch the pounds just fall away.

☾

THE NEXT DAY, my third day at work, we close my first issue. It takes nineteen hours. Yet I am not unhappy, even with the overwhelming amount of work to do. The thing about being at the top of the masthead is there is never any question of leaving early or leaving anything undone. I find something very comforting about succumbing to this total commitment; it eliminates all other choices. I'm going to make this a better paper or die trying. I have nothing else to distract me. I am free of an intimate relationship, having just ended a turbulent on-again, off-again romance in New York; I haven't time to socialize outside of work; and I have no other deadlines. I can give the paper everything. I will have to.

I wake at six A.M. and walk to work. Men stare at me as I pass—it's unusual to see a woman walking alone, particularly one with blue eyes and uncovered hair—but their comments are mostly benign. Everywhere I go, I am showered with "Welcome to Yemen!"s and "I love you!"s. I stopped covering my hair after I realized it made no difference in the amount of attention I attracted and because Yemenis kept asking me, "Why do you cover your hair? You're a westerner!" The morning is deliciously cool and crisp. Sana'anis are not early risers, so the streets don't get busy until close to eleven A.M.

When the women get in, I consult with Zuhra, who is fast becoming my right-hand woman, and send Najma and Noor to cover a Japanese flower-arranging demonstration. Hardly real news, but it's a nice easy way to break them in and get them used to reporting outside of the office. I have to send them together, so that neither has to travel alone in a car with a man. It can damage a woman's reputation to be seen alone in a taxi with a male driver. There is no *Yemen Observer* driver available, so I have to wheedle the taxi fare out of the Doctor, who vigorously resists all attempts to draw down his allotment of *riyals*.

The Doctor. Everyone lives in terror of this tall, bespectacled man, who is not actually a doctor but the person in charge of administration and finance. He doles out salaries, takes attendance each morning, and serves as Faris's iron fist of enforcement. The Doctor never speaks; he shouts. He shouts at Enass the secretary, he shouts at my reporters, and, inevitably, he shouts at me. Shouting in the newsroom does not always suggest displeasure, however. Many of the men shout as a matter of course. Often I run out of my office thinking I am overhearing a fierce argument, when really the men are saying to each other: "FANTASTIC NEW CAR YOU HAVE! WHERE DID YOU GET IT? HEY, DO YOU WANT SOME OF THIS *QAT*? IT'S DELICIOUS." But when the Doctor shouts, it generally means trouble.

So far he is trying to be nice to me, so I get the taxi money for the women. I have to talk to Faris about providing transportation for our reporters; they do not have enough money to pay for these things themselves. I am amazed that Faris fails to provide his staff with so many essentials. My reporters are not given business cards, telephones, or press IDs and are even required to buy their own notebooks and pens. But they cannot afford these things on their salaries of $100 to $200 per month. No wonder they make a notebook last for weeks. I buy a stack of notebooks for them. I would buy them phones too, but my salary does not stretch that far.

I spend the morning editing the Panorama page, a collection of editorials from other Yemeni papers, and Najma's article about a course that trains women to manage money. It's an interesting story, but she hasn't talked with any of the women at the workshop, other than the instructor. "You should have talked with a minimum of fifteen women who participated in the workshop," I say. "Their personal stories are what would really make this interesting." Too late for this issue. (I have to let a *lot* of things slide in this first issue.) But Najma seems to understand. So. It's a start.

I write and edit all day, with no break, save for the twenty minutes I spend walking to the Jordanian sandwich shop with Zuhra. "You need to take a breath," she says. Back at the office, Zuhra helps me figure out which pages are missing stories. Farouq still hasn't turned up, so we have nothing for the front or local pages. I try not to panic. I ring Ibrahim at his home office to ask him about the election page, and he sends over two stories, promising a third by noon. Al-Asaadi promises at least one front-page story. Clearly we need more staff.

Luke swings around my doorjamb toward lunch, flushed with excitement. "Did you hear?" he says. "The crocodile hunter died."

"No! Steve Irwin?"

"Yes."

"What killed him, a crocodile?"

"Stingray. Right through the heart."

"Jesus."

"So—front page?"

"Perfect. We have nothing else."

"It's definitely of global significance."

Luke pops into my office often, to chat or to trade stories. A half hour later, he walks in holding an enormous jar of amber liquid. "I just accidentally bought thirty dollars' worth of honey," he says.

"Accidentally?"

"Well, I was with al-Asaadi, and there was this guy he usually gets honey from, so I ordered some too, but I didn't realize it would be this big! Or that it would cost thirty dollars." He looks forlornly at the enormous jar in his hand. "I have enough honey to last me a year."

"Well," I say, "I guess you'd better learn to bake."

"You don't bake with Yemeni honey! It's too special for that."

"It can't be *really* good Yemeni honey," says Zuhra, who has just walked in. "If it were *really* good honey, it would have cost you eighty dollars. At least."

Later in the afternoon, al-Asaadi pops his head into our office. "How about we don't have a front page this issue? What do you think?"

I shrug. "I can live without it."

But the banter hides a growing panic. The later it gets, the more we shuffle stories from page to page. We don't have enough local stories, so I suggest we move a story on the back page to the local page and that I quickly write the story on the batik exhibit to replace the back page. It is infinitely easier to churn out a story myself than to rewrite one of theirs. I feel some guilt over this, but not much. It's just one story.

☾

ZUHRA LEAVES WORK around three P.M., as she and the other girls must be home before dark. She is distressed to leave me on my own, worried I will never survive without her.

"I'll be fine," I say with a complete lack of conviction. "We just might not have a front page."

She looks at me with concern.

"Do you maybe need to swim?" she says.

I laugh. "Not today," I say, gesturing toward the stack of pages waiting to be edited. "Tomorrow."

☾

AL-ASAADI RETURNS from a long lunch around four P.M. and throws a handful of *qat* next to my computer. "This will help," he says. My energy flagging, I follow his lead. The *qat* tastes extra bitter, and the shiny leaves are hard to chew. But I imagine that al-Asaadi knows where to buy the best *qat,* so I assume it is a good vintage. It must be, given how much I immediately perk up. With newfound vigor, I whip out a 955-word story on the batik exhibit in less than an hour. No wonder everyone loves this drug.

I file the story and run upstairs to choose photos with Mas, the paper's precocious nineteen-year-old photographer. When I return, a pile of new things to edit is waiting on my desk. Ibrahim's election stories are thin; everything I edit ends up half its original length. My reporters repeat themselves ad nauseam.

Around ten P.M., when I finally start to crash from the *qat,* dinner arrives. We all eat outside in the courtyard, standing around a table piled with *roti* (Yemeni baguettes) and plates of *fasooleah* (beans), eggs, *ful,* cheese, and tea. We fall upon the food like a pack of wolves. I am the last to leave the table, reluctantly, with a fistful of bread.

My energy is back. Good thing, too, given how much is still left to do. The flash-drive-passing between me and Luke accelerates. I edit the stories, then he edits them, then I see them again on the page, and then he sees them one last time. I don't take a step out of the building from the time I get there—eight thirty A.M.—until the time I leave, in the early hours of the following morning. Yet I am so busy that the day feels short. So many times in those first few weeks, when my reporters come to me with a question, I instinctively think I should run it by someone else. Someone in charge. But slowly, it begins to sink in that the only person responsible for these decisions is me.

☪

MIRACULOUSLY, BY THREE A.M. we have a front page. And a Local page. And an Election page, a Health page, a Reports page, and Panorama and Middle East and Op-Ed. In fact, we have an entire newspaper! We all high-ten each other and say, *"Mabrouk!"* (Congratulations!). I am briefly euphoric before a terrifying thought occurs to me: We have to do it all over again. Starting in about six hours.

SEVEN

my yemeni shadow

Zuhra has adopted me. Never mind that she is twenty-three and I am techni-
cally old enough to be her mother. When she isn't out running after a
story, Zuhra is chronically at my elbow, asking me what I need. A back-
page story? The telephone number of the foreign minister? Lunch? She'll
help me get it. When I head to the small grocery store at the end of our
block in search of matches, milk, and peanuts, she won't let me go until
she has written me a shopping list in Arabic—even though I have become
quite capable of asking for what I want in Arabic.

"Zuhra, I already have a mother!" I protest. "Really, I can manage."

"Motherhood is a feeling," she says. "It is not an age."

When other people try to take me tea or walk me to the sandwich
shop, she bristles. "You are *my* Jennifer," she says. "I want to be the one to
take care of you."

All of my women must be home well before dark, and so their work
day ends earlier than the men's, at one P.M. But this stretches later and
later throughout the year, until the women only rarely leave before three
P.M. and sometimes stay until five P.M. It makes Zuhra anxious that she has
to leave me alone at night, especially when I am closing an issue. She
wants to be there to help me. When I arrive at work the day after my first
endless close, Zuhra is waiting. "I can stay with you until three P.M.!" she

announces with as much excitement as someone who has just been awarded the Nobel Peace Prize.

It is a long time before I truly understand how much it means to Zuhra to be in the office of the *Yemen Observer* at all, a long time before I understand her improbable journey to me.

The other reporters tease her for her possessiveness and call her Jennifer's Shadow. She is certainly dressed for the role. Her sisters, she tells me later, also tease her about her newfound passion for work. "When are you and Jennifer getting married?" they ask. It takes Zuhra months to tell me this, because she is afraid I will think they are implying I am a lesbian and that I will be offended.

She is just as energetic about chasing stories as she is about following me around. While Noor and Najma are timid about leaving the office and cling to each other for support, Zuhra often waltzes off on her own. She takes the *dabaabs* (small buses) around town, walks, or cajoles a friend into giving her a ride. When I am at a loss for a back-page story, Zuhra always finds one. Rummaging around in the back alleys of Old Sana'a, she comes up with, say, a story on the demise of Yemeni lanterns called *fanous,* which are being replaced by electric lights. Zuhra's story-shopping in the *souqs* of Old Sana'a also results in pieces on jewelry and fashion fads, the persistence of the illegal trade in rhinoceros-horn *jambiyas,* and the increasing popularity of Indian goods over Yemeni products.

She is even better at finding front-page stories. I like to have a minimum of five on every front page, and this always involves a lot of last-minute scrambling. When I need hard news, Zuhra heads to the courts. Or to the streets. Or to anywhere she can find a bit of news to bring triumphantly back to me.

☪

I FIND OUT Zuhra's personal story gradually. Not until late fall, when she and I are curled up in my *mafraj* looking over her essays for an application to graduate school, do I finally piece together the general outline of her life. This is a different Zuhra than the little black shadow who trails me around the office. In an aqua jogging suit with her hair in a ponytail, she looks like any Western girl kicking back at home on a weekend afternoon.

I try not to stare. Though I've seen her a few times without the *abaya* and veil, I'm still not used to seeing the contours of her body, the strands of hair falling across her dark eyes.

We sit side by side on my red and gold cushions as the late afternoon sun streams through my jeweled windows, sending bits of colored light cavorting around the room. My laptop is propped in front of us, and slowly we read through her application. In her personal essay, she describes her long battle with her family to seek education and eventually a career. Her written English still confuses me, so we go through each line together as she explains how she came to work at the *Observer*.

"My father died when I was ten." This is the centerpiece of her story. It is the root of all of her pain, the beginning of her struggle, and the explanation for her loneliness. "I get depressed because I have an unbalanced life," she says. "I have no men in my life."

Her father, Sultan, lost his own father when he was twelve and took off alone for the southern port city of Aden, then part of South Yemen. He was a socialist, a revolutionary against the British, and a supporter of unification. In Aden, Zuhra told me, he arranged many secret meetings. Yet the details of this part of his life remain a mystery to her. After marrying and divorcing his cousin, Sultan met Zuhra's mother, Sadira, a young teenager known for her beauty, who hailed from his home village of Ammar in Ibb Governorate. They married. But she became increasingly worried about her husband's political activities and the safety of her family. After the first three children were born, the family moved north to Sana'a and Sultan took a job with the government water corporation.

Zuhra is the fifth of eight children, two of whom are dead. One was miscarried, and the other died in her first few years of life. The surviving six are tight. Zuhra worships her oldest brother, Fahmi, thirty-five, who lives in Brooklyn, and her sisters are her dearest friends. Their early life, Zuhra says, was idyllic. "My father treated us equally, girls and boys. He insisted that the younger respect the older, not that the girls have to respect the boys. Maybe for that we have some kind of problems in our life, because this was the way our father raised us. This is why we have trouble with the restrictions of society. He hates us to wear a veil."

Because Sultan never had the chance to finish his own schooling, it was deeply important to him that his children receive an education. "He was desperate to make all of us study," said Zuhra. "He wanted Fahmi to be a doctor. He was amazing. He really fight for us. To be educated. He was a very modern man."

Nearly all of Zuhra's siblings have a university education, except for Ghazal, who is still at school, and Shetha, who married young. But it was a condition of Shetha's marriage that she be allowed to finish her studies. Sultan refused many suitors who came calling for his daughters' hands. "He yelled at the suitors and said, 'Are you crazy? They are too young! They must finish school!'" said Zuhra. "He was so protective, but not authoritarian."

Everything fell apart when Sultan died from a heart attack while visiting his home village.

"He went to attend a funeral of my young cousin. Then he died there, alone," said Zuhra. "He went there alone, and for lack of treatment—his brothers never got him to the hospital—he died. They lied and said our aunt died and that we had to come to the village. Then when we got there, all of us knew it was our father who died. He died without anyone next to him, even his brothers. It was really horrible."

"My mom, for twenty days she didn't speak. She cried day and night. She did not sleep. We were all afraid that she will die. She knew that. She held on because she felt that the uncles might try to take the children, so she became strong. She and Fahmi."

When Yemeni women and girls have no father or husband, their lives are handed over to their uncles or brothers. Women cannot be trusted with the reins of their own lives. This Yemeni emphasis on controlling and defending women is a result of the importance of *sharaf* (honor) in society. Nothing is more important to a Yemeni tribesman than his honor. Honor is communal as well as individual; when one man is shamed, his whole tribe is shamed. An assault on honor is called *ayb*, meaning shame or disgrace. Honor is a vulnerable thing; a man's honor depends heavily on his wives and daughters. When a daughter misbehaves, particularly if that misbehavior is sexual, she damages her father's honor. It is wise, therefore, for men to keep a close eye on their women.

So without Sultan, and without her oldest brother, Fahmi, who had found work in the United States, Zuhra's fate was left to her uncles. When she reached seventeen, she told them she wanted to go to medical school. Impossible, they told her flatly. They convinced her second-oldest brother, Aziz, to forbid Zuhra to attend. Zuhra's theory is that her uncles were jealous of how clever she was and how well she performed in school, because their sons did not do as well. Even Zuhra's mother, Sadira, who had supported her daughter's education, acquiesced.

Not only did the uncles refuse to allow Zuhra to go to medical school, they would not let her attend any kind of university. "They claimed that an educated woman would not find a husband and would become rebellious. This is the fear of most Yemeni men," she says. "They say college will corrupt girls and they will not get married."

So she studied on the sly, hiding her schoolbooks in magazines so her family would not see that she was reading medical books. On the day of the exam, she veiled herself and sneaked out. Her heart pounding with the fear of discovery, she finished the exam. "I remember that while taking the exam, looking at my watch, I felt like Cinderella, afraid of being revealed." A few days later, she found that she was one of twenty-nine people admitted to medical school.

Her family was furious. Immediately, her brothers and paternal uncles forbade her to go. Zuhra was so desperate that she contemplated sneaking out to attend classes. But she knew that she would eventually be caught, and her motives for her clandestine outings could easily have been misconstrued.

Thus began her darkest days. She was so angry with her family she decided to stop speaking. "I was locked up at home for an entire year. I waged a silent battle against them and refused to talk to them. I became ill and was close to death, making many more people support me. These people knew that if my father were alive, he would support me.

"During this period of my life, I have realized lots of things and built lots of things. And lost lots of things. One of the things I built is that I know how to be strong. And that sometimes in your life you will be alone and nobody next to you," she said. "And then I felt how horrible my father's death was, because if he were alive this wouldn't happen. So I learned how to be strong and not emotionally dependent on anybody in this world."

One of the things Zuhra lost during this time was belief and confidence in herself. To this day, insecurity plagues her.

"I feel I am a second-class human, that I am not important. Because no one cared about my priorities, which really hurts," she told me. "I know it's not my fault that I can't study, but I start to blame myself."

Soon, Zuhra had stopped doing any of her normal activities. She wasn't allowed to go to work. She began to believe that she was a horrible person.

"It was almost a prison. When you are an active person and smart and have many things in life waiting for you, but then you are stopped like a machine . . .

"I still remember one day, I was taking some garbage outside the home. I saw my friends that day, they were going to their college, and then I felt it is the worst feeling ever when you really feel pathetic to yourself. I felt how horrible it was—I knew I was smarter than all of them, and there I was throwing garbage."

She became embarrassed to appear in society, worried that she would be thought pathetic and helpless. Because of this, she even lied sometimes and said that she didn't want to go to college, just so no one would think she was controlled by other people.

At her nadir, discouraged and friendless, she became religious, but in a different way than she had been before.

"I established a new relationship with my God. I was praying alone. I started to feel like there was someone next to me, and that is what makes me strong. I started to feel I am not alone. Felt there was someone in this world loves me. I felt how important it was to have faith. One day, the room was dark and I was so hurt, it was close to my trauma, I started to pray and I felt something was going to happen. I remember that at the beginning I prayed all the people that hurt me to go to hell. Then I realized that I don't want this. I forgave all these people. I said this to God. All I want is to finish my education; the rest doesn't matter to me. I realized it wasn't my real battle, to pray against these people. Then, when I started to do that I felt that I am stronger."

One day, having noticed Zuhra's decline, one of her maternal uncles persuaded her other uncles to work together to convince Aziz to let Zuhra go to school. One of these uncles had consulted a religious scholar who had said that it was forbidden to stop her from an education if she wanted one.

At first, Aziz refused. He didn't want to admit he was wrong. By that time, Zuhra's health was in danger. She had lost weight, was often faint, and had developed eye problems and allergies. Her family was afraid for her.

Fear at last prompted Aziz to relent. "He said that it seemed like I was going to die, and he didn't want anything to happen to me."

Zuhra still wanted to study medicine, but her brother said that was out of the question. If she insisted on going to college, she would go to the College of Education, which was a more suitable place for girls.

Hardly daring to believe she had been reprieved, Zuhra began classes, majoring in English. But still she struggled, feeling that she was being forced to study at a place she did not freely choose. The only thing she chose was English. "I chose this field because I knew that the English language would empower me," she says "Most of my diaries are in English, because I can speak freely. And through English I was exposed to another culture that I was curious to know."

Her college years were difficult socially. Many of her peers were more conservative than she was, with rigid ideas about how to dress, how to study, and how to express an opinion. But Zuhra refused to be cowed. She spoke often in class and was not afraid to debate the professor. She worked feverishly, constantly fearful that her brother would change his mind and pull her out of school.

Despite the fact that she was training to be a teacher, Zuhra had nightmares about joining the profession. "I remember after I graduated I was praying day and night not to be a teacher. But it was hard for me to look for another job."

When she was offered a teaching post at a school, she panicked and confessed her fears to her brother Fahmi. The school was run by religious zealots from the Islah (Reform) Party, she said. "They impose their opinions on others and I told Fahmi I hated that."

Her supportive older brother told her that it was okay to follow her heart. But she didn't know of an alternative to teaching. Her career choices were restricted by the fact that her family did not want her working with men.

Not knowing what to try, Zuhra put together the best résumé she could, adding a note at the bottom saying, "I know that I am not qualified, but I have what it takes to be successful." And she set out on a quest.

Clutching this piece of paper, Zuhra walked into the offices of the *Yemen Observer*. It was the first place she tried.

At reception, Enass took her résumé and said she would show it to al-Asaadi. "I waited. Al-Asaadi came in. You know him, he likes to show off. But I still remember that I was very confident and he was saying to me, what do you want to be? And I said I want to work as a journalist, if not, then as a translator."

Al-Asaadi told her that he would speak to Faris. Zuhra didn't hold out much hope. Not only was she inexperienced, but she was sure that her family would not allow her to be a journalist. "It was a huge fear. Exactly like when I go to my college. As important as that."

She was unaware of how much she had already impressed al-Asaadi, who saw her potential immediately. "Journalism isn't a job; it's a passion," he told me. "Zuhra had that passion. Even the first time I met her, I could tell how much she wanted to *work*." She was also unafraid to admit how much she didn't know, a rarity in the male reporters. Zuhra could kill you with questions—but they helped her to learn her job faster than anyone else.

When al-Asaadi told her she had the job but had to work evenings as well as mornings, her heart sank. She told him that she could not work nights. "He told me, you won't be a good journalist. And I thought he was right. I can't do work if I can't be available all the time."

But a week later two things happened. Al-Asaadi decided he could allow Zuhra to work only mornings, and Aziz realized how much it meant to Zuhra to have this job. "My brother said, 'I trust you like a blind person.'"

She began work. Her first hurdle was a fear of talking with men. Not because she was shy—not Zuhra!—but because she feared that the men would lose respect for her if they saw her speaking to other men. Never before had Zuhra mixed with men outside her family. "The nightmare of being a woman followed me when I started my career. Men do not say openly that we cannot do the job; they say it behind our backs and amongst themselves." I nod. I've seen the men do this.

"I felt like a cripple when I first started the job, since such weakness is expected of a Yemeni woman. Even more difficult was interviewing Yemeni men in such a conservative society. It was a hard time for me. I was fighting the many ideas of what constitutes a woman's role that were planted in me."

When Zuhra arrived at the *Observer,* she heard rumors about the women who worked there. "They are killing their reputation by working with men," people whispered. One girl in particular was derided for talking and laughing with men. "The men said she wasn't a good girl and she was having affairs outside of the job. That scares me," says Zuhra. She made herself strict rules to protect herself from gossip. She never laughed with men. She never gave out her phone number. She never got into cars with men. "I didn't want anyone to say anything bad about me," she says. "I lived in horror all the time."

Only slowly did her nervousness disappear. "When you came, I don't know what happens to me, but you take off some of this fear," she tells me. "I was asking you about objectivity. If you have belief in what you are doing it gives you more strength. Because I know what journalism can do and why it is there." She came to believe that it wasn't she who should feel ashamed—it was anyone who would give her a hard time for following a noble calling.

At the same time, Zuhra was grappling with the rudiments of journalism. "I had no real model. I didn't know what was good journalism," she tells me. "I got to know that when you come. Do you remember what I first told you? It was very eye-opening for me when you told me we had to be objective. When you said that, what made me believe was that you said [if you report objectively] then people will believe you."

Zuhra has an instinctive distrust of partisan media, because she loathes other people telling her what to feel or think or do. She would rather be presented with all of the facts in as balanced a way as possible and make up her own mind than read an editorial.

So when I began to define objective journalism for her, she was immediately attracted to the idea. "It seems the highest way of thinking," she said. "I met you, started thinking about going to the Columbia University Graduate School of Journalism, and my dreams started to have a face and legs."

EIGHT

kidnappings, stampedes, and suicide bombings

It is late on a Sunday afternoon when we hear about a kidnapping of French tourists in Shabwa Governorate. First we hear there are five hostages, then four. Then we hear that only two are French. Then we hear that three are French and one German. Such is the accuracy of reporting in Yemen.

We at least know who the kidnappers are: the al-Abdullah tribe. The kidnapping is a result of a long-running feud with the neighboring al-Riyad tribe. The al-Abdullah are the same tribe that kidnapped five Germans the previous December. Apparently, the government didn't keep the promises it made to get those Germans released, so tribesmen took a few French people to underscore their disappointment.

I'd heard a great deal about the kidnappings before I came to Yemen, as it was one of the few things westerners seemed to know about the place. "Aren't you worried you'll be kidnapped?" was one of the first things people asked me. That is, if they had heard of Yemen at all.

I wasn't worried that I would be kidnapped. Most kidnappings don't have anything to do with hostility toward foreigners. Tribesmen just see tourists as handy bargaining chips in their disputes with the government. Thus they sometimes capture a convoy or two to pressure the government to, say, build a school or improve the water system. (My parents, being parents, did worry I would get kidnapped. When I explained that my kidnappers would probably just want a mosque or a school in return for me, they fretted that they couldn't afford a whole building. "We could afford a stop sign," they said. "Tell them that.") Almost all of the approximately two hundred tourists kidnapped in Yemen in the past fifteen years have been treated kindly by their captors and released unharmed, though there are a few exceptions. In 1998, sixteen westerners were kidnapped by a group called the Aden-Abyan Islamic Army. Four were killed during a botched rescue attempt by the Yemeni government. Another tourist was killed in 2000, again as a result of a shootout between the government and the kidnappers. "If I ever get kidnapped," I say to al-Asaadi, "don't let the government try to rescue me."

Another reason I don't waste too much time worrying about kidnappings is that they very rarely happen to foreigners in Sana'a. Most attacks occur as tourists travel in conspicuous convoys through more remote parts of the country where there are active tribal conflicts.

Now that the al-Abdullah tribe has the government's attention, it is demanding that some of their incarcerated tribesmen be released in return for the French tourists. Al-Asaadi gives me ten stories he wrote about the kidnappings last year to get me up to speed. He also draws me a chart of the tribes and their various disputes, which started with the murder of some members of the al-Abdullah tribe years ago. My head reels.

Yemen is home to hundreds of tribes, which play an integral role in Yemeni politics and lives. Divisions among tribes are largely territorial. Before 1990, when Yemen was divided into North and South Yemen, both the British and the Communists in turn endeavored to weaken tribal allegiances in the South, in an effort to create a more cohesive society. But in the North, tribal ties remain strong.

President Saleh belongs to the Sanhan, a Hashid tribe from near Sana'a. The Hashid and Bakil tribal confederations are the most powerful in the country. But Saleh's control over tribesmen diminishes the farther one gets from Sana'a. Rural people are far more likely to turn to their tribal leaders, called sheikhs, than to the government to resolve disputes over land, grievances, or natural resources. Sheikhs serve as spokesmen for their tribes, arbitrating conflicts, helping parties agree on appropriate amends, and wielding political influence. For example, oil companies working in Yemen often must negotiate separate deals with the government and with the sheikhs of tribes upon whose land they are working. Otherwise they can find their buildings suddenly surrounded by angry, AK-47-wielding tribesmen.

Most Yemenis' first loyalty is to tribe and family rather than to their country. Whenever I get into a taxi with my reporters, the first thing they do is figure out what tribe our driver belongs to. Mohammed al-Matari, my elder-statesman reporter, is the most adept. He can find out the tribe, hometown, and family of a driver within the first three minutes of the journey. All of this has to be ascertained before conversation can continue.

☪

I CAN'T FIND ANYONE free to work on the kidnapping story, so when Farouq —the paper's main political reporter—walks into the office that day for the first time since my arrival, I nearly weep with joy. It is a struggle not to hug him; his face is pale with sorrow over the death of his daughter. The skin is pulled tight across his skull; Farouq is so skeletally thin that my first impulse every time I see him is to hand him a sandwich. "I am so sorry, Farouq," I say. "I am so sorry to hear of your tragedy."

He blinks back tears. "Yes, I had something very bad happen in my life," he says, unable to look at me.

"I am so, so sorry."

He shows me photos on his cell phone of the infant daughter he just lost and kisses the small screen. I ask if he needs more time off, but he says he wants to work. We go over what stories I need, and he says, "Do not worry about the front page. I will take care of the front page. It is my specialty."

There's a catch, of course. Farouq writes only in Arabic and requires translators for all of his stories. We have no good translators. Bashir and Talha struggle along, but often I cannot understand the results of their labor. I'll need to hire at least one translator in addition to several more reporters. If Faris will let me, that is.

Farouq asks me to call the French embassy, because I'm the only one in the office who speaks French. I speak to both the ambassador and the press attaché, but they have no new information. So Farouq taps his sources in the security department in the region and we get most of the story from them.

I end up writing the piece myself, based on Farouq's notes and al-Asaadi's background, and get it on the Web by ten fifteen P.M. the same day. This is thrilling, but I wish I could travel south to where the kidnappings happened to do some real reporting. It's tough to be stuck in the office, orchestrating coverage. None of my journalists can go either. No one has a car, enough money to get down there, or—most significantly—the drive to get the story in person. Not one of my reporters has expressed the slightest interest in trying to get face-to-face interviews. But how else can we get to the truth about what happened?

I'm learning that in Yemen the truth is a slippery thing. Two days after the kidnapping, fifty-one Yemenis are killed in a stampede at one of Saleh's election rallies at a stadium in Ibb, a city a couple hours south of Sana'a. As usual, the number of victims reported fluctuates throughout the day, from hundreds to dozens. Both the *Yemen Observer* and the *Yemen Times* report more than sixty dead, until the government news agency announces the official count as fifty-one.

The exact circumstances of the stampede depend on which newspaper you read. We report that the stampede was caused by overcrowding, as more than a hundred thousand people were crammed into a space meant to hold half that. Exits were poorly marked, and when people rushed out at the end of Saleh's speech, they trampled each other. The *Yemen Times* reports that two hundred thousand people were packed into a stadium with a capacity of ten thousand. People were crushed when fences installed to control the crowd's movement collapsed, trapping people underneath as the crowd swarmed over them. Still other reports say a hundred and fifty thousand people had been crammed into the stadium. The truth is elusive.

When Farouq asks the deputy security manager in Ibb how such tragedies could be prevented in the future, the man shrugs. "We don't have another rally," he says. "So it's not really a concern."

I am struck by the casual, fatalistic view Yemenis take of tragedy. Stampedes, car accidents, kidnappings, and terrorist attacks rarely seem overly to trouble anyone or trigger societal self-analysis. A stadium collapse and stampede in New York would provoke public outcry and a demand for improved safety standards and crowd control, but this doesn't happen in Yemen. Perhaps it is simply that they believe all catastrophes are Allah's will. For example, few Yemenis see any point in seat belts. If Allah decides it's time for you to go, it's time for you to go.

President Saleh issues a statement offering condolences and cash to the bereaved families, calling the deceased "martyrs of democracy." Opposition parties, eager to use the tragedy to their political advantage, rush to blame Saleh, decrying his shoddy security and criticizing him for busing groups of students from schools to the rally to support him, contributing to overcrowding and putting young people in danger.

This stampede followed a smaller one in Ta'iz, a hundred and fifty miles south of Sana'a, which killed four or five people. Several papers report a third stampede, rumored to have killed five or six people in Zinjibar in Abyan Governorate in the south, but government spokesmen vigorously deny this. An auto accident killed a few people, they say. Not a stampede.

The kidnappings and stampedes, happening right on top of each other, underscore the near-impossibility of squeezing facts out of the Yemeni government or any other sources, although perhaps this isn't surprising in a culture that values belief over empirical evidence.

Farouq keeps busy trying to sort out both tragedies. Big stories like these, I know from experience, are good at staving off grief. At least until deadline.

☪

ONE GOOD THING the kidnapping brings us is Karim, a Belgian-Tunisian photographer on freelance assignment for *Paris Match*. When I run up to Faris's office with a lengthy list of demands—a residency visa, more staff, business cards, toilet paper—I find Karim sitting there. Tall, with dark curling hair and mischievous eyes, he's possibly the most attractive person I've seen since arriving in Yemen. I am suddenly acutely aware of my untidy braids and spinsterish skirts.

Karim hopes to get photographs of the kidnapped tourists, so he'll be staying in Yemen until they are released. I immediately want to go with him, though Faris tells me in no uncertain terms that I am not to endanger myself. "Maybe you can do some reporting for us then," I say to Karim. No one seems to worry that any violence will befall the hostages. Farouq's source says that they are being fed well. Yemen will not attempt to use military might to get them back; a new sheikh has begun mediating.

I linger in the office until Faris invites me to join them for dinner. "Faris says he's taking me to some sort of five-star restaurant," says Karim.

I laugh. "That would be Zorba's."

☾

WE CHOOSE AN OUTSIDE TABLE, overlooking busy Hadda Street. Karim, I discover, has been everywhere. He has been embedded with the U.S. military in Afghanistan, traveled with the Taliban, covered the Iraq war, explored Iran, and written features on the nightlife of Beirut. Of all of the countries he has visited, Yemen is the most beautiful, he says. Karim's impressive résumé includes freelance work for the *New York Times, Time, Newsweek,* the *International Herald Tribune, Geo,* and various German magazines. He is planning to go back to Afghanistan next month to be embedded and then to go on a night raid against the Afghan National Army with the Taliban.

"That's just crazy," says Faris.

"That's just responsible journalism," says Karim.

I could use him on my staff. He tells me stories about smoking opium in the mountains with the Taliban. One morning, he woke up to find his socks missing, only to find out that the Taliban soldiers had washed them for him. I'm impressed by his fearlessness and a bit dispirited that I'll probably never have *my* socks washed by the Taliban.

Talk turns to the hostages down south. While the kidnappings don't make Faris worry about my personal safety in Yemen, he does fret that violence could break out around the upcoming elections and that westerners could be targeted. Yemen is home to myriad groups of extremists, among them al-Qaeda, which has been growing in strength in recent years.

"Jennifer," says Faris. "Do me a favor. Don't leave your house at the same time every morning." Predictable routines make one an easy target for terrorists. This is the same warning offered by the U.S. State Department website. Of course, if I believed everything I read on the State Department website, I would never leave home.

But I don't need encouragement to vary my route; boredom keeps me from ever walking the same streets two days in a row. This means that I often end up lost and add an extra half hour to my travel time just trying to get back to a major road. But at least I'm not predictable.

"Faris," I say as we stand to go, "are you worried al-Qaeda will come for me when they find out a New Yorker is editing the paper?"

He hesitates. "I don't *think* so."

☾

BUT AL-QAEDA HAS APPARENTLY set its sights on targets more strategic than me. It's a Friday, our only day off, when it next makes the news. Several oil installations have just been attacked by al-Qaeda operatives, and Faris wants the story on the website immediately. In the South, two terrorists drove car bombs at high speed toward oil storage tanks at al-Dhaba plant, Yemen's main export terminal on the Gulf of Aden. Guards managed to detonate the bombs before they reached their targets, but one security officer was killed in the explosions. Less than an hour later, two other cars loaded with explosives headed toward the oil-gathering and gas-oil separation plant in Ma'rib Governorate. Guards shot at the men, and only the attackers were killed when the car bombs exploded. Neither attack damaged facilities, but they are dramatic evidence that al-Qaeda has been resurrected.

Al-Qaeda in Yemen grew out of militant Islamic campaigns overseas. Yemenis flooded to Afghanistan in the 1980s to fight the Soviets, and many stayed through the 1990s to train. Others returned to Yemen to fight in the 1994 civil war against the "godless Socialists" in the South. Osama bin Laden, whose father was born in Yemen, recruited Yemenis to train in al-Qaeda's camps in Afghanistan. After the U.S. invasion of Iraq in 2003, large numbers of Yemenis traveled there to fight U.S. forces.

Until the late 1990s, Yemeni terrorists stuck to a deal they had made with the government: they would be allowed sanctuary and freedom of movement in Yemen in return for not staging attacks within Yemen's borders. But by the end of the decade, militant groups, frustrated with government negotiations with the United States for military basing rights in Yemen, opened training camps in the South and launched a campaign of attacks on government offices. And in October 2000, a group of al-Qaeda veterans launched a suicide attack on the USS *Cole* in Aden harbor, killing seventeen American seamen. The MV *Limburg*, a French ship, was hit two years later. These attacks prompted the government, with U.S. support, to crack down on terrorists. Nearly a hundred were arrested by 2003.

But al-Qaeda continued to grow, inside and outside Yemen. The September 11, 2001, attacks on the United States vaulted al-Qaeda into public consciousness. Before then, the terrorist organization was relatively obscure. But the massive publicity it received in the wake of the attacks suddenly made it a global brand. Afterward, any self-respecting terrorist group with Islamic credentials and aspirations to bring the West to its knees began claiming to be part of al-Qaeda.

In the Central Prison of the Political Security Organization (one of Yemen's domestic intelligence services), in Sana'a, several key al-Qaeda leaders continued to plot. On February 3, 2006, twenty-three prisoners, some of whom had participated in the *Cole* and *Limburg* attacks, escaped the maximum-security prison through a tunnel to the al-Awqaf Mosque. Since the prison break, al-Qaeda in Yemen has organized a series of terrorist attacks on Western and Yemeni government targets—the latest of which is today's assault on the oil installations. Al-Asaadi reports the story, and we get it online that evening.

It's only my second week at the paper, and already we've had kidnappings, stampedes, and suicide bombings. This is a news junkie's paradise.

NINE

the front lines of democracy

I'm still adjusting to my new role. One night at a party to celebrate Ethiopian New Year's, someone refers to me as Luke's girlfriend. Luke is quick to correct him. "She's not my girlfriend," he says. "She's my *boss.*"

I like the sound of that. I've never been anyone's *boss.* That is, I like the sound of it until we get back later that night to the work I abandoned earlier on my desk.

Even without the recent catastrophes, we'd have no shortage of news. Hardly have I had time to learn the intricacies of Yemeni politics when I am plunged into orchestrating coverage of the September 20th presidential election. The elections are an excellent opportunity to drive home to my reporters the importance of fair and impartial journalism. Almost as important is that I am anxious to prove to our readers that the *Yemen Observer* is not a tool of the regime. Because of Faris's work with the president, many Yemenis assume the paper is simply a government mouthpiece.

Thus, in the days leading up to the election, I am careful to include coverage of all of the candidates. We split the front page equally between Saleh and bin Shamlan, the major contenders, but also include at least one story on each of the other candidates.

But while we are not short on news, we *are* short on people to write it. I don't have enough staff to cover the elections while still producing the regular Culture, Business, and Health and Science pages. Only Ibrahim and Farouq seem capable of writing political stories, but they can't fill the front page alone. How can I create a revolution without an army? If only I had arrived to find a full newsroom, what a world of difference that would have made! But Faris seems intent on running the paper with as few people as possible. This baffles me, because reporters' salaries cannot possibly be one of Faris's main expenses. My journalists earn between $100 and $200 per month and have no health insurance or any other benefits. How can a man who drives a Porsche and lives in a mansion with alabaster windows refuse to adequately staff his own paper for financial reasons?

I brainstorm with Luke and Zuhra for solutions to our dearth of staff. We decide to run an ad in the paper and to put up fliers in the university at the school of journalism. Al-Asaadi concurs with this decision but cautions me against hope. "The problem with hiring staff is that none of the graduates of the journalism school can write in English," he says. "And we can't hire translators for everyone. But if we hire people who can write in English, they have no journalism experience." I have no choice, really; I am going to have to train English majors. It irks me that Yemenis seem to believe that if they can write in English, they are qualified to be a reporter. It doesn't occur to them that other skills might be necessary for the job.

We also have copy-flow issues. I want to get reporters to file some stories on the first day of our three-day cycle, so not everything is coming in just before deadline. Ideally, the features pages would be filed to me Saturday; the Business, Panorama, and back pages would be filed Sunday; and only the front, Local, and Election pages—which need to contain the latest news—would be left to edit on Monday, a closing day. But this seems impossible. I'm lucky if I get any copy by midday on the second day of the cycle. This means I spend days worried sick that we won't have enough to fill the issue.

It bewilders me that al-Asaadi is unconcerned about the lack of a schedule. He seems perfectly happy to have everything come in at the last minute and to stay up all night closing each issue. In fact, he rarely bothers to come in before eight P.M., thus *ensuring* the lateness of our close. Our closing days continue to run from eight A.M. until three or four A.M.

the next day. I am exhausted, and the irregularity of my hours means that when I am home, I often cannot fall asleep. My body has no idea what time zone it is in. The irregular hours don't seem to bother any of my male staff—but then again, they're all on drugs. They chew *qat* every day. Like al-Asaadi, they are never in any rush to get home and seem to be quite content to spend all night in the office chewing with their friends.

"It doesn't speak highly of their wives that they never want to go home," I say to Luke.

"Well, if your wife was uneducated and illiterate, with no interest in politics and no conversational topics beyond the children and the next meal, would *you* be in a rush to get home?" he says.

☪

ONE FRIDAY, I have a chance to work on my delicate relationship with al-Asaadi and learn a bit more about Yemeni politics when he invites me to a journalists' *qat* chew. The focus is to be democracy and the imminent elections. This group of journalists chews together every week, in rotating locations. This week it is in the tented *mafraj* on the roof of the *Yemen Observer* building, which disappoints me as I am not anxious to spend any more time at work. Al-Asaadi picks me up at Sabri's, and we arrive at the office to find Faris's car outside.

"Great," I say. "He's going to try to make us work!"

I run up to the roof and take my seat next to al-Asaadi. Ten journalists are seated in the tent, all men. They work for a variety of media outlets, including al-Jazeera, several Yemeni Arabic-language papers, a Saudi paper, and the *Yemen Observer*. On the way there, I had asked al-Asaadi if the men would mind having a woman join the group. "They loooove having a woman join the group!" he said. Ibrahim, whom I've come to think of as Mr. Front Page because he reliably helps fill page one, sits on the other side of me. None of the other journalists speaks English, but al-Asaadi and Ibrahim translate things I don't understand.

Al-Asaadi has brought *qat* for me and shows me how to pick only the tenderest and prettiest leaves to chew. The big glossy leaves are too tough and hurt the gums.

Before the session, I run into Faris, who pulls me aside. "Jennifer, don't chew too much *qat*," he says, looking grim. "It isn't good for you. There are pesticides, and it's bad for your teeth."

"Don't worry," I reassure him. "I don't do too much of anything."

After some initial persiflage, the men fall into serious, focused discussions about the elections and *fatwahs* and democracy.

On paper, Yemen is a constitutional democracy, with executive, legislative, and judicial branches of its government. The president is head of state and the prime minister head of government. A 301-seat elected parliament and a 111-seat president-appointed Shura Council make up the legislative branch. Yemen has notional separation of powers. It has regular elections to the presidency, parliament, and local government. It has genuine pluralism. Any constitutional change requires a popular referendum. Which is more democracy than exists in any other country in the Arabian Peninsula.

But all is not quite as it seems.

While Yemen's government has many superficial resemblances to the checks and balances prevalent in developed Western democracies, in practice, parliament is little more than a tool of the executive. Saleh's party, the General People's Congress or al-Mu'tamar Party, wields nearly all of the power. Saleh uses parliament to stall legislation he doesn't want. The judiciary is corrupt and manipulated for political purposes by the regime. Big decisions are made by the president and not by ministers. A small ruling elite prevents decisions that are in the best interests of the country from being made, so as to protect their own vested interests. For example, costly fuel subsidies encourage oil smuggling, from which corrupt presidential allies benefit. Oil subsidies also help big *qat* producers, who include friends of the president, as diesel pumps are used for water to irrigate the crop.

There's no question Saleh will win reelection, though he is campaigning with the ruthlessness of an underdog. I'm amazed at the bitterness and viciousness of his attacks on his opponent. Does he truly believe negative campaigning is necessary when he has the election all but sewn up?

True, things are a bit tougher for him now than they were in the 1999 election. The second-most-important party, Islah, the Islamic reform party, has joined forces with the Yemen Socialist Party and other opposition parties to form the Joint Meeting Party. The JMP's presidential candidate is Faisal bin Shamlan, a former oil minister campaigning on an anti-corruption ticket. While no one thinks bin Shamlan has a chance, it would be a hopeful sign for Yemeni democracy if he could draw, say, 30 percent of the vote.

The journalists gnawing on their *qat* leaves are pessimistic about the chances of a completely fair election. Saleh has a near-monopoly on media time and resources. All broadcast media is government controlled and airs nonstop coverage of Saleh's rallies around the country. Even Sheikh Abdullah bin Hussein al-Ahmar, the head of the Hashids and the chairman of the Islah Party, endorses Saleh at the last minute. "Better the devil you know," he tells reporters.

Some Salafi clerics go so far as to contend that democracy is un-Islamic. The ultra-traditionalist Salafis believe that Islam has strayed from its roots since the Prophet Mohammed's day and desire a return to a "purer" version of the religion. "To compete with the ruler is an illegitimate act; this is un-Islamic," says scholar Abu al-Hassan al-Maribi at an election rally. Naturally, the government broadcasts his speech.

In this last month before the election, there is hardly a surface in Sana'a that isn't plastered with Saleh's stern, mustached face. Posters paper the walls of the Old City, fill shop and car windows, and hang from bridges. I've begun to feel like I know the guy personally. My reporters tell me that the shopkeepers who put Saleh's face in their windows aren't necessarily supporters; they are merely trying to stay out of trouble with the ruling party.

The political talk at the chew eventually subsides and is followed by the inevitable Solomon's Hour of Zenlike quiet. I find myself feeling rather depressed as I stare into the carpet with nothing to say. I'm not sure Yemen is ready for true democracy. How can a largely illiterate people with no access to independent broadcast media make informed choices about their future? I wonder.

☾

AS PART OF MY EFFORTS to encourage impartial reporting, I am trying to keep the advertising department from telling my reporters what to cover.

When I say advertising department, I mean Qasim, whom I originally found so charming. He constantly steals one or two of my reporters and sends them off to cover one of his advertisers or stands in the newsroom trying to dictate a positive story about Saleh. He fails to grasp that the editorial and advertising departments of a newspaper must be discrete entities. I explain that what he is doing is unethical, that a thick wall must be maintained between editorial and advertising. "We lose all of our credibility if our readers think we are reporting something because advertisers are paying us to write about it," I tell him. "Besides, I am trying to teach my reporters how to do real reporting, and you are confusing them."

He nods and smiles, and then goes ahead and sends one of my reporters to cover a fund-raising event for one of President Saleh's charities.

(☪

THESE TENSE DAYS have unpredictable moments of brightness. One night, I am scrambling to edit a couple of election stories before closing day when Luke comes running into my office. Luke never runs. "Jennifer," he says. "Come out and see the moon!"

I follow him outside, and we stand in the middle of the street, gazing up as the dark shadow of the sun creeps across the moon. A lunar eclipse! Farouq joins us and we all stand around with our faces to the sky and our mouths open. I run back in to fetch al-Asaadi. We stand in the courtyard breathing in the fragrance of jasmine and marveling.

"Call Mas," al-Asaadi says. "Tell him to get photos of it."

"Mas isn't here," I remind him. "He's traveling with the president."

"Jennifer," says al-Asaadi. "Tell me where is Mas that he cannot see the moon?"

(☪

ON SEPTEMBER 11, I wake up in tears. I never anticipate how much the anniversary of the attacks on my city brings all the grief and horror back to the surface. Overwhelmed, I cry straight through my shower, coffee, and the walk to work. I am dressed all in white, in honor of the Ethiopian New Year (which falls on the same day) and because I am tired of dark colors and need to cheer myself up. I wear a floor-length white skirt, a white cotton Indian shirt, a white shawl, and, in a particularly daring move in this dusty city, white socks.

"You look like an angel!" Zuhra says when she sees me. Ha! Everyone comments on my outfit, even al-Asaadi, who tells me that white becomes me. Compliments from al Asaadi are rare and precious things. Zuhra and I draw stares when we walk down the street for lunch, negative images of each other.

"Together, we're a penguin," I say. "Or a nun."

"Or I am your shadow!"

"That, we knew."

September 11 is a Monday, and thus a closing day, so work and its frustrations divert me from personal sorrow. I'm a wee bit exasperated with the three-and-a-half-hour lunch breaks my male reporters are taking. If they could cut their lunch break down to even an hour or two, we could get out of the office much earlier. However, I know I can never suggest this ridiculously American idea without a mutiny.

In an effort to help me with election coverage, al-Asaadi hands me a new intern, a tall, broad young man named Jabr. Jabr wears his hair slicked back and dreams of becoming a movie star. In the meantime, the *Yemen Observer* will do. He has no experience, but I can't afford to turn away able bodies.

I send Jabr out to poll people for our opinion poll column, in which four ordinary people answer a question such as "Can democracy work in Yemen?" "What is the first thing you want the new president to tackle?" or "Do you think the newly released bin Laden video is real?" This should take about half an hour, tops.

Jabr disappears before lunch and is gone for six hours. I'm wondering if maybe he has decided to quit when he returns to tell me he has quotes from only three people, and they are all men. I had told him explicitly that we must always interview two women and two men.

"Jabr," I say, "you've been gone from the office for *six hours,* and you're telling me you couldn't find four people to talk to? In all that time?"

"Some of the women wouldn't talk."

"So ask more of them."

"Where am I supposed to go?" He stands there looking large and helpless.

"Walk out to Algiers Street. Hundreds of people walk by every minute. Surely you can find *one* who will talk. And we need women. We *are* half of the population. And I would like to know what *both* halves of the population have to say." Representative democracy begins here.

He nods and backs out of the room.

Two hours later he comes back to tell me that he can't find anyone.

It would be generous to call Jabr a slow starter. Luke and I become so frustrated with his inability to perform even the simplest of tasks that we begin referring to him as the Missing Link. I can't fire him though; we're hardly paying him anything, and I suppose (though sometimes I have doubts about this) that having him around is better than having no one.

Adding to our woes, the Internet connection goes down regularly, usually on closing days, when we most need it. Ibrahim e-mails me his election stories from home on closing days, and all of the op-ed pieces and Middle Eastern news must be drawn from the wires. With the Internet connection down, we cannot finish an issue. No one seems to know what to do when this happens. Everyone stands around and complains, but no one *does* anything. The Doctor is supposed to help, but he is either out on a four-hour lunch break or useless. He will shout at people and then come tell me it's all taken care of, which it rarely is. Only one technician can help us with our Internet, Enass says. But often when we need him, his phone is off.

Faris has promised me an Arabic tutor, who has yet to materialize. I've taught myself enough to get around on my own, but here are a few phrases I'm desperate to know:

"None of the power outlets in my office is working. Can someone fix them?"

"Can you tell me when the toilet will be functional?"

"There is no water in the entire building."

"There will be no newspaper if something isn't done about the Internet."

"Am I ever going to get the key to open my desk drawers?"

☪

ON OUR NEXT CLOSING DAY, Zuhra finishes her stories before three P.M. and makes her reluctant departure. It occurs to me that *she* should be the person I train to take over the paper when I leave. This is one of my main goals: to train a successor to carry on my work when I leave. But Zuhra is a woman and thus cannot stay late in the office (or, probably, command the respect of the men). It's early to be thinking about my successor, but it could take the rest of the year to properly train someone.

At three A.M., we're still working, although I am having trouble reading the words on the page. I give the last of the front-page stories to our designer Samir and am about to call it a wrap and escape when I see al-Asaadi typing away on the pages I have already finished. "I'm just moving a few stories," he says. It turns out he has also rewritten several critical election headlines, none of which is grammatical. I am convinced he is only making these changes for the same reason a dog pees on lampposts. But I have no choice but to stay until he is done; my eyes *must* be the last to see the paper before it hits the printer. Sighing, I set down my bags and pick up the pages he has altered to do one last edit.

☪

THE PREELECTION DAYS turn quickly into newsprint. I am now beginning to realize the peril of trying to change everything at once. I've been trying to get the paper on a schedule, hire staff, train reporters, edit the entire paper, write some pieces of my own, and earn the respect of my staff all at the same time. But despite my growing awareness of the impossibility of this task, I haven't figured out yet how to do one thing at a time or what should come first.

I don't have enough time to sit with my reporters as I rewrite their pieces and explain to them how to do better. So I am happy when I get all three health and science stories early enough in the last preelection issue not only to edit them but to discuss with Najma, Bashir, and Talha what is missing from each of them. Bashir, for one, wrote about the accelerating melting of the Arctic ice without mentioning two major studies just conducted by NASA. I am trying to get my reporters to read all of the background stories on a subject before they begin reporting the news. But they resist and don't seem to understand why it is important. Farouq has flat-out refused, saying that he has his own reporting, so why does he need to know what everyone else is saying? When I explain that he can write a better story knowing the whole background, he simply tells me that I should read the background and fill it in myself.

Production has been slow this week, because every single staff member has had to take time off to care for a sick relative. Al-Asaadi's mother has a snakebite on her foot that has turned into a cyst that won't heal. Bashir's mother is ill. Farouq's brother is in the hospital. So is Hakim's wife, who has stomach problems.

We are also burdened by a love letter that the minister of health has written to President Saleh for our last preelection issue. Faris insists that we put it in the paper, saying it will encourage other officials to talk to us and write for us. He also insists that it be on the back page, which he considers prime real estate. This is all communicated to me by al-Asaadi.

"I won't do it," I say. "Opinion does not belong on the back page."

"*You* tell him that." Al-Asaadi is unwilling to argue with Faris over anything.

I run upstairs and explain to Faris that an opinion piece belongs on the Op-Ed page, which is widely considered the most powerful page in a newspaper.

"That is not true here," says Faris. "Here the back page is most important."

"Really?"

"Arabic is read right to left. So Arabs will naturally turn first to what for you is the back page."

This hadn't occurred to me. "But we're an English paper. And even if that is true, we lose legitimacy when we publish opinions in the regular pages," I say. "Opinions and news must be kept separate."

Finally, Faris suggests a compromise. "I will let you put it on the Op-Ed page," he said, "if you will put a mention in the banner on the front page, with a little photo."

"Done!" I say, greatly pleased.

I run back downstairs. "It's going on the Op-Ed page," I tell al-Asaadi, who looks at me in astonishment.

The minister's piece, it transpires, is utter garbage. Al-Asaadi gets stuck translating it and moans the entire time. "Jennifer," he says, "you know what it's like when you are forced to eat something that makes you gag? That is what I am doing." The heavily edited piece is then thrust upon Luke, who wrestles with it some more. And I still have to do further edits. It tortures all of us.

Faris stops by in the late afternoon with his friend Jalal. On their way to a *qat* chew, they're clad in long white robes. "Faris," I say with mock sternness, "you shouldn't chew too much *qat*. It has pesticides and isn't good for your teeth."

"But I am Yemeni!" he says in defense. "Whereas *you* are soft and tender."

"*Soft?*" I flex a bicep.

Faris pinches my arm and agrees that there is nothing soft about it. "It's just that when I see your face, I think of meditation and tranquility," he says. "You're like a calm angel."

Luke laughs so hard he almost chokes. "Come back and see her at two in the morning."

☪

ON ELECTION DAY, I walk to work, disregarding all warnings that it is un-safe for westerners to be outside. I just can't get through such a busy day without a bit of exercise. If I don't burn off some energy, I'll need to be peeled off the ceiling by noon. The streets are deserted. All of the shops are dark and shut with steel gates, except for a few juice places. Even the big Huda supermarket is closed. To keep a low profile, I wear all black, plus sunglasses to hide my blue eyes, but I'm conspicuous no matter what I do. This is driven home when just a few blocks from my office, a filthy man I pass on the sidewalk invites me to suck his cock. Who taught him this English?

I arrive at work to find the gates locked and no one there. I pound on the doors, trying to wake the guard, to no avail. Dear god, does everyone think this is a holiday? Our biggest reporting day of the year? I mean, it *is* a holiday for the rest of the country, but we work for a *newspaper!* Surely my staff knows that they must show up? It hasn't even occurred to me that this is something I needed to tell them.

Desperate, I ring al-Asaadi. He doesn't have keys but makes a few phone calls to try to find someone to let me in. In vain. "You shouldn't stand around in front of the newspaper," he tells me. "It isn't safe."

"Al-Asaadi, there is nowhere else to *go!*" I am so frustrated that I kick the gate, and to my great surprise, it swings open. Now I am in the courtyard but still can't get into the building. The welcome mat that usually hides the key is missing. So I pound on the door to the guard's hut until I finally rouse him. Rubbing his eyes, he stumbles out to open the building.

I worry that no one will show up. It is unusual for the women reporters not to be here at this hour. Enass is also missing from the reception desk and there's no sign of the Somali cleaning lady. So it is an enormous relief when I see Zuhra bustling into the courtyard. "Please call everyone else and tell them to get their butts to the office," I say.

Noor and Najma say that their families won't let them out of the house. "It's too dangerous." The usually reliable Hassan is spending the day working for the EU election observers. Talha, who has no phone, is MIA. We also have no secretary, Doctor, or drivers.

Trying not to panic, I send Zuhra out to the polls. As soon as she is gone, Farouq shows up. He promptly heads out to report from the Supreme Council for Elections and Referendum (SCER) and to visit other polling sites. Two reporters in action!

Jabr, the Missing Link, shows up an hour later, and I send him out to the polls as well. I hand him a notebook. "Don't come back until you fill this," I say. He looks terrified. I soften a bit. "Here, I will write you a list of questions to ask."

Luke arrives next, followed by Qasim, who waves his dark purple thumb—proof that he has voted. I beg him to take me to the polling sites. I don't want to sit in the office missing all of the action. He insists on calling Faris to get permission to take me out, and we finally head to the SCER. It's housed in a massive building filled with scores of hustling and bustling Yemeni officials and local and international reporters dashing about looking important and typing up stories in a computer room. On the first floor, reporters run in and out of the smoky restaurant, holding glasses of *shaay haleeb*—tea with milk.

We head to the Ministry of Information to get my press ID. This is no simple task. Qasim asks me to lie and say that I am a reporter for *The Week* in the United States, because an international press pass apparently grants greater freedom. I don't want to lie. I'm going to be living here for a year, and I will be found out sooner or later. But it's illegal for a foreigner to be running a Yemeni paper, Qasim reminds me. We compromise and put both the *Observer* and *The Week* on my tag, which is pink for "international reporter."

We hear rumors of election-related violence and killings in Ta'iz and other governorates, but most remain unconfirmed. It's funny how fast the news of these alleged incidents spreads. I even hear from several people that a man was arrested with explosives in Tahrir Square, just down the street from me. Misinformation seems to move much faster than fact.

My pink tag dangling from my neck, I climb into Qasim's car and we head to a nearby polling place. In the courtyard of the al-Quds School for Girls on Baghdad Street, a long black column of women stretches all the way down the hall leading to their voting rooms. Though it's now noon, many of them have been standing there since the polls opened.

Across the courtyard, men do not have to wait in line. They dart in and out, completing their votes in five minutes or less.

"The women take longer to vote because they are not educated," local election supervisor Ameen Amer explains. "Many are illiterate."

To assist the illiterate, the presidential ballot has color photos of each candidate, as well as his party's emblem, next to his name. A rearing horse symbolizes Saleh, while a rising sun is the sign of the Islah Party.

"Most of the women just registered this year and haven't done this before," says another election supervisor. "It's a matter of education, and now, democracy is proceeding, day by day, and getting better and better."

Others we speak to in the sunny courtyard suggest that men vote later in the day, after work, while most women vote in the morning. It's a frustrating wait in the hot sun for the women, who grow restless and shout out their complaints. "We have a crisis!" one woman cries. "Nobody is moving!" Yet they admirably do not give up, and most wait patiently for their turn in the voting booth.

As voters file into each room, they are given one presidential ballot, two ballots for governorate councils, and two for district councils. They then secrete themselves behind the gray curtains of a small booth, where they mark their chosen candidates. As each emerges, she stuffs her papers into the plastic ballot boxes, before dipping her thumb into the well of purple ink that brands her as a voter.

A row of seated representatives from each party observes the voting, often erupting into arguments but not becoming violent.

"Nobody is cheating," says observer Hanan al-Jahrani, who is representing the GPC (the ruling party to which President Saleh belongs). "We have had no problems."

For the most part, the process is going smoothly, concurs Amer. But at least fifteen people have come to the polls wearing T-shirts or hats emblazoned with their favored candidates, which is against election law.

A businessman tells us that the voting process has improved. "We have seen the competition getting stronger, and each party is more nervous this year, which means we are getting closer to democracy. If a voter senses this, he will be more likely to vote."

Outside each room stand two armed men in green camouflage and red berets. Despite the threat of violence, I don't see any reason to feel uneasy. Things seem to be moving more or less smoothly and thankfully the guns remain unused.

Back at the office, I write up my notes. Zuhra and Jabr bring me their stories from other polling centers, and I tuck them into my reporting. Farouq runs around between the SCER and polling centers all day, so I don't see him. Al-Asaadi is allegedly doing something similar.

Election results won't come in until the next morning, so I am able to leave work by eight thirty P.M. The next day will be long; I had better escape while I can.

The results trickle in all the next day, with Saleh unsurprisingly winning 77.2 percent of the vote. It's a disappointing anticlimax after the frenzy of the last few days. No serious election violence is reported, no riots, no major problems at the polls. And privately we had all hoped bin Shamlan would do a bit better.

On the upside, it's a bizarrely calm day. I sketch out the issue on my dry-erase board and get al-Asaadi's approval. He hasn't eaten breakfast so

I offer him some of my oat cookies. He takes four. "My food is your food," I say.

"My office is your office," he says, his mouth full of oats.

I am pleased that he's so cheerful, and even more pleased that he gets his pages to me on time. So does everyone else. It's not a perfect issue, but some of my ambitions for the paper will have to wait. When al-Asaadi leaves early to let me finish the issue on my own, I am downright astonished. Without his last-minute headline changes and layout shifting, we finish all the pages by midnight and I am out of the office by one A.M. Some nights, it feels good to be boss.

TEN

homemaking in the holy month

After a month in my little suite at Sabri's, I still haven't unpacked my suitcases. My two rooms are certainly adequate, but they do not feel like home. I have made no attempt to decorate the walls, put up photos, or stock my kitchen. It seems a waste of effort when I know I am leaving. Living in a dormitory with Sabri's young Arabic students has its perks, but I want a place of my own. Once I have a house, I can get myself sorted. I can unpack, decorate, invite people over for tea. *Then* I can truly begin my Yemeni life.

So far I have had no time to look. Faris found a house he thought I might like, but it was far away from everything—far from the Old City, shops, and my office. I want to be able to continue walking to work. Karim gives me the number of a Yemeni man he knows, Sami, who can find me a house in Old Sana'a. I tuck it in my purse and plan to call. Just as soon as I have a free minute.

Work is beginning to follow something of a schedule when Ramadan arrives abruptly. I am dining at Zorba's with Shaima, my worldly World Bank friend, when she gets a text message from a friend telling her that Ramadan will begin the next morning. She immediately texts others to spread the news. I wonder how this was all done before cell phones.

No one is entirely sure when Ramadan will start until the evening be-

fore, as it depends on the first sighting of the crescent of the new moon.
The Islamic calendar is lunar and shorter than our solar calendar. Islamic
months thus rotate through the seasons, with Ramadan falling about
eleven days earlier each year. Yemen turns upside down during this holy
month. One of the Five Pillars of Islam is that Muslims must fast from
sunup until sundown during Ramadan to burn away their sins. But in
Yemen, after breaking their fast at sunset, everyone stays up until four
A.M. binge eating and then sleeps half the day away. It seems a bit like
cheating to me, to sleep until three P.M., when only three hours of fasting
are left before sundown and *iftar*, the fast-breaking meal. But who am I to
judge?

At the *Yemen Observer,* we don't go completely nocturnal, but our hours
change dramatically. I have only just begun to inch our deadlines earlier
when our Ramadan hours throw everything off kilter again. Our official
hours during the Holy Month are ten A.M. to three P.M., and then nine
P.M. until one A.M. (except on closing nights, when we're often there until
five A.M.). But in reality, the men never straggle in before eleven and
seem to find it a struggle to get back by nine, despite the six-hour break
for *iftar.*

Unsurprisingly, everyone is much more productive in the evenings.
During the day, they are cranky with hunger and thirst. My original impulse is to fast along with my staff. It seems like the right thing to do. I
want to squeeze myself into as much of Yemeni life as possible. But at the
moment, fasting is inconceivable. I am already losing weight and am constantly so tired I can barely stay upright. I often go days without eating
meals—I have no time to cook or go out—but forgoing water just seems
unhealthy. Fasting throughout Ramadan would indubitably weaken me
too much to run this newspaper properly.

Al-Asaadi is quick to reassure me that no one will judge me. "We are
open-minded," he says. "We understand you are being true to your own
culture."

But I am careful not to eat or sip from my water bottle in front of my
staff. Only when my office door is firmly shut do I delve into the secret
stash of dried fruit, nuts, and oat biscuits I keep in my desk drawer for
emergencies. Luke isn't fasting either and comes into my office to sneak

food. Occasionally, a reporter will burst in and catch us with our mouths full and our hands dirty with crumbs. Like guilty children, we hide our hands under our desks and swallow hard. But our reporters never seem to mind; we are not Muslim and are thus held to different standards.

Luke and I have grown much closer as a result of an intimate hour we spent in my office while closing the election issue. This was when he finally confessed to me that he is gay, which I had suspected all along (the *Will and Grace* videos on his laptop, his love of *Project Runway*, etc.). I am curious about what it is like for him to live here, in a country where homosexuality is punishable by death.

Yet homosexual acts between men are hardly rare in Yemen, he tells me. A large percentage of the male population has sex with men. Luke, for one, is propositioned regularly. This doesn't surprise me; he is blond and blue eyed, attractive, and speaks charming Arabic.

"But how does it work?" I ask. "I mean, how do you know who it is safe to hit on?"

"Well, once in Aden a guy cruised me in an ice cream shop. When I left he chased me down, and I got his number and he came over later that night. Easy."

"Very interesting."

"Naturally, this does not leave this office."

"I wouldn't dream of saying anything."

In return, I confess my past romantic relationships with men and women alike. This is an enormous relief. I hadn't realized just how half-alive I was feeling, unable to be my full self with anyone here. Suddenly I can tell someone the truth about my sexuality and not risk punishment or judgment. I am so grateful for Luke I want to hug him. I feel lighter than I have in weeks.

☾

ONE BENEFIT of our Ramadan schedule is that I actually have free time during the evenings. On the first day, I head home a couple hours after my staff have fled and make myself dinner for the first time since arriving in Yemen nearly a month before. I boil water and cook whole-wheat pasta. This feels like a major achievement. I take my bowl of pasta into my bedroom and eat it while watching a DVD on my computer. This is the first truly relaxing, nonproductive, leisurely thing I can remember doing in weeks.

But this would be more satisfying if I could do it in a real home. Maybe if I bought some spices and flour, I might start cooking for myself. I could fill a corner of my kitchen with water bottles so I wouldn't have to stop and buy water every day. I could make friends with my neighbors. I really have to ring Karim's friend Sami soon. I'm tired of living in between places; I want to be *here*.

Salem comes to take me back to work at eight thirty. My reporters arrive enormously cheerful after their massive *iftars*. Ramadan fasts are traditionally broken with dates, with which the Prophet Mohammed broke his fasts. These are followed by deep-fried samosa-type potato dumplings called *sambosas*, yogurt drinks, fruit juice, a pale wheat porridge, and then meat, rice, and bread. Before sunrise, everyone eats again to store up for the day. Ironically, many people complain that they actually gain weight during Ramadan.

Final election results are declared on the first day of Ramadan. We knew them already, but now it's official. The city goes wild with joy. Firecrackers explode the whole evening, and men on neighboring roofs empty rifles into the air. The country has been saved from a tricky transfer of power, saved from unpredictability.

I run out to go buy some gum and candy for the office, wanting to give the staff a treat after their day of fasting. Farouq stops me at the door. "Why don't you send someone to the store?" he says. "You are the boss; you don't have to go yourself."

"Because it's right there," I say, pointing down the street. "I can walk."

"But you don't *have* to walk."

"But I *want* to walk."

"Send someone! Someone can go for you!"

"Farouq! *I like to walk!*"

We both start laughing, and he finally moves aside and waves me down the steps. My days are filled with plenty of these small, happy moments with my staff, enough to keep me fond of them even when they are thwarting my deadlines or returning late from lunch.

☪

One of the most striking things about Ramadan is how clearly it illustrates the cohesiveness of the culture. I have never in my life lived anywhere where everyone belonged to the same religion (although Yemen is divided between Sunni and Shia Muslims, and within these groups are scores of subgroups). I have never lived in a country where everyone is doing exactly the same thing at exactly the same time. For example, at sunset during Ramadan, every single Yemeni is eating a date. This alone is remarkable. At this time, there is no one, *no one*, on the streets. Every single Yemeni man, woman, and child is home breaking his or her fast. No stores are open and no taxis are on the streets.

I don't find this out until the second day of Ramadan, when I go to the Sheraton in the afternoon, emerging from the hotel just before six P.M., in time to see a spectacular sunset over the city. The Sheraton is perched on a hill over the bowl of Sana'a, and the purples and pinks descending across the mountains above and valleys below take my breath away for a few moments as I stand on the totally abandoned street. But my awe is short-lived as I look up and down the hill. Not a car in sight. No taxis, no *dabaabs,* no trucks, nothing. How will I get home?

Fortunately, just as I am despairing of a ride, a Sheraton taxi driver who remembers me from June passes by and sees me standing in the empty road looking bewildered. He mimes eating gestures to explain where everyone is and drives me swiftly home. We make it from the Sheraton to Sabri's house in about three minutes—without stopping once—a miracle! Sana'a is a ghost town. We do not pass a single car or person. My driver speeds away as soon as he drops me, no doubt late for his own feast.

☪

ON SEPTEMBER 25, the kidnapped French tourists are finally released. Karim gets photographs of them as they disembark at Sana'a airport, and we run them on our front page. I'm relieved, although the Yemenis have all been predicting this outcome, so they didn't worry. While I am upstairs with Karim, Faris stops by. I tell him again how much I need more staff and that I can't hope to get the paper under control until I have an adequate number of reporters. I mention the hours I am working.

"Jennifer," he says, looking concerned, "I don't want 100 percent from you. Do this gradually. Aim for 40 percent improvement or 60 percent improvement. I am afraid you will burn out if you try to do too much."

Fine, I think. It's good to know his expectations are low. But how do I *do* that? I don't know *how* to give less than 100 percent.

Because I end up working until *iftar* most Ramadan days, I walk home for dinner. It's too hard to find a taxi. Besides, it's so lovely to walk home when the streets are near-deserted. As I pass the restaurants along Zubairi Street, I see men poised to break their fast. Some even have plates of food in front of them, which they poke at hungrily as they wait for the cannon to go off so they can eat. The expectation in the air accompanying the approaching *iftar* always feels festive. Watching them makes me wish for a kitchen of my own, an *iftar* dinner waiting for me. If only I had a wife!

One of these solitary nights, I finally ring Karim's friend Sami about apartments. A slender, handsome twenty-four-year-old who studies English and works as a fixer for foreigners living in the Old City, Sami does a small business in tourism, arranging drivers to take people around the countryside, finding homes for expats, running errands, and generally being the most helpful person I have ever met. He is enthusiastic about meeting me and finding me a home. It doesn't take long. In the last few days of September, at our third meeting (having looked at a house that was too vast and one that was too tiny), we find my gingerbread house in Old Sana'a.

☪

THE HOUSE SAMI FINDS for me is not just any house but my *dream* house. It's a three-story, boxy stone house of my own, tucked behind a pale blue fence overflowing with pink flowers. I know I want it after just having seen the kitchen. It is vast, with a long counter, a small table for eating, a stove, a refrigerator, and antique Yemeni bread-baking ovens (in case I get *really* ambitious). On the same floor are a bedroom and a small laundry room/bathroom. On the way up the uneven stone stairs to the second floor is another small room, about the right size for an office. The next floor holds a large bedroom, with Star of David *qamaria* (Jews built this house 350 years ago, the landlord, Mohammed, tells me) as well as a couple of circular alabaster *qamaria*. I immediately decide this is where I will sleep. On the same floor is a large, airy *mafraj* lined with red cushions and adorned with several half-moon *qamaria,* a guest room, and a Western-style bathroom—with a tub!

And there's more! The top floor includes a tiny jewel of a room that looks out over all Sana'a, a storage room, and a door to a wide roof.

A whole house! I have never had so much space in my adult life. Mohammed and his entire family follow me as I admire the house, and then we all take off our shoes and sit down in the *mafraj* of the neighboring house to sign the lease. The rent is $300 a month. Expensive for Sana'a, but worth every penny to me. Sami and Shaima translate each line of the lease. Ever since I moved here, Shaima has been my most loyal friend. We eat together once a week or so; she helps me run errands and introduces me to her family and friends.

Several westerners have warned me away from the Old City, the most conservative part of town. Here, people keep a very, very observant eye on their neighbors. I will be watched, and all my guests will be duly noted. But what is the danger in that? I don't have time to behave badly. Besides, there is nowhere else in Sana'a I can imagine living. I can think of no greater bliss than to inhabit these thick gingerbread walls in the cozy warren of cobblestone streets. In fact, I long for nosy neighbors. I am so incredibly lonely that the smallest kindness from strangers makes me teary. Sami lives right down the street and says he is willing to help me with anything, anytime.

I sign my name to the lease, in both Arabic and English. I have a home.

The morning I am to move into my new house, an exploded cyst in my ovaries sends me to the hospital. I've been bleeding, feverish, and in pain for days with no idea why. A female doctor assures me I'll survive and sends me away with antibiotics. I'm too weak to carry anything, so Sabri's guards kindly transport all my possessions to the Old City.

But I can't rest yet. I have no bed! I am so tired I can barely walk, but I head out shopping with Sami. The Old City streets are thronged with people; it is just before *iftar* and everyone is buying provisions. Around Baab al-Yemen, the main gate to the Old City, the ground is covered with cross-legged merchants selling heaps of dusty plastic sandals, pyramids of raisins, and bright red pistachios. Crippled children sit in cardboard boxes, their big dark eyes eloquent with despair; dwarves stretch out their palms for alms; and deformed children are pushed by their parents to beg for cash. The high rate of birth defects in Yemen is visible every-where. I feel much less sorry for myself.

Sami weaves through the clusters of men as I hurry in his wake, breath-ing in a soup of male sweat, cumin, and exhaust. I am struggling to catch up when, a few blocks from the gate, a man grabs me hard, squeezing my left side and breast. My scream carries. Some 150 people turn around to look. Sami whips around and takes a step toward the man, intending to hit him.

But the man is clearly crazy. He is half-dressed, in what looks like a large white diaper, with no shirt. His arms and legs are bent and wiry; his shoulder-length hair is dirty and wild, sticking out from his head in all di-rections; and his grin is toothless. Madness glazes his eyes. When Sami re-alizes this, he lowers his arm.

"I would hit him," he says. "Only it wouldn't do any good because he is insane."

I concur, but the attack has shocked me into tears. Sami tries to find something comforting to say but is obviously unequipped to do this. Real-izing how uncomfortable I am making him, I pull myself together. By the time we get to the mattress store, my eyes are dry. We pick out my bed things, and Sami negotiates the price. Finally, I have a place to lie down.

☪

SAMI HELPS ME furnish my house, fixes electrical and plumbing problems, and runs errands. Both he and Shaima are constantly trying to feed me. One night I enjoy a massive *iftar* at Sami's house, and the next day I am in-vited to Shaima's.

Shaima and her sister Nada live in Hadda, the fancy part of town, in a large, two-story home with vast carpeted rooms and a kitchen big enough for a sit-down dinner for twelve. A froth of flowers surrounds the house.

Shaima's father, currently away in Germany receiving treatment for lymphoma, was a diplomat. When he was posted to Algeria, he fell in love with an Algerian woman, taking her as a second wife, much to the distress of Shaima's mother, who stopped talking to him for a couple of years.

Shaima's stepmother (whom she despises) has children by Shaima's father, but she has not been told about his lymphoma.

Nada is married to an Italian man, Desi, who has also fallen in love with another woman. When he told Nada he wanted to make this woman his second wife, she was grief-stricken. This is why she is now living with Shaima. Desi comes to visit his daughters Ola and Mumina but doesn't want to give up the other woman. It all sounds horrible and painful. Shaima says that if he were her husband, she would have drawn and quartered him by now. Throughout the year, I hear many more stories like this one. These multiple wives cause immense pain. Yemeni men seem to be about as faithless as American men—only instead of keeping their mistresses secret, they marry them. Islam permits up to four wives, as long as the man commits to treating them all equally. But this is impossible. Even the most perfect of humans cannot love four women equally. And in reality, this is rarely how it seems to work out. The women always suffer.

Shaima herself was once briefly engaged to a man with a first wife in Aden. But she backed out of the deal after three days. "I am just too jealous to deal with another wife," she tells me.

When she was at university in Jordan, Shaima received several marriage proposals, which she turned down because she thought she wanted to marry a Yemeni. But when she returned to Yemen, she found Yemeni men not up to her standards. "They are not polite to women," she said. "They do not hold doors, they do not want to chew *qat* with their wives, they don't want to spend time together." Now she is hoping to marry a Muslim foreigner, like her sister. "Jennifer, I am an atom bomb for Yemen," says Shaima bitterly. "I am an educated woman. I won't stay home. I work with men."

I ask her if there is really no contact at all between men and women before marriage. "Oh, everyone here is in a relationship," she says. "They are just underground. Like people everywhere, they find a way."

"What kind of relationship?"

"Like by texting. People have relationships by texts or by e-mail. Or they Bluetooth each other."

This intrigues me. I wonder if Shaima has such a relationship, but she assures me she doesn't.

☾

WE START THE *IFTAR* MEAL with dates, of course. Then comes *shafoot* with salad, and *sambosas* filled with vegetables and cheese. Shaima has made the whole meal vegetarian on my account, which touches me. No one seems to mind—there is such a vast amount of food. After *shafoot,* they go one by one to pray before eating the rest of the meal.

Shaima serves us bowls of Ramadan soup, which is made from coarsely ground wheat, milk, and onions. "High in fiber," Nada tells me.

I am already getting full. But there are still roasted vegetables with cheese, couscous and yogurt, and several breads. I keep protesting they are feeding me too much. Yet somehow, when Shaima brings out the crème caramel, I manage to squeeze it in.

Desi interrogates me in a friendly fashion. He's very interested to hear everything about my life and work. I'm curious about him, because of the other woman. He makes us Italian coffee after dinner, and he and Nada compete to see whose coffee I like better—Nada's Yemeni or his Italian. I pick Nada's in solidarity.

After dinner, he heads to work teaching English. The rest of us have just retired to the living room when all of the power goes off. This happens every day during Ramadan, often for hours at a time. Nada is on her feet in a shot. "Ola will cry," she says. "She hates this."

Sure enough, a second later we hear a wail from upstairs, where the girls are playing. I dig a flashlight out of my purse for Nada, who runs upstairs to fetch the girls. Once they join us, Mumina starts to dance. She is wearing a long, pink princess dress with spaghetti straps. Ola, who is wee at a mere one and a half, dances with her, making me want to kidnap them both for my own.

☾

I HAVEN'T BEEN in my new house for a week when I slip on my uneven stone stairs and crack two ribs. I am carrying my computer in my arms, and when I fall my only thought is protecting it. My ribs catch the edge of the stone step so hard that I cannot move for nearly half an hour. I lie sprawled between my kitchen and the second floor, stunned with pain, thinking that it might be a good idea to have a roommate. Someone to call the ambulance. Were there any ambulances. At last, I roll onto all fours and crawl up the stairs to bed. There's nothing to be done about a rib anyway, even if it is broken. I take four ibuprofen and try to sleep on my left side.

This puts an end to my swimming for several months. Every time I try—which, given my obsession with exercise, I often do—there is such searing pain in my ribs that I end up in tears. How on earth will I cope if I cannot swim to release stress? I walk to work every morning, but it is not enough to ease the strangling amount of tension that builds up in me each day.

It doesn't help that I've been suffering from a flulike Yemeni virus for more than two weeks. Al-Asaadi and I have been sneezing so much we finally conclude we're allergic to each other. I've already had to make one trip to the hospital, and I am not keen to make another.

I keep thinking that I should go out on my days off, or call someone, or try to meet new people, but I am just too tired and sick to do anything. Hope begins to desert me. I worry I will never be healthy, never be without pain, never get the newspaper on a schedule, never teach my reporters anything. Work is an unending struggle. Reporters are constantly missing, our Internet connection goes down every few minutes, and photographers refuse to show up when I need them.

I want to believe that there has been some progress, that something good is coming of this. My standards for success have dropped dramatically. Give me just one grammatical headline. One issue closed before midnight. One day when my male reporters get to work on time. But I am still fighting simply to fill pages—forget trying to fill them with good reporting or decent writing. I still have no one to whom I can delegate any of my work and no one to cover for Luke over Christmas when he is gone for a month. Talha vanished from the office after I caught him plagiarizing an entire story from the IRIN news service and has not been seen since. Zuhra is out sick until after Eid al-Fitr, the festive holiday celebrating the end of Ramadan. Her doctor told her she has exhaustion and must rest. Whom can I turn to now to find stories at the last minute? Who will make me laugh when I am feeling cross? Who will walk me to the Jordanian sandwich shop? I miss my little shadow.

Giving up isn't an option. After all, I have no backup plan. But I feel so tapped out I just don't know where to turn. Everything overwhelms me. I remember that Faris gets back from a trip to Washington the next day, and I decide to talk to him. Maybe he will know where I can find good reporters. The number of applications I get from people with master's degrees in English who can barely write astonishes me. The résumés and cover letters are riddled with typos, malapropisms, and grammatical mistakes.

I've just reached the nadir of my despair, however, when I have my best closing night yet. Al-Asaadi is away, so I pull the entire issue together myself, and my skeleton staff pulls through for me. Thilo, a German freelancer I hired in desperation without ever having read his writing, turns in a wonderful piece about antiquities smuggling. Hassan writes several news stories. Ibrahim sends front-page stories from his home office, and I realize I will have enough stories to fill the paper after all.

I whip out my editorial in fifteen minutes and even enjoy the process. When no pressing issue is begging to be editorialized, I indulge my pet peeves. Tonight, it's honking.

Excessive, ear-ravaging honking of automobile horns is a pervasive problem in Sana'a, but perhaps never quite as terrible as it is during Ramadan. During the holy month of fasting, everyone in the city rushes home for iftar to break his or her fast at exactly the same time. The ensuing gridlock only aggravates the frustration of drivers, who turn to their horns to express their dissatisfaction with the situation.

But these are futile gestures. Blaring horns are powerless to move heavy chunks of automobile. Making screeching noises that harm the ears of passengers, pedestrians, and bystanders alike will not make the cars in front of you move any faster. Nor will it make other drivers behave any more kindly toward you. . . .

Scores of medical studies have found that exposure to elevated noise such as loud horns causes a range of physical and psychological problems, including: hearing loss, high blood pressure, stress, heart problems, increased levels of aggression, as well as vasoconstriction, which can lead to erectile dysfunction. Before leaning on that horn, perhaps a man should think about what it could do to his reproductive capabilities.

(This prompts an e-mail from my mother, who is concerned that perhaps attacking men's reproductive capabilities isn't a wise move on my part. "But, Mom," I protest, "that's a surefire way to get their attention.")

With much cajoling and limping up and down the stairs, I manage to squeeze all the photos I need out of the often-elusive Mas. He complains, but cheerfully. Noor surprises me by turning around a quick story on Eid al-Fitr, which she reports and writes in one day. It is a miraculous night all around. Perhaps I do better when I am not relying on al-Asaadi to do anything for me. We finish laying out the last page of the night at two forty-five A.M.—our earliest Ramadan close ever! I am jubilant. Luke looks at me with suspicion. "You're doing unusually well for three A.M.," he says. "What kind of cold medicine are you taking?"

I finish the last few captions and catch Farouq's eye. "What?" he says, alarmed. "What do you need from me?"

I smile and make a zero shape with my fingers. *"Nothing."*

Farouq raises his eyes and hands to the ceiling. *"Al-hamdulillah!"* he whispers thankfully. Praise belongs to Allah.

My neighborhood is silent as I unlock my gate and tiptoe through my courtyard, a slip of moon lighting my way. A cat darts across my feet and disappears under the water tank. I wonder if anyone is watching me, wondering at the hours I keep. I climb the stairs, shed my shoes, and turn the lights on in my kitchen. Boxes of tea and cereal line my counter, next to an enormous bowl of oranges, apples, and grapes. I flick the switch on my electric teakettle and pad upstairs (slowly!) to change into my pajamas. Ten minutes later I am curled in my bed, a cup of mint tea by my side and a history of Islam in my hands. I am home.

☪

AS SUDDENLY AS IT BEGAN, Ramadan is over. During the last few days, traffic comes to a complete standstill, as everyone in the city is out every night shopping to prepare for Eid. Old Sana'a is thronged with five times the average number of people, and the markets stay open until nearly dawn.

I have never been so happy to see a holiday. For the first time, I have more than one day off in a row! For the first time in nearly two months, a piece of unscheduled time! My first morning off I sleep and sleep. Eid has quite literally saved my life. It makes me feel so festive it's like Easter and Christmas all rolled into one. The little girls tear around the streets dirtying brand-new princess dresses, men fit themselves out with upgraded *jambiyas,* and women bake sweet cakes to feed visiting family and friends in preparation for these four days of celebration. Every single one of my journal entries during this time begins with "Eid is the best holiday *ever!*"

Now I finally have time to enjoy my new home. Solitude is a luxury after long days with my staff. I like the freedom to read over dinner. I like to take my clothes off and dance around my rooms to Fountains of Wayne and XTC. I like to write in my journal in bed. I like sprawling in my *mafraj* with a chunk of dark chocolate and a pile of books and magazines. I still long for more companionship, but I trust that it will come.

My Yemeni friends have trouble understanding why anyone would choose to live alone. For instance, when Shaima drives me to the super-market one day, I tell her I need to find a little coffeemaker. I'm desperate for real coffee—I've been drinking the ubiquitous Nescafé since I moved here. But all I can find are giant, exorbitantly expensive family-size Mr. Coffee–type coffeemakers. Even I could not drink that much coffee. "No one lives alone here," Shaima explains. "They all live in big families. No one *needs* a little coffeepot." I hadn't thought about this. It's true; no one lives alone. Yemeni people live with their parents until they marry, and often married people stay in the same house as their parents. The concept of "alone time" does not exist. When I tell my Yemeni friends that I wish I had a bit more time to myself, they are baffled. *"Why?"* they say. "Why would you ever want to spend a minute *alone?*"

☪

ON THE FIRST MORNING of Eid, my elderly neighbor across the street, Mohammed, invites me over. He calls my home phone, waking me. I have no idea how he got my number, but he says he has seen me unlocking my gate, and won't I come for an Eid visit? I have a friendly neighbor! So I dress quickly and run across the street. Everyone in the Old City is so kind to me that it never even occurs to me to be afraid of strangers. Mo-hammed ushers me through halls hung with oil paintings of landscapes to a *mafraj* done all in blue, with white lace draped across the cushions. Across the carpet are scattered several little silver tables covered with dishes of pistachios, raisins, pastries, and chocolates. Mohammed pushes one of these little tables in front of me and tells me to eat. I nibble on raisins and almonds while he calls for his wife and daughter. "I've been to Arizona," he says. This is evidently a great source of pride.

His wife, a rounded, wide-hipped, hook-nosed woman with an enormous smile, comes in and sits beside me. Their daughter sets a glass of lime juice in front of me and settles on the other side of her mother. She's around twenty and rather plain. Both women, according to Mohammed, speak English but are too shy to speak it around me. Mohammed does most of the talking, telling me how much he loves America and Americans.

"Do you like Kenny Rogers?" says Mohammed. "I *love* Kenny Rogers." He gets up and puts on a cassette. Somehow I failed to imagine that an Eid celebration would involve suffering through "Coward of the County." Whenever his wife leaves the room, he turns it up. When she returns, she turns it back down. Eventually, when the first side of the cassette ends, she gets up and replaces it with a tape of Yemeni *oud* music.

"She *likes* this kind of music," says Mohammed disapprovingly.

"It's pretty," I say. "I like the *oud*."

They keep encouraging me to eat and ask me about my life. Mohammed hands me a large, illustrated book about Yemen and tells me all the places I have to visit.

"You must go to Soqotra," he says. "Or you have only half lived."

They ask if I have a husband and I lie. They ask if I have children and I tell the truth. "But maybe I would like some," I say.

This sends Mohammed's wife into fits of laughter. *"Maybe!"* she says. "Maybe!" I wonder if she simply thinks it is ridiculous for someone as old as I am—I've gotten so much more white hair since I got here—to consider children or if it is funny that I am not sure.

A similar scene repeats itself at Sami's house later that day. Sweets are served, tea is poured, I am again forced to explain my childlessness, and my teeth ache with all of the sugar. But I am grateful. For the first time, I feel a sense of community. I belong to my neighborhood.

☾

EID ALSO BRINGS ME the gift of Anne-Christine. A German woman about my age who has worked in Sana'a for several years in hospital management, Anne-Christine is living in a small flat under my house when I move in. But when its tenant returns from Denmark in October, she finds herself suddenly homeless. I discover her in tears one night on my stairs. Though I hardly know her, I invite her to live with me. I have so much space, and she is so distressed.

The arrangement works out marvelously for both of us. Anne-Christine is not only a vegetarian, and so shares my eating habits, but she is also a talented cook. She is happy to have someone to cook for, and I am ecstatic to eat something other than salad and bread, which is all I can ever muster the energy to throw together. For the entire two months she lives with me, Anne-Christine makes dinner every night. Even when she goes out to dinner with friends, she still cooks me an eggplant curry or stewed lentils and leaves the dish for me with a note. As if I couldn't possibly manage to fend for myself.

On nights that I fail to come home for dinner or am late because of work, Anne-Christine is distraught. "Oh, I just *wish* I knew when you would be home!" she says to me one night. Feeling a bit like a 1950s husband, I start to leave work earlier, so as not to upset her.

Al-Asaadi finds this greatly amusing. "You have a wife!"

"Yeah," I say, shutting down my computer. "She's the best thing ever. I can see why you guys would want four of them."

After she's been living with me a few weeks, I cannot imagine how I ever survived before Anne-Christine. It makes such a difference to come home to someone. I've also begun to recognize that it is a matter of survival to have a few non-Yemeni friends to whom I can confess the whole of myself. This keeps me sane and keeps me from overconfiding in people who do not have the cultural context to understand some of the decisions I have made. I am still feeling my way toward the boundaries of what I can tell and what I need to keep secret.

Anne-Christine is so integrated into the fabric of Yemen that she has a Yemeni lover, Yahya. I cannot hide my astonishment when she confesses that he is married. I wonder if she is risking her life with this relationship in a culture where adultery can be punishable by death. The night I meet Yahya for the first time, he's terribly shy and worried that I will think poorly of him, though Anne-Christine reassures him that in Germany and the United States, it is perfectly normal for a man to visit a woman in her home. When he rings to say that he is on his way, she becomes giddy as a schoolgirl, running around the house fixing her hair and changing her dress. I've never seen down-to-earth Anne-Christine like this. Her face has flushed crimson, and she looks pretty and all of sixteen.

Yahya is tall for a Yemeni, attractive, and very soft-spoken. He speaks English, though slowly. I speak too quickly for him, and Anne-Christine tells me to slow down. He seems kind and not at all the sort of man to take the risks he is taking. But people here, I am learning, are rarely what they seem.

☾

NOT ONLY DO I now have someone cooking for me and a few friends in whom I can confide, I also have what I consider the ultimate luxury: a cleaning woman. I've never had one before. No one but me has ever scrubbed my bathroom or washed my dishes. In New York, it was so expensive to hire someone to clean that I didn't even know anyone who had a cleaning woman. But Shaima has insisted that I have someone. "I don't know what we'd *do* without a housemaid," she says. She sends me Aisha, a Somali woman desperate for work.

Yemen is home to some 150,000 Somalis, most of whom have fled to Yemen to escape violence in their homeland. They are granted automatic refugee status in Yemen—as long as they can reach the country alive. Thousands of Somalis save their money to buy passage on tiny, overcrowded smugglers' boats across the Gulf of Aden. Many don't survive the journey. They are often victims of violence on the boat, and many of the smugglers transporting the Somalis dump them so far from Yemen's shores that they drown. But Aisha has survived. She doesn't speak a word of English, so I uncover her story gradually, as my Arabic improves. She lives in Sana'a with five children and a husband. A tall, heavy woman, Aisha wears a *hijab* but doesn't cover her face. When she smiles, she reveals a mouthful of enormous teeth. At first I ask Aisha to come just once a week—I don't make much of a mess given that I am rarely home. But she is so desperate for work that I relent and have her come twice a week. I pay her $10 per visit, which Shaima tells me is the going rate. This seems staggeringly little to me, but Aisha accepts it without complaint. She leaves my house gleaming, with the smell of bleach wafting up from my stone floors.

After the first couple of weeks, I start to give her things to take home, usually food. I give her whole cakes, boxes of cookies, chocolates, and even some jewelry and clothes, mostly gifts I have received for which I have no need. A few weeks later, I give her the keys to my house. I trust her.

☾

DESPITE THE REST and nutritious meals, my ribs refuse to heal. I still cannot laugh without agony, so finally our photographer Mas takes me to the hospital for X-rays. I don't know quite what the point is, because if they are cracked there is nothing I can do but rest. But it couldn't hurt to see a doctor.

We walk into an office in the emergency pavilion of the Yemeni-German Hospital, where three men sit idly shuffling papers. The one in the middle is apparently the doctor. I explain my problem, and he gives us a written order for an X-ray. We then find our way to Radiology, up and down stairs and through doorways. The technician ushers us right in and has me change into a hospital gown (even more modest than ours). I change in private, but during the actual X-ray, he allows Mas to stay in the room. Does the technician not know that he is exposing Mas to radiation? Or does he just not care? No one even asks me if I am pregnant. Do they know that pregnant women shouldn't be X-rayed? Maybe they just think I look too old to be pregnant?

We have to go to a different department to pay. It costs a whopping YR800, or about $4. We return to the doctor, who takes me to a room where a woman sits next to a tiny infant attached to an IV. It is screaming its lungs out.

The doctor sits me on another bed and draws a screen around us. My heart thuds nervously. I have not been to a male doctor in at least a decade. This man pokes and prods my rib cage, making me yelp with pain, and then moves his hand higher. I draw back in shock. "That is *not* my rib." I am too stunned to get up and walk out.

"I think you are having pain in your liver and gall bladder," he says. "You might have a liver disease."

I glare at him. "*I fell down my stairs and landed on a rib.* There is nothing wrong with my liver!" I struggle to pull down my shirt and stand.

He *insists* that I have a liver function test and asks me if I have been sick. Yes, for nearly three weeks, I say, desperate to escape him. He hems and haws and hands me over to the phlebotomist. I figure there is no harm in having the blood tests, so I let a gloveless woman take a couple of test tubes of my blood. She hands these to Mas and tells us to go to the lab. Clearly, there's no chain of custody for blood samples. I could stick any sort of substance in my test tubes, or even trade them for someone else's on the way to the lab. But I'm in a Third World country, I remind myself. I should know better than to have First World expectations of the medical care.

The lab is in a different building. We hand the unlabeled test tubes to a man behind a glass window, who struggles to write my name on them. He tells us they will be ready the next day and that the test will cost YR 4,300, nearly $25, a fortune here. I don't have that much left, so I will have to dig around the house for loose change. I don't get paid until next week.

A couple days later, Mas and I go back to the hospital, which is much more chaotic in the daylight. We want to pick up my X-ray as well as the test results, but the X-rays are nowhere to be found. The men in the emergency room walk about their office, looking under piles of paper. Then one of them finds a stack of dusty X-rays sitting unprotected on top of a metal filing cabinet.

"Here," he says, handing me the stack. "See if you can find one of ribs."

I stare at him in disbelief but thumb through the transparencies. There are legs and arms and collarbones. Finally, I find one rib cage and hold it up. The doctor looks at it. "It *could* be yours," he says. There is no name on the film.

We give up on the X-ray and go to fetch my blood test results, which of course show that I have the healthiest and happiest of livers. The entire experience has been nothing but a monumental waste of time.

☾

WHEN I RETURN to work after Eid, I am told that Hadi will be replacing our designer Samir, who is being moved to *Arabia Felix*. Despite my sadness at losing Samir, I quickly realize that Hadi is a big improvement. Samir is a lovely designer but slow. I like a pretty front page as much as the next editor, but newspapers are ephemeral things, and what's most important is that the news gets printed in a timely manner. With Hadi laying out our pages, we close earlier than ever. By eleven P.M., all of the pages are closed and we are in a van home, the men stunned to be heading out so early.

All of the hospitality I experienced around Ramadan and Eid leaves me feeling curious about something. Total strangers often invite me to their homes for meals or tea or *qat* chews, but my staff members never do. At first I take this personally. I figure that it isn't that they don't want to spend time with me. After all, al-Asaadi and Qasim have both invited me out several times. But I am never invited to their homes. Even odder is that Faris has never once invited me to his home.

I bring this up with Anne-Christine one night over dinner. She has lived in Yemen for much longer and is much more knowledgeable. "It just seems so un-Yemeni," I say, "given how hospitable everyone I meet outside the office has been."

"But they are afraid to bring you home," says Anne-Christine. "They are afraid of their wives. They cannot introduce them to you."

"Because I am a Western woman?"

"Because you are a beautiful woman. And women are very jealous. They would not allow their husbands to work—and until such late hours!—with a woman like you."

A woman like me. I'm not sure I even know what that means anymore.

ELEVEN

the trials of mohammed al-asaadi

The fanatics are calling for our heads. They've been calling for our heads since last February, when the *Yemen Observer* republished controversial Danish cartoons depicting the Prophet Mohammed, one of which shows the prophet with a bomb tucked in his turban. The paper reprinted three of the cartoons on the Op-Ed page, alongside an editorial condemning them. A large black X obscured the cartoons, yet this did nothing to temper their inflammatory impact. Islam considers even respectful depictions of the prophet to be blasphemy. The *Yemen Observer* and Mohammed al-Asaadi have been on trial for nearly ten months.

The twelve cartoons, originally printed in the newspaper *Jyllands-Posten* in September 2005 and reprinted by scores of Western publications, sparked outrage. Muslim protestors staged violent demonstrations throughout Asia, Africa, and the Middle East, during which at least fifty people were killed. The cartoonists received death threats, editors went into hiding, and Danish goods were boycotted.

Despite the *Yemen Observer*'s explicit condemnation of the cartoons, the Yemeni government insisted that the mere reprinting of them constituted an unforgivable offense against Islam. Fanatics called for the execution of al-Asaadi, and the courts shut down the paper for three months. Al-Asaadi spent twelve days in prison before he was released on bail. Yemeni prisons do not provide inmates with food and water, so reporters and family ensured al-Asaadi was fed during his internment.

Court date after court date passes without a final ruling. If we are convicted, the paper could be shut down. We could all lose our jobs. But the judges keep postponing the sentencing. The wait is taking a toll on al-Asaadi, who by November looks exhausted and drawn.

Al-Asaadi has worked for the *Yemen Observer* since 1999, when Faris plucked him out of an Internet shop in Ta'iz. "It was always my dream to be a journalist," al-Asaadi told me. "Since seventh grade. Either a journalist or a diplomat." But he was unable to study for either of those careers. Al-Asaadi grew up in the village of Ramadi in Ibb Governorate, the greenest, most fertile part of Yemen. He headed to nearby Ta'iz for university, where there were no courses in media studies or international relations. Media courses were offered in Sana'a, but al-Asaadi had no money to travel. So he studied English.

Just a couple months after graduation, al-Asaadi was working in an Internet café in Ta'iz when Faris walked in to check his e-mail. He was sitting there reading the *Yemen Times,* and Faris asked if he ever read the *Observer.* Al-Asaadi said he did. Faris then quizzed him about a recent issue, asking him what he thought of various stories, including one that he himself had written. Al-Asaadi gave his opinion, not suspecting he was speaking with the publisher of the paper. Faris said, "I am Hessam, the brother of Faris. If you want a job at the *Yemen Observer,* maybe I can talk with him."

"Yes!" cried al-Asaadi, feeling lucky indeed. The two men exchanged phone numbers and Faris went on his way.

Two days later, al-Asaadi rang Faris at the *Observer.* "I met your brother," he said. "And he said you might have a job."

Faris then confessed his true identity. "I just wanted to see how interested you really were," he said.

Al-Asaadi began working as an office assistant. Faris helped him to get training, and al-Asaadi received several grants to study journalism abroad. By the time I came to the paper, al-Asaadi had risen as far up the masthead as it is possible to go.

☪

I first accompany him to court in early November. "I just want a *verdict,*" he says. "But I know they are just going to postpone again." Faris claims that the delays are beneficial because they give the fanatics time to calm down and lose interest in the case. I repeat this to al-Asaadi, but it doesn't seem to quell his anxiety. Though al-Asaadi and I are increasingly at odds over how to run the paper, we put aside our differences when the trial date comes up. Neither of us wants to lose our job and I certainly do not want al-Asaadi sent back to prison—or worse, put to death.

One of the *Yemen Observer*'s early stories on the case (the paper continued to publish on the Web after it was shut down) reported that twenty-one lawyers for the prosecution called for the death penalty for al-Asaadi, as well as the permanent closure of the newspaper and the confiscation of all of its assets. The lawyers "recounted a story in which a lady was killed during the Prophet's lifetime after she insulted him, and that the Prophet then praised the killer. They said that they wanted the same punishment to be applied on 'those who abuse the Prophet' (PBUH)." This drives home to me the very real risk my reporters are taking by attempting to report what goes on in the world.

My reporters always follow the name of the prophet in their copy with PBUH, for "peace be upon Him." I am unsure how to deal with this. To me, newspapers are secular, reporting objectively on all issues, including religion. So for the paper to wish peace upon the prophet at first strikes me as editorializing. The articles about the cartoons naturally include scores of "PBUH"s in a concerted effort to prove how unlikely it is that the paper would insult the prophet.

The first few times I encounter "PBUH," I delete it, and no one complains. But eventually, this strikes me as overly pedantic. I am living in an entirely Muslim country. Does it hurt anyone to allow the "PBUH" to stay? Will this put the paper on the slippery slope to promoting a religion? My fears that the paper is biased toward religion feel slightly ridiculous in a uniformly religious society. I resolve to overcome my knee-jerk secularism. Besides, until our court case is over, I'm not taking unnecessary risks.

According to the *Observer,* lawyers for the prosecution also demanded "personal financial compensation for the psychological trauma they claimed they suffered by the actions of the newspaper, which they said has impaired their ability to do their jobs and follow their normal daily lives."

This is laughable. Reprinting the cartoons has psychologically dismantled the extremists? How mentally healthy can they have been to begin with if a mere cartoon can unhinge them? I despair of the Arab world ever achieving press freedom.

The defense team pointed out that the newspaper had condemned the cartoons, had defended Islam and the prophet, and had reported the different reactions from all across the Arab and Islamic world. But the prosecution said their case rested on the cartoons alone and that the accompanying articles were irrelevant.

The Ministry of Information first revoked the newspaper's license on February 8, 2006. At the same time, *al-Rai al-'Aam,* another weekly that reprinted the cartoons, was also shut down. And *al-Hurriyah* weekly not only lost its license, but its editor was jailed along with his assistant.

Prison had a profound effect on al-Asaadi. The following is an excerpt from a personal account he wrote of his incarceration, which we published on the anniversary of his arrest.

I held my breath as I was locked in a dark room in the basement of the same building, where I was interrogated. . . . Fifteen people were in that dark and dirty room. Some people, who were still asleep, though it was midday, were interrupted by noise. The inmates recognized that the new comer was a high-profile person as a result of the protest that could be seen from the only window in the room. "Who are you and why are you here?" I was asked by the inmates. I revealed my profession but concealed my name and the reason of my imprisonment. I dared not tell them that I republished the cartoons. Whatever was the context of my story, I would not be welcome. I was really afraid . . . that I might be attacked by the prisoners. That fear was justified the second day when two bedouins from Ma'rib were jailed. They asked about everybody. I was pretending that I was asleep. They asked about me and the inmates told them that I was the journalist who republished the Danish cartoons. They jumped and said, "This is the dog, then." They were calmed down by others who told them that I was defending the prophet. . . .

I was asked to pay YR 200 for the toilet water, like any new comers to the cell. Then my family sent me a mattress, blanket and pillow. My colleagues from my

newspaper and other friends flooded me with food, fruit and all edibles. I offered
my fellow inmates food and other stuff. They appreciated my offer and started asking seriously about my case. I put off telling them the story until after the prayers.
I wanted to assure them that I pray like all good Muslims. It worked out and they
trusted me. . . .

Mosque preachers and religious fanatics launched severe attacks against us.
Many of our relatives and friends boycotted us, believing we really were offenders. Obviously, it was not only the government against me in this ordeal, but also influential Islamic hardliners. The latter, who proved to be the toughest, collected millions of rials
to prosecute us. . . .

After 12 long days, painfully as long as 12 years, I was released on bail. Everybody
was happy for my release except the inmates. . . . They told me that they would miss
the food, lectures and the cleanliness of the room. I was released, but the trial continued and the newspaper continued to be suspended from printing, but continued to be
updated online. The staff and top administration's determination to continue online
was great. Their work during my stay in jail helped a lot to raise the profile of the case
in the international community and contributed to my release.

When al-Asaadi parks his car near the courthouse for our November
court date, at first I am unaware that we have arrived. The building, set in
a dusty, rock-strewn courtyard, doesn't resemble any courthouse I have
ever seen. It is devoid of grandeur and looks to me like an ordinary modern Yemeni house. A crowd of men bustles around the entrance, and we
have to push our way through. All of the guards kiss al-Asaadi hello. Even
the prosecutor on his case comes over to kiss him several times as we arrive at the gate. The prosecutor tells al-Asaadi that his sentencing has been
postponed yet again, to December. This was just what al-Asaadi feared. To
make absolutely sure that we cannot get a verdict, we push our way into
the building. The prosecutor tells me that there are three similar cases
going on, involving the other newsmen accused. "None of the judges
wants to be the first to rule," he says. They are afraid of the response of the
fanatics.

If al-Asaadi were not dragging me behind him into the building, I am
not sure I would make it through the throngs. There are too many people.
Too many men. Guards pat men down at the entrance to the building, but

they have no female guards and so they don't search me, despite the fact that I am toting an enormous bag. I see no other women.

We pass through a grubby narrow hallway and start up a filthy set of stairs at the back. At the top, we pass from small square white room to small square white room, greeting people and moving on. I have trouble keeping up with al-Asaadi, who is tiny enough to slip easily through crowds. I am also very busy trying to keep from brushing against any of the men, which is no easy task. When we at last reach a small square white room with a judge, al-Asaadi is unable to persuade him to issue a verdict, and we are turned away. On our way out, al-Asaadi stops to kiss a few hundred more men.

"Do you want to see the prison cell where I was?" he asks me.

I do.

Al-Asaadi greets (and kisses) one of the guards and convinces him to unlock the prison underneath the courthouse. The low-ceilinged room is crowded with men. They have been sitting on their thin sleeping mats, but most spring to their feet when they see us. They stare at me.

"Salaam aleikum," says al-Asaadi.

"Aleikum salaam," they chorus back.

I gaze around. The dingy yellow walls are scrawled with graffiti. On my right, the entire corner is littered with empty water bottles. Just beyond them is the toilet. It doesn't smell all that horrible, though I have a cold again, so I'm not smelling much in general.

"That's where I used to sleep," al-Asaadi says, pointing to a corner toward the back.

The men continue to stare at us, silently, until we turn to go.

"They never let anyone in there," al-Asaadi tells me as we walk back out into the sunshine and the guard locks the door behind us. "But I formed a good relationship with the guards."

"I can see that." We climb back into his car and return to the office to work. And to wait.

When the next court date rolls around in December, everyone feels certain we will finally get a verdict. The day before, the Yemeni Journalists Syndicate, an advocacy group for journalists' rights, holds a rally to support al-Asaadi and the paper. I meet al-Asaadi and Farouq in the courtyard of the YJS first thing in the morning, and we mingle with the journalists trickling in.

The rally is held outside, under a blue-and-white-striped tent. Pro-press slogans demanding the unshackling of journalists have been printed on sheets of white paper and pasted on all the walls of the courtyard. The crowd of sixty or so journalists is almost entirely male, with two Yemeni women sitting quietly toward the back. Because the sexes are almost always segregated in Yemen, it is unusual for a woman to sit near men. But I take a seat in one of the front rows. I'm the editor of the paper, damn it. A series of journalists then make impassioned speeches in Arabic for about an hour (Ibrahim translates). It's all preaching to the choir—everyone present is on the same side. I wonder if the rally would be more effective if it were held, say, in front of the courthouse. This doesn't seem to have occurred to anyone.

Kamil al-Samawi, the lawyer representing us in court, makes a speech in defense of press freedom. He works with HOOD, a nonprofit, nongovernmental human rights organization. HOOD reports human rights violations and defends victims, offering free legal assistance. It is unpopular with the government, which doesn't like to be reminded of its shaky human rights record. A short, stocky man with glasses and a broad smile, Kamil is a passionate speaker, and the crowd murmurs its assent as he talks.

I am particularly fond of Kamil for helping Zuhra overcome many of her initial fears about becoming a journalist. She first met him at the courthouse when the *Observer*'s trial began, and they became friends. He was close to her oldest brother, Fahmi, so Zuhra felt comfortable with him. "I liked the way he speaks about human rights. He is very open-minded," she said. "He feels it is important for victims to speak up. I have never seen a man that respects people like Kamil."

She had always thought she was "a coward journalist" because she avoided controversial stories. "This was before you came," she says. She worried that covering provocative topics would make her a target. "I remember Rahma Hugaira [a female Yemeni journalist]—her reputation was assassinated because she attacks the government." Rahma was called a whore and worse, just for having the courage to speak out. Zuhra was terrified of suffering a similar fate. But when Kamil took her to court to meet Anisa al-Shuaibi, Zuhra knew she had to write about her case.

In 2003, Anisa was accused of killing her former husband but was acquitted of the crime when no evidence was found against her—and her ex-husband was found to be living. At the time of her arrest, she was brutally dragged out of her home at night and locked in prison, where she was raped. When she was released, more than a month later, she accused the head of the Criminal Investigation Unit, Rizq al-Jawfi, and the head of the CIU's investigations department, Saleh al-Salhi, of illegally imprisoning her and of being responsible for her rape and torture in jail.

Zuhra interviewed her, as well as her two small children, and was shocked by the tale. "The Anisa case represents in all ways part of what we are suffering here as women," says Zuhra. The men who put her in prison knew that no one would support Anisa, she continued. "If you are being raped and speak out about it in Yemen, you are going to be scandaled and face social denial." It is unacceptable to talk about rape, and any woman who claims to have been raped is blamed for the crime and ostracized. Zuhra admires Anisa's bravery and hopes she will inspire other women to speak out. Since Anisa's protest, Zuhra adds, fewer women have been put in jail, because officials became afraid that they would be accused of abuse.

Zuhra's stories on Anisa have prompted threatening letters from readers. But while these frighten her, she has no intention of silencing her pen. "I was afraid to cover it, but it makes me feel good about myself," she says. She doggedly follows the story, never missing a court date and filing several front-page pieces on Anisa's plight. "I have started my war and I have decided not to stop."

☪

DECEMBER 6 IS D-DAY for al-Asaadi and the *Yemen Observer*. I am at the office by eight thirty A.M. to check in with my staff before heading to the courthouse. Najma and Noor are late with the Culture page, so I tell them they must stay and finish it. But I am forced to relent when Mohammed al-Matari says he has spoken to Faris, who wants everybody there. Al-Matari colors his graying hair black and dresses in suits that fit him the way a refrigerator fits a stick of butter. His lapels are often stained with something, spots of tea or dried beans. There's a kind of old-world gentlemanliness about him, a persistent chivalrousness.

Al-Matari's insistence that everyone attend the trial shames me—I should not have tried to make the women stay in the office on such an important day. Of course they should come with us. We should be filling the courthouse and squeezing out the fanatics who will be there in the hopes of seeing al-Asaadi laid low. I am surprised when Faris himself does not show. Since the fate of his paper hinges on this trial, one would think he might want to attend. When he doesn't appear by nine A.M., we all pile into the *Yemen Observer* van.

At the courthouse, Zuhra glues herself to me. We push through the mobs at the gate and building entrance and up the stairs to the courtroom.

"I haven't missed a single court date for this trial," says Zuhra. "Even al-Asaadi missed one date when he was sick, but I have never missed one!"

Zuhra makes Najma change places with her so she can sit next to me on the wooden bench lined with splitting, chocolate-colored cushions. The narrow courtroom fills up quickly, mostly with fellow journalists. My women are the only women in the room. I am the only westerner. I take several photographs of the crowd.

Faris never arrives.

☾

AL-ASAADI IS LATE. He told me on the phone earlier that his lawyer had advised him to be a little late, to make a dramatic entrance I suppose. But he is so late that his lawyer finally calls him and says, "Where are you? Do you want to just go straight to jail?" (The lawyer is standing in front of us, and Zuhra translates.) He and Qasim and several other men in the front row laugh. There is much nervous laughter and chatter, but the anxiety in the room is palpable. We are all journalists; we all have a stake in this. If the *Yemen Observer* is shuttered, my staff and I will be jobless. I have no idea what I will do if this happens. I suppose stay and fight to get it reopened. I couldn't possibly go back to New York now. To return to New York would be admitting defeat. Besides, I have grown attached to my reporters. I cannot imagine abandoning them.

A cheer goes up in the courtroom. Al-Asaadi has arrived, making a grand entrance from the judge's end of the room. Men rush to the front of the pews and surround him, kissing him and squeezing his hand. He looks very sharp in a black suit and striped tie. I feel an impulse to hug him, but naturally this is impossible, so I settle for a wave and an affectionate nod.

By the time the judge arrives, the room is filled to overflowing. The back of the room is so packed that guards have to push people to keep them from surging forward. A dozen or so men dressed in army green and wearing red berets watch us intently, their hands fiddling with the triggers of machine guns and pistols. Their presence reminds me that violence is expected. If al-Asaadi and the paper are not convicted, the fanatics could go mad. Fortunately, there isn't much room in the courtroom for fanatics; we journalists take up almost all of the benches. I crane my neck to try to spot them. Zuhra says they are in the back, but I can't tell who they are.

Several more guards stream in with the judge, who takes a seat at the head of the bench.

I am so anxious I might throw up. My heart pounds so loudly I have trouble hearing Zuhra, and my hands tremble as I scribble notes.

Al Asaadi stands at a small, low lectern on our right. His supporters close in, hovering protectively around him, clinging to each other's hands. I find it touching that Yemeni law allows someone about to be sentenced to stand surrounded by dozens of his closest friends.

His face solemn as death, the judge—gray hair, glasses, green sash—begins to read from a paper. Zuhra whispers a translation of his words while furiously taking notes. He begins by recapping the cases of both the prosecution and the defense. The only sound in the room other than his words is Zuhra's occasional "Oh my God!"

I hardly dare to breathe. Not knowing exactly when the sentence is coming, I watch the audience closely for clues. The men look stern and frightened. Al-Asaadi is slumped against his lectern, as though he can't quite hold himself up.

Finally, a murmur goes up from the crowd, and I hear the words "YR500,000." "Is that a fine?" I whisper to Zuhra. "Are we getting a fine?"

She nods and tells me that al-Asaadi has been convicted. I draw a sharp breath.

"Of insulting Islam?"

"Yes, by republishing the cartoons. The judge just confirmed that it was a crime."

But al-Asaadi will receive no jail term, she tells me. Even better, the paper will stay open!

There is a collective release of breath. Men begin to whisper to each other and shuffle their feet.

When the judge finishes reading, there is scattered applause. Along with relief for al-Asaadi, however, comes concern that this conviction makes him more vulnerable to being attacked by extremists. A conviction of insulting Islam is a serious thing, and the fanatics might just take it upon themselves to punish him, now that his crime has been confirmed.

Guards whisk al-Asaadi away to a holding cell until a guarantee can be deposited. We quickly follow, streaming down the stairs and out into the sunshine.

A Reuters television reporter has grabbed me in the courtroom and asked if he could interview me, so I follow him to an area away from the crowds. He asks my opinion of the verdict and the Yemeni courts, while al-Matari translates. A crowd gathers to watch.

"I am very pleased that the paper will remain open," I say, squinting in the bright sunlight. "That is a victory for freedom of the press. But I am very disappointed with the conviction. I am concerned that it puts our colleague Mohammed al-Asaadi at risk."

The men around me murmur to each other and ask al-Matari what I have said. Several of them seem to nod in agreement. When I am done, I turn and scan the crowds for Zuhra. She is busy interviewing people, darting from man to man. It's easy to spot her; she's the fastest-moving object in the courtyard.

Al-Asaadi has appeared in a window of the courthouse and is making the most of his audience, clinging to the bars of the window and posing for photographs. He calls out to me.

I climb up the embankment under his window.

"Mohammed! What are you doing in there?"

He looks awfully cheerful for a convicted man. "I'm in prison!" he chirps.

"How do I get you out?" This is a serious question. I wonder if I should pay the fine myself, so that we can take him back to the paper with us. But I don't have enough *riyals* on me. Where the hell is Faris?

"I will be out in a little while, after we make the guarantee. Go back to the paper and get the story online."

"Of course. Zuhra is on it. Do you need money?"

"No, not now."

"Well, I can get you some if you need it."

"Thank you."

I find Zuhra and try to take her to the van, but she keeps spotting new sources to tackle. We are about to make it out of the gate when she sees one of the men who want us dead.

"There's one of the fanatics!" she cries, recognizing a man she met in court before. "I have to get a quote!" I watch her flap away, bursting with pride.

Finally, we all pile into the van to go back to the paper. Zuhra and I decide that it will be fastest to write the story together. She has all of the quotes from the judge and other sources, and I have descriptions of the proceedings and quotes from al-Asaadi. We run to my office, and Zuhra pulls a chair up to my desk. We send someone out for tea.

"Have you had breakfast?" I said.

"No."

"Eat this. We can't have you falling over before deadline." I hand her an energy bar, a package of peanuts, and a parcel of toast from my secret food drawer.

We are a good team, working fast and efficiently, me typing, Zuhra reading and translating her notes for me. Our story is online within an hour—and we are the first to break the news, beating Reuters, Agence-France Presse, and the BBC.

I am very pleased and flushed with manic energy. Zuhra and I high-five each other and toast ourselves with sugary tea.

Ibrahim calls in the afternoon to congratulate me. "It was so brilliant, so professional, and you even got a quote from a fanatic!" he says.

"That's all Zuhra," I say. "She did all the real reporting."

"I called al-Asaadi to tell him what a wonderful job you did."

"You did?"

"I said, 'She even mentioned your tie!'"

"Well, it was a very nice tie!"

Al-Asaadi sends me a text later to thank me for my support and the story. I glow with happiness.

☪

OF COURSE, our busy morning means that we fall behind with the rest of the paper. So, feeling quite like Sisyphus, I put my shoulder to the stone and begin, slowly, to roll it back up the hill.

TWELVE
tug-of-war

Unfortunately, the solidarity al-Asaadi and I experience during our day in court is short-lived. Now that we have been reprieved, we resume our slowly escalating power struggle. I've tried my utmost to avoid conflict, but it's hard when al-Asaadi refuses to acknowledge deadlines. By now, I've realized that the first thing I need to achieve is a proper schedule. Not until I get the paper moving in an orderly way, with pages coming in at predictable times and issues closing on time, will I be able to turn my attention to the development of my staff's journalistic skills.

By December, the only thing standing between me and a regular schedule is al-Asaadi. The rest of my reporters now turn in their pieces on time, so we *could* close every issue by eight P.M. But al-Asaadi purposely withholds his stories until the last minute and drags out our closes for hours. To make a point, Luke and I finish absolutely every page, send everyone else home, and ring al-Asaadi to tell him we are just twiddling our thumbs waiting for his story, which is the last thing we need in order to close. This has little effect. Al-Asaadi still refuses to come to the office before eight P.M. on a closing day. He doesn't seem to care that he is holding us all hostage. Thursdays are particularly bad, because he spends all afternoon chewing *qat* with his friends and is reluctant to come to the office at all. When he gets there, he is so wired that he is perfectly happy to stay up all night—and keep us up with him—closing the paper.

Things come to a head during the Consultative Group for Yemen's donors' conference in London, held to encourage foreign aid to Yemen. Yemen is the poorest country in the Middle East, but it receives surprisingly low levels of development assistance. Now Western and Arab countries are meeting to discuss Yemen's development challenges and to pledge financial support. This is intended to help Yemen develop its economy, improve its infrastructure, and battle poverty and illiteracy. The money comes with strings attached, however. Donors insist that Yemen forge ahead with anticorruption reforms, bolster democratic institutions, create a more independent judiciary, and increase government transparency. Yemen has vowed its dedication to these reforms, but whether it will be able to fully realize them remains a great unknown.

Al-Asaadi has traveled to England with Faris to attend the conference and has promised us a front-page story. The biggest news, that a total of $4.7 billion has been pledged, breaks on a closing day. This is a major increase over amounts pledged at previous donors' conferences. Yemeni officials (and Faris) are euphoric.

But we hear nothing from al-Asaadi. All day, I edit the rest of the issue and wait for his news. We cannot run the issue without it; the donors' conference is the biggest story in the country. By seven P.M., we have edited everything else. I grow anxious. Just in case, I tell al-Matari to start putting a story together from the wires and calling local officials for comment.

We are still waiting when Luke begins vomiting. He thinks it's the pesticides on his *qat*. Pesticides illegal everywhere else in the world have a way of sneaking across Yemen's borders and ending up on *qat* plants. Luke chews Yemeni quantities of *qat* and by deadline can hardly speak, his cheek is so packed with greenery. "He's more Yemeni than most Yemenis," Zuhra says.

I send him home. Manel, a twenty-four-year-old Senegalese-American I recently hired to share the copyediting, stays to help me. Manel speaks fluent Arabic, French, and English and brims with infectious good humor. His copyediting is patchier than Luke's, but he has such a sunny attitude that his mere presence in the office inspires all of us. Handsome, with a lean wiry body and neatly cornrowed hair, Manel is particularly inspiring to the women in the office. But *everyone* loves Manel, who wouldn't even know how to go about getting stressed out. I'm hoping some of his Zen will wear off on me.

I have already written several e-mails to al-Asaadi, asking him how the conference is going and when I will receive his copy. No reply. When the rest of the issue is done, I write again to tell him that if I don't hear from him in the next half hour, I will have to run a wire story.

He rings me in response. "Zaid and I will have the story to you in a couple of hours," he says.

"A couple of hours? Al-Asaadi, the rest of the issue is completely done! Please get it to me in the next hour."

Our conversation is cut off just after that, and I get an e-mail from him that says, "I am the editor in chief, and if I tell you to hold the paper until I send you the story then you have to hold the paper. I don't have to answer to you."

Actually, I want to say, you *do* have to answer to me. It is in my *contract* that I am to have *complete editorial control* over this paper. Thus far, I have purposely avoided saying such a thing. I have never pulled rank on him, in an effort to preserve his dignity and our diplomatic relations.

Even Faris has warned me about al-Asaadi. "He doesn't like it when anyone else gets too good," he told me. The reason al-Asaadi has been sabotaging every issue, Faris believes, is that he can't stand to see me get the paper on a schedule. To see me succeed where he failed.

I do not respond to his e-mail. I sit and stew, while Manel holds my hand and tries to keep me from erupting into flames. As it becomes clear why we are stuck in the office so late, my staff also grow impatient. It's midnight by the time we get the story and photos from al-Asaadi. He fails to send me photo credits and doesn't respond when I ask for them by e-mail. I am forced to run the photos without credit and send everyone home. I've been at work for twenty hours.

I indulge in revenge fantasies all the way home. I imagine calling al-Asaadi and saying, "Why do you think they hired me? Because you were running the paper perfectly?" But I do no such thing. I go to bed with an aching stomach and dream that al-Asaadi is livid with me for not waiting in the office all night for him to send me photo credits.

(⋆

THINGS CONTINUE in the same vein after he returns from London. The very next issue, he e-mails me that he wants to write the editorial. So I save him that space. Luke and I finish every other page by seven thirty P.M. Al-Asaadi waltzes into the office at seven forty-five P.M. He hasn't even started his editorial. It's *textbook* sabotage.

I have been in a sunny mood all day, but now clouds are gathering. When he finally finishes his editorial, al-Asaadi decides to rearrange the entire front page and suggest additions to the Local page. I fight to keep my voice steady.

"I would have loved your feedback—*at four P.M. this afternoon*," I say. "When we had plenty of time to rework things before deadline."

"I can't come in at four P.M.," he says.

"Why not? Everyone else does. That's our work hours."

We are interrupted by his phone. Al-Asaadi has two mobile phones, both of which ring constantly. He chats for several minutes, his cheek bulging. While the entire rest of the staff has been hard at work, he has been at a *qat* chew with his friends.

Al-Asaadi seems to believe that holding the title of editor in chief entitles him to do less work than the rest of the staff. His time in prison has made him a bit of a celebrity. He's Yemen's poster boy for press freedom, and he milks this so much that Manel takes to calling him the "Boy Wonder" or the "Ghetto Superstar." He loves to go out to embassy parties, to meet and greet dignitaries, but isn't all that interested in the day-to-day sweat and toil of editing a paper. He spends no time training the staff to become better reporters, though they could use his help, and is impatient with their mistakes.

Luke and Manel and I confer about al-Asaadi's obstructiveness after we finally flee at eleven P.M. Compared to our first two months, this is still an early close, and I have worked a mere fourteen hours instead of twenty. Luke, who worked for the paper for several months before I arrived, says that before I came there was no order at all and they were often there all night. "We were here until five or six in the morning," he says. "You've done an amazing job."

Luke offers to come with me to talk to Faris, to support my complaints about al-Asaadi. "He has blatantly sabotaged you for the last three issues," he says. "All three issues would have closed at eight if not for him."

Faris, as is too often the case, is out of town. So we wait.

The weird thing is that I know al-Asaadi likes me in spite of himself. And I like him. He brought me a pretty souvenir candy dish from London, and on days we are not closing an issue, we often talk and laugh together. But throughout the fall, the tension has escalated. When he is in the office, he entertains a constant stream of visitors, who sit a few feet from my desk talking loudly and slurping tea. The incessant racket is deleterious to both my patience and my editing. If al-Asaadi isn't with a guest, he is shouting on the phone.

In Yemen, no one ever makes an appointment. People visit the editor of a paper when they feel like visiting, with no regard for the fact that she might be on deadline. Yet it is the height of rudeness to turn anyone away. I make this mistake one day, when a Yemeni reader drops in to talk with me about the paper just as I am editing several stories on a closing day. "Look, I'm really sorry, but I just don't have time right now," I tell him. "I am trying to close an issue. Could you please make an appointment next time?"

As soon as he leaves the office, al-Asaadi berates me. "You cannot *do* that," he says. "You must *always* offer them a seat and at least a glass of tea. That is how things are done here."

I feel terrible guilt for being so culturally insensitive. But I am also frustrated. If I am required to entertain endless visitors, as al-Asaadi does, how am I ever going to get my work done?

Yet sometimes, my visitors delight me. I am busy editing one afternoon when a tall, blue-eyed cowboy walks into my office. A real cowboy. From Arizona. This is Marvin. He steps hesitantly across my threshold, looking as though he's just been peeled off a Marlboro billboard. His gray hair is cropped short, and he sports a big mustache, jeans, and bowlegs.

I'd heard of Marvin. He is running a livestock program on Soqotra and splits his time between the island and Sana'a. Thinking that I could get an interesting story, I invite him to sit.

Goats run loose across the pristine island of Soqotra, he tells me, and they are slowly destroying its unique and delicate ecosystem. Marvin's plan, yet to be put into action, would help the local people learn how to keep their animals healthy, manage foraging, open a sanitary *halal* slaughterhouse, and sell meat to the mainland.

We commiserate about the difficulty of getting anything done here, the malingering of our workers, and the disorder of the country. Marvin tells me that one of his workers refused to come in one day because he'd skipped breakfast and his stomach hurt, while another didn't show up because his left pinkie finger had a paper cut.

"You know the Spanish word *'mañana'*?" says Marvin.

"Of course," I say. "Tomorrow."

"It doesn't really mean 'tomorrow,' " he says. "It means 'definitely not today.' "

I could see where this was going.

"And here, it's the same thing with *'insha'allah.'* "

"I know! It's the universal excuse for everything. If my reporters don't get a story done on time, well, it just wasn't *meant* to be done on time." This absence of personal responsibility bothers me. The general attitude of my male reporters seems to be "Why should I worry about it, when I can just leave it to God?" While my women will work themselves to exhaustion, refusing even to eat until a story is done, my men spend the bulk of their time justifying their minimal efforts. This is the result of privileging one half of society over another, I think. The men feel the world owes them a living and work only to get more money for *qat,* whereas the women work three times as hard in an effort to prove that they can do what everyone tells them they cannot.

Yet the men treat the women with condescension. One afternoon, al-Matari, who is Noor's cousin, comes into my office to tell me that Noor has gone home crying. "It is Farouq," says al-Matari. "He yelled at her."

This is not the first time this has happened. Zuhra recently ran into my office trembling. "Can I talk to you?" she said, closing the door and throwing back her veil. She was in floods of tears. Farouq had been taunting her, she said, accusing her of spending too much time talking with westerners, as if this were a betrayal of her people. By "westerners," he meant Western men, which meant Luke and Manel. Zuhra sees Luke as a brother and is nearly as comfortable talking with him as she is with me. Because Luke is Western, she knows he won't mistake her friendliness as a sign of loose morals. Over time, she has come to feel the same way about lovable Manel. It's agonizing to have these relationships misconstrued.

Today, it's been Noor's turn to play punching bag to Farouq. As she is already gone, I send her an e-mail saying that I am sorry Farouq has upset her and that she shouldn't hesitate to come talk to me if he bothers her at work.

The next afternoon, I pull Farouq into my office. He claims that Noor yelled at him first (which I doubt). "Farouq. You are an adult. No matter *what* Noor said to you, I need you to try to be kind to her in the office. If you have a problem with her, come talk to me about it, and I will deal with her. But this isn't the first time you've upset someone in the office, and I don't want my reporters leaving here in tears."

"I will have nothing to do with the women!" he says angrily. "I will never speak to them!"

"Well, you may *have* to, for work. So I need you to please try to be nice. And professional. Come to me with any problems. Okay?"

He gives me a curt nod and leaves my office.

I tell all of this to Marvin, who nods sympathetically. "Well, if you need to get away, come see us on Soqotra," he says. "There are plenty of stories for you to write there."

☾

I KEEP MARVIN'S INVITATION in mind as I redouble my efforts to work with al-Asaadi. The tension is not constant, and he can be quite charming. In late November, our relationship gets a boost from an out-of-town field trip. I haven't left Sana'a since I arrived (other than a long weekend in Istanbul) and am aching to see the countryside. Al-Asaadi says he wants to take me somewhere in honor of my birthday, which I think is the best gift possible. So one Friday in November, he and his two eldest daughters come to pick me up in the Old City to take me out to Wadi Dhar, a valley about a half hour from Sana'a.

Hulud and Asma, ages four and six, both tiny and shy with identically braided hair and long, curly eyelashes, stand in the backseat of the car for the entire ride, staring at me silently. I cannot get used to seeing parents fail to buckle their children safely into cars. There are no child safety seats, and older children never wear seat belts.

It is a bright, sunny morning as we head out of Sana'a, past the sprawling fruit and vegetable markets on the fringes of town and increasingly ramshackle homes, into the mountains. We are heading to Dar al-Hajar, the imam's palace built on top of a rock in Wadi Dhar.

On the way, al-Asaadi pulls over at a scenic overlook, where hundreds of tourists, both Western and Yemeni, mill around the edge of the cliff overlooking a deep, green valley. The four of us walk to the edge and stand looking down at the patches of *qat* and the squat homes beneath us. Mountains fill the horizon. Yemeni men sell trays of bright pink cotton candy, fruit, and nut brittles. A man with a falcon on a rope lets foreigners take pictures for a price. We take photos of each other and talk with a German family standing near us. Al-Asaadi is happy to see tourists in his country. "When bad things happen, like these terrorism things, it makes me worry about their future," he says, tapping his girls on their heads.

I want to say that one of the best things he can do for their future is to make them wear seat belts in the car, but I bite my tongue.

It is hot and dusty when we arrive at the palace. Just outside, men dance in a circle with unsheathed *jambiyas*. Even knee-high little boys wave their daggers around in the air as they try to follow the steps of the men. No one seems concerned about trusting preschoolers with lethal weapons. I am reminded of my sister's horrified reaction when, after my first trip to Yemen, I gave a tiny *jambiya* to my four-year-old nephew, Noah. "I can't let him have a *weapon!*" she scolded me.

We wander over to the entrance and make our way up the many flights of stairs, pushing through throngs of people. The five-story medieval Dar al-Hajar (Rock Palace) was expanded in the 1930s into a summer residence for Imam Yahya, who ruled Yemen from 1918 to 1948. It is a maze of gypsum-walled rooms, riddled with *qamaria* and nooks and crannies for children to crawl into. We lean out windows to gaze at the valley below. Hulud and Asma are interested in everything, touching the walls and looking around them with big eyes, but are almost entirely silent. They don't even jabber with each other.

When we're done exploring, al-Asaadi is in a hurry to get home in time for noon prayers. The dirt track winding back to the main road is lined with fruit sellers offering pyramids of plums and pears. I buy a kilo of tight-skinned purple plums and we eat them as we drive back, the sweet juice running down our arms and chins. When Al-Asaadi drops me home, he runs to the Qubat al-Mahdi mosque across the street, as he doesn't have time to get to his mosque. I ask if he is taking the girls, and he says no, they will wait in the car. The afternoon heat is sweltering and the car is overly warm. Trying to hide my horror, I ask, "Why don't they come stay with me until you're done?"

"Oh no," he says. "They're used to it." He opens a window and shuts them in the car.

I stand next to the car for a moment as al-Asaadi hurries across the street to pray. The girls sit quietly. It feels unconscionable to walk away and leave them there, but I don't have a choice. I turn to head toward home, hoping that al-Asaadi prays quickly.

☾

AT THE END OF NOVEMBER, two men from the South African embassy visit me. These men actually made an appointment, only I have completely forgotten. When they arrive, I am buried in work, but I set my editing aside to talk about the recent elections and press freedoms in Yemen. Ambassadors often drop by to quiz me about the Yemeni press. They want to know "where my red lines are"—what limits are put on free expression. I normally enjoy these ambassadorial briefings, but I am so overwhelmed by the work I have left to do that their visit sends me into a panic. Exacerbating matters, I return to my office to find a group of women students sitting there, waiting for al-Asaadi. Struggling to be polite, I chat with them briefly before he arrives.

Now I am even more behind, so I ask al-Asaadi to please take the students to a conference room, so I can catch up with my editing.

"No," he says with a note of defiance in his voice.

I look up from my computer, startled. "Why not? The conference rooms are both empty, and I have to be in the office to edit on my computer and e-mail questions to Hakim on his story."

"No. *You* go someplace else."

I am stunned, not just by his irrational obstinacy, but by the fact that he is arguing with me in front of a room full of women.

"Mohammed, I need to be in this office and you know that. Why do you need to be here to talk with these women? This is why we have conference rooms! For meetings like this!"

He refuses to leave. I attempt to work, but it is impossible with him talking at top volume to the students right next to me. Faris, for once, happens to be upstairs, so I run up to solicit his support. I interrupt his meeting with Jelena, the temperamental advertising coordinator for *Arabia Felix,* who has just had such a vicious fight with Karim that he threatened to quit.

"What is it?" says Faris, looking annoyed.

I explain the situation, and Faris immediately phones downstairs to tell al-Asaadi to take the girls to a conference room. I am well aware that tattling on al-Asaadi to Faris sounds the death knell of our relationship, but I don't know what else to do. I have five pages left to edit, and most of the day is gone.

I run back downstairs, but al-Asaadi, in defiance of Faris's orders, still refuses to leave. Faris sends down the big guns, in the shape of the formidable Doctor. I hide out in the newsroom with Luke while he goes to oust al-Asaadi and the girls from our office.

When at last they are gone, I go straight back to work. Al-Asaadi promptly returns to yell at me. I yell back.

"Why are you being so stubborn?" I say. "You know I have to be here for work. Why do you have to be here, when both conference rooms are free?"

"Because it's *my office!*"

"That is not rational! There is no reason you cannot talk to those women in the conference rooms!"

Al-Asaadi picks up things from his desk and throws them down again. "This isn't even an *office* anymore," he says. "It looks like a *grocery* store!" He waves angrily at the orange sitting on my desk.

"You know I keep most of my food in my desk drawers," I say, my voice starting to tremble. "And I *have* to keep food here, because I don't have a *wife* at home to cook me lunch." (Anne-Christine has moved to Syria, and I've gone back to a diet of cereal and salads.) "*This* is where I eat my lunch. I have too much work to finish to go home. What do you want me to do? Stop eating?"

Silence.

"Al Asaadi, if you want me to move, I will try to move to a different office. Then you can do what you want. It is your office, after all."

"No," he says, relenting a little. "It is your office too. I am sorry. I want you to stay here."

"I am sorry too. I really didn't want to get into a huge argument about this, but you have to understand that I really need to get work done!"

I turn back to my computer, and al-Asaadi taps away at his keyboard, for once in total silence.

I finally get caught up on my editing, after skipping both the gym and lunch, enabling us to close by the not unreasonable hour of ten thirty P.M. I'm pretty pleased with the front page, although nervous about what Faris will think, as it is packed with what he is sure to see as negative stories. Headlines include QAT-CHEWING DOOMS YEMENI FOOTBALL TEAM, GUN-TOTING YEMENIS DISCOURAGE INVESTMENT, and ATTACKS ON JOURNALISTS CONTINUE.

I am even more nervous about my editorial, in which I attack President Saleh for not standing up for journalists. He has said nothing to condemn the imprisonment and harassment of journalists, and I think this is disgraceful, particularly given all his big talk about how Yemen is such a swell democracy.

Yet Faris doesn't notice. I start to suspect he doesn't even read the paper unless someone makes a complaint. I never hear a single word from him about anything we publish.

Qasim has begun giving me almost as much trouble as al-Asaadi. Noor comes to me one morning to say that she wants to cover a big concert for her Culture page. This sounds fine to me, so I agree to write her a letter confirming that she is a journalist. Faris is still refusing to give my staff press IDs, which means they are constantly getting thrown out of government buildings and hospitals for lack of credentials. He claims that my reporters must prove themselves trustworthy before they deserve IDs, although I point out that it is nearly impossible for them to do their jobs without identification.

Just after I give Noor permission to go to the concert, Qasim storms my office. "You cannot let Noor cover the concert!"

I am bewildered. "I want this story for the Culture page," I say. "Why shouldn't we cover it?"

"*Arabia Felix* is writing about it."

"*Arabia Felix* is a *magazine* and comes out twice a *year*. It's not exactly a conflict of interest for us both to write about it."

"Well, Noor can't get in. I only have two passes."

"I'll get her press passes then. Who is the press contact?"

"He only speaks Arabic."

"Fine. I'll find someone to call him."

Qasim is beside himself. "No! A professional journalist should cover this concert."

I stare at him. Noor is standing right in front of him.

"Noor *is* a professional journalist," I say coolly. "And I am sending her and Najma to cover the concert. I will buy their tickets with my own money if I have to."

I do have to. Qasim persists in refusing to help the women, so I give Noor and Najma enough cash to cover both their tickets and transportation, along with a letter stating that they work for me. They are delighted, thank me effusively, and write a colorful feature about the event. I wonder sometimes how much more we could get done if men were not constantly trying to stand in our way.

☪

I HAVE BEEN at the paper for three months when the Ministry of Information telephones to ask about my specific role at the paper and for my visa number. Enass comes into my office to take my passport, sending me into a panic.

"Am I going to be thrown out of the country?"

She laughs and shakes her head.

Al-Asaadi says I must write a letter to the ministry saying that my title is merely honorary and that I make no editorial decisions at all. I agree to do this because it is illegal for a foreigner to run a Yemeni paper. But I am suspicious of the ministry's sudden interest. Why now, when I have been on the paper's masthead for three months? Have they just not been paying attention, or has someone tipped them off? I wonder briefly if my editorials criticizing the government are to blame, but they are unsigned.

The letter does the trick, and the ministry backs off. My title, however, has slipped down the masthead and been changed to consulting editor. Al-Asaadi must be thrilled. But it doesn't bother me. As far as I'm concerned, they can call me staff janitor as long as I can do my job.

C*

MY NEXT TACTIC in my campaign to get everyone, including al-Asaadi, meeting deadlines is a written schedule. In late December, I pass this out, along with a style guide I have been compiling since my arrival. We have already begun to close pages on a somewhat regular timeline, but too many of my reporters seem consistently surprised when their deadlines arrive. Now, with a written schedule in front of them, they cannot claim to be ignorant of when their pages are due. I have made a point of making al-Asaadi's pages due before lunch on closing day, given that he can't be trusted to get back to work after lunch. I'm hoping this will help keep things on track when I go off to Cairo for ten days' vacation over New Year's.

On Christmas Eve, I decide to leave work early because it's a holiday for me and I have an out-of-town guest. I edit manically to finish by eight P.M. I've already told al-Asaadi that I won't be coming in on Christmas, which falls on a closing day. For once, I am going to play the Christian card and claim a religious holiday of my own.

But when al-Asaadi shows up in the office close to eight P.M. on Christmas Eve, he tells me that he has decided to finish the paper that night, a day early.

"Why?" I am bewildered. "There's no reason."

"Tomorrow's Christmas!" says al-Asaadi.

I stare at him. "Mohammed. This is a Muslim country. There is no reason not to work on Christmas."

"We're all going to take a day off in solidarity with you."

"Why?" I ask again. "Do you feel like you won't be able to close tomorrow without me?"

He insists and says he will keep Manel with him in the office until the issue is done. This is incredibly unfair to Manel and the rest of my staff, but there is nothing I can do. I can't stay in the office myself when someone has traveled all this way to be with me. Just as I am about to pack up to go, al-Asaadi hands me several stories to edit.

"Al-Asaadi. It is Christmas Eve, and I would like to be able to go home and spend some time with my guest," I say.

"But I need you to edit these before you go."

"Why don't you just save them for tomorrow and have Manel do them?"

"We're closing the issue tonight!"

"Look, I *never* ask for time off. Just this *once,* I want to go home and spend time with someone who is in this country for only ten days and whom I will not see for months."

Al-Asaadi then informs me that not only has he decided to close this issue a day early, but he has decided that we should put out one more issue before Eid al-Adha, which falls just after Christmas this year. We have already decided, *together,* that we would not publish another issue before the holiday. Now everyone will have to work on Tuesday and Wednesday in order to put out that extra issue, when they have counted on having a holiday. What's even worse is that the reason we have to publish this extra issue is that Qasim has already sold advertising for it. Qasim had done the same thing during Eid al-Fitr, and I had made him promise me that he would never again sell advertising for an issue that would have to be put out over a holiday.

Fuming, I quickly edit the stories al-Asaadi has given me and am walking out the door when he says, "So, I'll see you here Tuesday!"

I whirl around. "Mohammed, I told you *a month ago* that I was taking time off this week. We also decided ages ago that this week was a holiday for all of us. So I am not coming in *at all,* except to collect my salary. It is nine P.M. on Christmas Eve, and this is the first that I have heard of this schedule change. If you want to do another issue before Eid, have fun. But I am not going to be here."

And with that, I leave. I cannot believe that al-Asaadi would behave so abominably on what—as far as he knows—is a holy day for me. He has done the barest minimum of work since I got to this country, and now he has the nerve to suggest that I am a slacker for taking time off? I fume all the way home and, despite a pleasant dinner, the Christmas spirit fails to materialize.

I throw a party on Boxing Day for those of my friends who didn't head westward for the holidays. Deputy U.S. Ambassador Nabeel Khoury, who has become a good friend, arrives first, with wine and flowers. Just as we've settled in the *mafraj*, Karim arrives, with several French friends, followed by the ever-charming Manel, a British journalist friend named Ginny, and several others. It's a low-key night, but to me the simple act of drinking wine and eating cheese in a room full of friends feels like an extraordinary luxury.

☪

WHEN I RETURN to Yemen after a brief holiday in Egypt, it doesn't take long for all of the familiar anxieties to catch up with me—as well as some new ones. I arrive home just after the second Eid holiday and Saddam Hussein's execution to find the entire country in mourning. More than half of Yemen's population is Sunni, and they *love* Saddam.

Yemen was one of the few Arab countries that refused to criticize Iraq's invasion of Kuwait in 1990. Every other Gulf state—Saudi Arabia, Bahrain, Qatar, the United Arab Emirates, and Oman—condemned the invasion. Yemen, the PLO, Jordan, and the Maghreb, areas with substantial Palestinian populations, abstained.

I've noticed a few correlations between Saddam and Saleh. Like Saddam, Saleh came from a military background and surrounds himself with a close circle of advisers who are military people. He places his trusted tribal associates in key positions of power, consolidating his control over the security apparatus of the state. In some ways, Saleh's Sanhanis are not unlike Saddam's Tikritis. But the comparison goes only so far. Saleh did not consolidate power by shooting family members who didn't agree with him, try to eradicate entire ethnic groups, or destroy the economy of Yemenis who didn't concur with his political or religious philosophy.

Saleh's support of Saddam during the invasion of Kuwait infuriated Yemen's neighbors. Every Arabian Gulf state expelled the majority of Yemeni expatriates working within their borders. Some two million wage earners were forced to return to Yemen jobless and unable to support their families, which had a hugely damaging effect on the Yemeni economy still felt to this day. It remains difficult for Yemenis to work in the Gulf. Kuwait has never really forgiven Saleh and has obstructed Yemen's attempts to join the Gulf Cooperation Council, the regional economic bloc.

In turn, Saddam expressed his appreciation for Yemen's solidarity by donating large sums of money to the country, both directly to Saleh and to the tribes. Members of Saddam's family have sought refuge in Yemen, which is home to an estimated one hundred thousand Iraqis. Not all of these were Saddam supporters; many came to Yemen to escape repression.

"Everyone in Yemen loves him [Saddam] because the official media told them to love him," a diplomat tells me. "And he was an important source of income to Yemen during a very difficult time."

Yemenis offer slightly different opinions. "He was good for Iraq because Iraqis need someone strong to keep them in line," a Yemeni Arabic teacher tells me. "Otherwise they are wild and difficult people." Posters of the dictator plaster storefronts and houses and the back windows of cars. Arabic newspapers sing his praises. Street vendors sell cigarette lighters that project an image of his face.

In the office, my men walk around with long, sorrowful faces.

"It's best if you don't bring it up," Manel warns me. "They're incredibly sensitive. Everyone here has been crying about him for days." He had made the indelicate suggestion that Saddam was a brutal tyrant responsible for the death of thousands, and was promptly abused. "They think he's a martyr." For once, I keep my mouth shut.

The video of Saddam's execution is disturbingly popular, and I keep catching the men watching it on the screens of their mobile telephones. I refuse to see it. Parents in Yemen apparently think it is appropriate to allow their children to watch such things, and in early January two young boys kill themselves in imitation of their hero. One hangs himself, and the other shoots himself. Their parents are quoted in the press as saying that their boys worshipped Saddam.

Angered, I spit out an editorial condemning the broadcast media for circulating the video and parents for letting children see it. We have just closed the issue when al-Asaadi demands to read my piece. With a sense of foreboding, I hand him the page. His face tightens as he reads. "You have to take out this part about Iraqis killing Saddam," he says. "Iraqis did not kill Saddam. Everyone knows Americans killed him."

He has a point. Americans have their fingerprints all over the execution, but it ultimately was Iraqis who hanged him, something no one in Yemen will admit. It doesn't even register in Yemen that the entire Iraqi population of Detroit danced in the streets at his death.

I am personally opposed to capital punishment, and I think that killing Saddam on the first day of Eid was a *terrible* public relations move. But it frustrates me that Yemenis refuse to acknowledge that Saddam did *anything* bad.

I keep all of this to myself. I tell al-Asaadi that I won't change anything that is factual.

"Your editorial isn't factual."

"It is."

"You need to say Americans killed Saddam."

"I am not going to perpetuate untruths."

"Then I will pull the editorial," he says imperiously, attempting to yank the paper out of my hands.

"You will *not* pull the editorial," I say, hanging on to the paper. "That is not your decision to make."

"Hadi, kill the editorial," he calls to our designer.

"Hadi, do *not* kill that editorial!"

Our reporters have all stopped working and turned around to watch us, their mouths hanging open. Their eyes are frightened, like those of children watching their parents fight. I'm glad the women aren't here to see this. They miss my battles with al-Asaadi because they're nearly always gone before he arrives.

We are both still tugging on the page. "Don't make me behave in a bad way," says al-Asaadi.

"You are responsible for your own behavior. If you behave in a bad way that's *your* decision, not mine," I say, refusing to loosen my grip.

He drops the page.

"You kill that editorial and I am going to Faris."

"Go ahead, call Faris."

I run to my office for my phone. My fingers are shaking as I dial. I have had it with al-Asaadi.

Faris, miraculously, answers his phone. I take the phone out to our courtyard and pour out my frustrations. I tell him about the editorial and about how al-Asaadi has been trying to sabotage every issue. I also remind him that my contract grants me total editorial control.

Faris tells me a story. "Jennifer, you know the tale of the robe?"

"No."

"A man went out shopping one evening, and his wife asked him, while he was out, to please pick up a robe for her. Well, when the man came back later, he had everything else but had forgotten the robe. And the wife was very angry and yelled at him, and they had a huge fight. But the fight was not about the robe; it was about everything else in their relationship. Do you understand me?"

I do.

Faris tells me to e-mail him the editorial. He reads it and rings me back immediately. "You can run this if you want," he says. "It would be best, however, if you run it as an opinion piece instead of an editorial. You see, I am trying to keep people from throwing bombs at the paper."

"This would get bombs thrown at us?" I have failed to consider this.

"It's possible."

"Which part?"

"You cannot say that there is any argument against capital punishment. It is part of Islam."

I am surprised. This is not the part of the editorial that I thought might get us killed.

"Oh," I say. "I hadn't realized."

"Other than that it's fine."

I think for a moment. "I think maybe I won't run it. Or I'll run it as an opinion piece in the next issue."

"It's up to you."

"I actually don't want to get the paper bombed."

Faris says he will sit down with us to talk this out on Saturday.

After I hang up, I tell al-Asaadi what Faris has said, adding, "You want a new editorial, you write it. I'm leaving. I've been here thirteen hours already and you've been here—what? Two?"

"Fine." He is sitting at his desk, waiting for me to leave. He often stays until I am gone so he can change things without me finding out until it's too late.

I pick up my things and go.

On my way out I stop in the newsroom, where only Hadi and Farouq are still working. I tell Hadi what we're doing with the page, thank him for his work, and say good-bye. When I thank Farouq, he says, "It will be okay. These things happen. Just be patient."

"Farouq," I say wearily, "I get tired of being patient."

He smiles at me. "Allah will help you."

"*Shukrahn,* Farouq, I hope so."

The worst thing about arguments with al-Asaadi is that by the end of them I feel as angry and disappointed with myself as I do with him. This is what I vowed I would avoid. The last thing I wanted to do was to come off like a patronizing, domineering, aggressive, culturally insensitive westerner steamrolling the locals. Yet somehow I too often end up in shouting matches with al-Asaadi, Qasim, or the Doctor. Given that *no one* ever shouts at the Doctor, there is great excitement in the office when this happens, and everyone gathers around to watch. I get the feeling that a few of them would cheer were that possible.

But I hate to shout. I've never been a shouter and I've certainly never yelled at anyone at work. I am uncomfortable with the discovery of this angry, frustrated, dictatorial part of me. After battles with al-Asaadi or the others, I am always in tears and full of self-loathing for losing control once again. Then I swear to myself that it won't happen again, that I will reason calmly with my staff and hope that I can cajole them around to my point of view instead.

Thankfully, I rarely have to yell at the women, mostly because they rarely argue with me. When I do raise my voice, I feel particularly awful because they would never do the same to me. This happened with Najma in the early months, and I called her into my office.

"I am sorry," she said as soon as she walked into my office. "I will do better."

"Najma, I am the one who should apologize to you. I should never yell at you; there is no excuse."

"No, you should. We deserve it." Her eyes are dark and earnest.

This breaks my heart. "You do *not* deserve it. No one deserves to be yelled at. I will try not to do it again."

"But you can—"

"I don't want to. I don't like to yell. I should be able to talk with you about work without getting upset. I make mistakes. I am sorry."

On Saturday, Faris finally appears at the office, and we talk about al-Asaadi. He does not seem surprised by his behavior and tells me that al-Asaadi has an ego problem. He wants to be a media superstar without doing any of the actual work. Al-Asaadi has the potential to become a really good reporter, I say, and a better manager. The problem is that he is unwilling to learn or to work within a schedule. Faris agrees that al-Asaadi is a poor manager and is better suited for a glad-handing job in public relations. He promises to have a word with him.

Then he introduces me to an attractive, charming young man named Ali who wants to join our staff. The product of a Yemeni father and American mother, Ali grew up in Oregon and speaks perfect English. I am thrilled to have him and put him straight to work. He immediately earns my undying gratitude by turning my reporters' stories into passable English.

The women are even more thrilled. They turn into adolescents around him, giggling and awkward and shy. When Zuhra comes to fetch her tea from Radia at reception, Radia tells her to go back into the newsroom. "I will bring you the tea," she whispers. "Just so I can come look at him again!"

Even Manel, a fine-looking man himself, is impressed. "He *is* the best-looking Yemeni I have ever seen," he says.

Ali is either unaware of the stir he creates or is simply accustomed to it. He types away at his desk, oblivious to the little black pillars of rayon swooning in his wake.

I'm feeling much more cheerful until Faris rings me again to tell me that al-Asaadi claims he cannot turn in his pages on deadline because he wants the news to be as fresh as possible. My dark mood instantly returns. "Look," I say to Faris, "if he cannot turn in his pages by one P.M., when precisely will he turn them in? The point is that I need him to pick a deadline that he can stick to *every single issue.*"

Faris suggests that I move into my own office. We could transform the conference room, he says. I remind Faris that al-Asaadi is due to leave the country in fourteen days, so it's absurd to move me now. I am thrilled that al-Asaadi has received a fellowship to spend four months studying in the United States, because this means that I might finally be able to do what I want with the paper.

(*

ZAID HAS RETURNED to the paper on holiday from his studies in London. He is full of enthusiasm, and I am grateful to have him. Still, it surprises me to read his stories and to see that his English has not noticeably improved in the four months he spent in England. I hope that this will change in the second semester. In fact, I am counting on it. Now that it is clear that al-Asaadi is uninterested in learning anything new and has no intention of carrying on my reforms when I leave, I have become anxious about finding a successor. I'm determined to create changes that are sustainable.

I figure Zaid is my best bet. He is due to finish his program in London in June, which means I will have at least two months to train him before I leave. When he is back in December, I sit him down and explain that I would like him to succeed me—assuming we can get Faris's support.

It distresses me deeply that I have failed to win al-Asaadi over, even after months of attempting to bond. No one else at the paper is surprised, however. Luke tells me that no other editor has survived even this long trying to power-share with al-Asaadi.

Al-Asaadi has promised me, as a result of his conversation with Faris, that I will have his pages by six thirty P.M. Despite the fact that he himself picked that deadline, he fails to show up at the office until eight P.M. When I open my mouth to remind him of the deadline, he shrugs.

"You only have six more days, *khalas.*"

Six days, two issues, one hundred and forty-four hours. Not that I'm counting.

(*

AL-ASAADI COMES IN the next day around eleven A.M., dressed all in black and looking somber.

"*Kayf halak?*" (How are you?) I ask.

He shakes his head. "*Mish tammam.* Not good at all."

"Are you going to a funeral today?"

He looks surprised. "You knew?"

"You're dressed in mourning."

"Yes, a friend of mine died."

"I'm sorry to hear that."

A little while later I find out a second reason for his distress. "I didn't get my visa," he says. "So I cannot go to the States."

My heart falls straight through the floor.

"*What?*"

No sooner are the words out of his mouth than I am e-mailing my friend Nabeel, the deputy U.S. ambassador. I am desperate. All of my hopes and dreams for this newspaper are at stake. "Please," I beg him. "Is there anyway you can fast-track al-Asaadi's visa? If he doesn't go to the States I will never be able to do anything with this paper."

Nabeel's response is prompt and reassuring. He tells me that he is aware of the delay and says they are waiting for Washington to give al-Asaadi security clearance. "Tell him not to fret," says Nabeel. "We will take care of him (and you)."

A few days later, al-Asaadi is on a plane.

Now, I think, the work can really begin.

THIRTEEN

pillars of rayon

I am impressed that Najma is still with us in January. During my first few months, she often appears in my office panicky and on the verge of tears. She can't finish her story on time, she says. There is no driver to take her where she needs to go. Or she can't find the sources I want her to interview. She becomes so hysterical about these things that it is difficult for me to reassure her that we can find solutions. I keep expecting her to give up, to decide it is simply too much to handle.

But she doesn't. No matter how traumatized she is over a story, she always perseveres. If anything, Najma works too hard. She stays in the office straight through lunch and sometimes into the early evenings, struggling to finish her page.

She has only just finished university and has no journalism experience. She also lacks a sense of what information is critical to a story and what can be left out. Almost everything she turns in is three or four times the length it should be. To be fair, she is not the only one with this problem. My reporters seem to think that it is perfectly reasonable to fill an entire page with one twenty-five-hundred-word story.

"No one reads stories that long," I tell them. "No matter how interesting. You're lucky if people read past the first few paragraphs." I want three or four stories on the Health and Science page instead of one or two.

In my first month, Najma turns in a story on children's health that is thirty-six hundred words long. Two full pages.

"There is a lot of important information in it!" she protests.

"I am sure there is! But people don't need to know *everything*." My reporters themselves would never read a story that long. In fact, they don't read. Almost no one in Yemen reads. Even the most educated people I meet have few books on their shelves. The only book anyone ever seems to pick up is the Qur'an.

Granted, Arabs do have a strong oral tradition, so poetry and other literature have historically been transmitted that way, rather than through written texts. And half of Yemenis are illiterate. Yemenis' resistance to reading may also be due to their experiences in school, which often drain the joy out of books. They are beaten and mocked when they fail and so live in terror of making mistakes. Zuhra tells me how a teacher once used her, when she was just five years old, to punish another little girl. The girl had been unable to read an Arabic word on the board, and the teacher had asked Zuhra to read it, to show the girl how stupid she was. She then forced little Zuhra to write the insult "donkey" on the other girl's forehead. Zuhra was so horrified by this experience that she lived in fear of meeting a similar fate for the rest of her school years.

Yemeni culture overall doesn't encourage reading as a pastime. Leisure time is instead whiled away chewing *qat* and gossiping. The women don't have as much free time for this as the men, given that they are generally kept busy at home with children and cooking—or out herding or farming—while their husbands gad about with friends. Even my women reporters, who still live with their parents and thus have fewer responsibilities, do not read. Their leisure time seems to be chiefly occupied with helping cousins or sisters or friends prepare for weddings.

I remind them that reading is the best thing they can do to improve their language and journalistic skills. "It doesn't matter what you read. Novels, cereal boxes, comics. Find something you enjoy. But *read*."

This learned aversion to education and absence of a culture of reading puts my journalists and the entire Yemeni population at an immense disadvantage when it comes to understanding the world at large and the range of human experience. How can people understand other ways of life and the world beyond their borders without the aid of books and newspapers?

How does one develop compassion for someone with a completely different set of values without reading something from their point of view? Books are one of the few ways in which we can truly get into the heads of people we would never meet in our ordinary lives and travel to countries we would otherwise never visit.

I suppose that the harsh existence of most Yemenis leaves them little time to contemplate other ways of life. Perhaps it is only when our own lives are comfortable that we can afford to look out at the world beyond our personal borders.

☾

GIVEN ALL OF THIS, one would think Najma would understand why our readers would be unlikely to make it through a thirty-six-hundred-word story. I explain to her how to pare down quotes to a sentence or two, eliminate redundancies, and delete irrelevant information. This is a significant problem for all of my reporters, who include paragraph-long quotations in their articles rather than selecting one or two meaningful sentences. They also frequently include information that bewilders them. When I ask questions, they look at me with wide eyes and shrug. My reporters assume that their readers are much, much smarter than they are and will understand things they do not—perhaps because it saves them the effort of figuring things out themselves.

Despite their challenges, it doesn't take long for me to realize that my women are the paper's most reliable strength. While they have no more training than the men—indeed, often less—they have the requisite *will*. They are harder and more persistent workers than the men, and none of them chews *qat* or smokes. They arrive promptly and do not disappear for three or four hours during lunch. They either eat sandwiches in the back room or wait until they finish their work to go home and eat.

The discrepancy between male and female work ethics is not limited to the *Yemen Observer*. Friends who manage oil companies, NGOs, or embassies often rave to me about their female Yemeni employees and decry the sloth of the men. This is partly because the women don't have the same sense of entitlement that the men do; they feel fortunate to have the opportunity to work. It is still unusual for women to work outside of the home in Yemen, and it takes a tough, driven woman to convince her family to allow her to pursue education and seek employment. By the time women get to the workplace, they are already seasoned fighters, whereas men are often handed jobs simply because of family connections.

Najma is lucky; her mother has always encouraged her to do what she wants. "And your father?" I ask. She hasn't mentioned him. She waves a hand dismissively. "He's not like my mother."

But she still has to fight to prove to the men at the office that she is as capable as they are. In fact, she is quickly growing *more* capable, solely as a result of her determination. By late autumn, her Health and Science page is at last improving. One Saturday, she turns in a three-thousand-word breast cancer story. I had told her that the story must be at most a thousand words. "Most readers won't read past five hundred," I say. "Please make this a thousand words and then give it back to me. I want you to make the cuts yourself. And I need you to put the news up front. We are not producing a medical textbook; you can leave out these lengthy and technical medical explanations. What I want to know is, what is happening *in Yemen?* How many *Yemeni* women have breast cancer? And what treatments are available to them *in Yemen?* This is what our readers care about—not women worldwide."

Najma looks at me as though I have just shot her mother.

"Okay," she says bleakly.

"And I want it back before you leave today."

Her eyes widen over her *kheemaar.*

"You can do it," I say.

And she does. It takes her until nearly six P.M., working nonstop, but she does it. When she hands it back to me, it is twelve hundred words long (close enough) and she has reworked the structure and reporting exactly as I asked her to do. How far she has come! And Najma has found some real news, in that Yemen has just acquired its first clinic specializing in the treatment and prevention of breast cancer.

I am so proud of her! I thank her for staying late, and she tells me her mother is very upset with her. "Please tell her it's my fault," I say. "I promise to send you home early tomorrow."

When I arrive the next morning, I make a beeline for her.

"Najma, I was really happy with your rewrite of your story. You did exactly what I wanted you to do. So *shukrahn.*"

Her eyes crinkle with happiness over her veil. That look is enough to make me think, Well, maybe I'll try to survive another month.

☪

I GIVE NAJMA her biggest challenge yet on World AIDS Day, celebrated on December 1, which hands us a news peg for writing an update on the progress of the disease in Yemen. This is Najma's first attempt at tackling this subject, and I am curious to see how she will handle it.

This is how Najma begins her story:

> A Muslim scholar has reached a result concluded by thought and study. AIDS is regarded as one of God's strong soldiers. Any people contradict God's right way are punished by a kind of torture. So AIDS is a torture firstly and violently infects some societies which have declared sexual revolution, allowed man to marry another man, and made the obscene acts as usual things.

It goes on like this for, oh, three thousand words or so and includes all kinds of misinformation, including the fact that Kofi Annan is the "secretary general of the United States." I am sure he would be interested to know that.

I don't know whether to laugh or cry. Particularly when I see passages like this:

> The first cases infected with AIDS in the world comes as evidence to prove what is told in the *Hadith,* Mohammed's prophetic tradition. The prophet Mohammed has told us . . . the bad results caused by appearing and spreading practicing the adultery in one society. Declaring carelessly practicing such things bring God's torture. God may send the plague disease as a torture on those people or some other strange diseases which are not known by their ancestors. So AIDS . . . comes to prove the prophet's speech and as a torture fallen down on the humanity that keeps away from God's right way.

The disease, she also informs us, "is not limited to the sexual odd people" and will spread more rapidly with the advent of the Internet in Yemen, because education is very dangerous.

I cannot possibly run the story. It's a judgmental rant and contains almost no facts. I am sitting at my desk staring at the piece when Luke walks in.

"What *now?*" he says when he sees my face.

"Believe me, you don't want to know." What would Najma say, I wonder, if she knew that Luke is gay? The cognitive dissonance might just do her in. Everyone loves Luke.

"Let me see the story," he says when I tell him.

I do, and a few minutes later Luke is back in my office, equally appalled. "Okay, I can see why we're not running it."

"On a technical note," I say, "if AIDS is meant to punish homosexuals, why is it that lesbians have the lowest infection rate?"

"God likes lesbians better?"

"Funny, I always picture God as a straight man."

"Straight men *love* lesbians."

"Incidentally, what's the Arabic word for lesbians? For some reason my dictionary doesn't have it."

"There are no lesbians in the Arab world. There are women who have sex with each other, but no lesbians."

The next day, I call Najma into my office and ask her to sit down next to me. I am so nervous that my hands tremble and I hide them in my skirts. It is important to me that I do this right. I do not want to risk offending her religious beliefs or losing my temper. Keeping my voice as calm and steady as possible, I explain to her that the Health and Science page is no place for opinion or judgment. What you have written, I say, is more a sermon than a piece of journalism.

"I have great respect for your beliefs, and naturally you are free to think what you want, but you may not put your personal beliefs in this newspaper. The only place in the paper that should show any evidence of personal beliefs is the Op-Ed page."

She listens and nods, her dark eyes serious. She does not argue or resist what I am telling her.

I go through her entire story, line by line, explaining to her every error. I explain which contentions go against science and which are simply unprovable. Education, I say, is much more likely to *prevent* the spread of AIDS than to increase it. I show her places where she is judging people.

"It is not our role to judge," I say. "It is our job to lay out the facts for people and let them make their own opinions. Let's leave the judgment up to God."

She nods and seems almost ashamed. We talk about the definition of the word "fact." We discuss the importance of studies being conducted by reputable universities and medical research centers, published in reputable journals, and peer reviewed. This is all news to her.

And oh! I can't help myself! I have to know what she will say! I ask her why lesbians so rarely get AIDS if it is meant to punish homosexuals.

This is obviously not a point she has ever considered. "I don't know," she says.

"Maybe something to think about," I say.

While she seems to understand, I won't really know if I have gotten through to her until I see her next story.

Toward the end of our talk, she looks up at me pleadingly. "I worked so hard on this—"

I stop her. "I *know* how hard you work. And I really appreciate that. This isn't at all about how hard you work. This is just part of learning how to do this work better. It's a continual process. We are all constantly learning. But I am well aware of how hard you work."

And we are through. She thanks me and leaves. I feel limp with relief and happy that I have managed to get through the entire conversation without once raising my voice or getting angry. Progress for both of us!

The next time Najma turns in a story on AIDS, it addresses the bias against victims of the disease and the misperceptions about how it is spread. It is full of factual information and accurate statistics and contains no preaching whatsoever. I very nearly kiss her.

☾

A TINY BESPECTACLED WOMAN shows up in my office one morning, unannounced. She wears a *hijab,* but her face is uncovered. This is Adhara. "I want to be a translator," she says.

I sigh. She and half the country. Everyone who speaks even a few words of English thinks they can be a translator, and they all show up at the paper sooner or later.

I politely inform her that we are not hiring translators—though we desperately need them—as Faris won't give me the money to pay one.

"But I need practice," she says. "I will work as a volunteer. My translation is very bad."

Hardly an advertisement for her skills, but I'm impressed with her honesty. Most would-be translators consider themselves quite brilliant, despite the fact that they can't put together a job application that isn't riddled with errors. Still, I worry that shoddy translations will only create more work for me. I send her away.

She is back in my office the next day. "Please," she says. "Let me translate something! I must learn!" She stands stubbornly on my gray carpet, refusing to be dismissed.

I believe in rewarding persistence. I relent and let her translate part of the Q & A for Jabr. She's right; she's not a good translator. But at least I can figure out what she means, and as we are not paying her, I can't complain. I allow her to stay.

When I get to the office the next morning, Adhara is waiting. She comes again the next day and the day after that. Her translation slowly gets better. I assign her the Panorama page, which contains translated editorials from Arabic papers. This used to be al-Matari's responsibility, but he has constantly been out sick. Adhara, on the other hand, never misses a day.

One afternoon, she walks into my office holding a flash drive aloft.

"Zuhra asked me to write a back-page story. She said you needed one," she says. "And I did it!" There is triumph in her voice.

"Fantastic!" I take the disk. I am desperate for a back-page story.

It's a piece about the conflicting views of the Internet in Yemen. It is crudely written, contains no real news, and is mostly made up of huge blocks of quotations with no transitions. But my standards are not what they once were. I decide to run it anyway. Together, Adhara and I rework the structure and impose some segues. She is immensely pleased. She follows this first story with a piece on a new course that trains women to paint on glass and sell their art. It needs massive work, but I sit her down and explain what to do. Now that the paper is on a schedule, I have time for training. It's thrilling to be able to watch and aid Adhara's diligent and measurable progress.

She begins to tail Zuhra, who takes her on reporting expeditions to the Old City and shows her how to conduct interviews. My women welcome little Adhara into their fold, thrilled to see their ranks expand. I tease my men by telling them that soon we will have an all-female staff—this seems to motivate them more than anything else.

By the end of my year, I will have to officially hire Adhara. There is nothing else to do. She won't stop *showing up* and we cannot in good conscience let her keep working for free, I explain to Faris. He finds the money to pay her.

One day Zuhra runs into my office, Adhara on her heels.

"Tell her," says Zuhra.

Adhara shakes her head, turning red.

"*Leysh?* It's okay."

"Please," says Adhara. "*Please,* Zuhra."

"What is it?" I say.

Earlier, I had told Adhara to give her story to Ali to copyedit. It didn't even occur to me that this might be awkward. But the prospect of talking to the handsomest man in the office overwhelmed Adhara, who is painfully shy. It was as if I had asked her to please interview Brad Pitt. Petrified, she had gone to Zuhra for help.

"Ali is very nice," I reassure Adhara. "You don't need to worry."

"I told her!" says Zuhra, who no longer fears men, handsome or otherwise.

Eventually, Adhara and Zuhra together get the story to Ali. And over time, Adhara's fear ebbs. One day, I walk out of my office and look out the front door to see Adhara and Ali sitting on the steps side by side. Ali is smoking a cigarette, and Adhara is talking easily to him. Almost as if he is just another human being. I can't stop smiling at the sight.

☾

LIKE NAJMA AND NOOR, Adhara is fortunate to have parents supportive of her ambitions. But this doesn't mean all three don't face barriers at work. The carefully cultivated modesty of women is at odds with the requirements of their profession. My women are often nervous about approaching men or about being perceived as too aggressive. Najma and Noor deal with this by working as a team. They accompany each other on reporting excursions, write stories for each other's pages, and edit each other's English. Rarely does one leave the office without the other. I'm impressed with their cooperation and the creativity they use to find their way around restrictions. The men could take a lesson.

Radia, whose official title is Faris's personal secretary, has also begun reporting and writing stories. Like Adhara, she doesn't ask me if she can become a reporter. She simply hands me a story one day. She writes in Arabic and gets one of the men or Zuhra to translate. Her reporting is good, though her writing and storytelling are weak. I spend hours with her, helping her find the news angles and fill in reporting gaps. One of her first pieces is a back-page story on the rising price of fabric. It sounds dull until she tells me that these rising prices are hurting brides in particular, many of whom have begun sewing their own dresses and settling for plainer fabrics. We refocus the story on the plight of brides, and it transforms into something eminently printable.

Soon, Radia isn't just writing back-page features. She is covering car accidents, human rights issues, and explosions, turning in several stories for each issue. One day she runs into my office to tell me that she has a good story about a "hot phone." I have no idea what she is talking about. When she can't make me understand, she fetches Enass, who laughs. "She means *hotline*," she says.

Yet she is not a reporter and continues to make the mere $100 a month Faris pays her to be his secretary. She asks Faris for more money, which he denies her, because she is "not a real reporter." Never mind that she writes more stories per issue than any of my men. She accepts this as something she is helpless to change. I've repeatedly tried to get higher pay for my women, but every time Faris just tells me he is paying the fair market wage. My hands are tied.

☾

ZUHRA IS ALSO FLOURISHING, largely because she asks more questions than anyone else and never leaves my side when I am editing her work. One day, Luke comes into my office after editing a raw story of Zuhra's. "I didn't realize how good her English has gotten!" he says. "It's been so long since I saw her raw copy. I'm amazed at how much better her stories are than they were in the fall."

Her stories are so intriguing that it is weeks before I realize how often she is quoting Kamil al-Samawi. It's clear why HOOD is such a crucial source of human rights stories, but Kamil can't be the organization's only lawyer.

"What's the deal with Kamil al-Samawi?" I ask her one day. "You've quoted him in your last three stories."

Zuhra smiles mysteriously. "He's the lawyer on all these cases. I have to quote him!"

"Well, try to figure out what cases the other lawyers are working on and write about them," I say. "You are banned from mentioning Kamil al-Samawi for a month."

(☾

DESPITE HER NEAR-CONSTANT PRESENCE in my office, Zuhra is still careful about what she reveals to me about her life. She tells me all about her career ambitions, her mood swings, and her physical ills, but when she falls in love in the middle of my tenure, she holds this secret close to her chest. It will be months before she can confess it all to me. For a Yemeni woman to admit to love before marriage is to risk social ruin. Women are not supposed to have friendly contact with men who are not close relatives, let alone spend enough time with one to fall in love. Very few Yemeni women choose their husbands, and most matches are arranged.

Thus, Zuhra has plenty of reasons to keep quiet. To confess to even one person is to risk exposure and censure. She lives in a conservative neighborhood, where her neighbors gossip, and the women are particularly vicious about each other. "Sex is the most important thing in all of our society," Zuhra tells me with bitterness in her voice. "Even homosexuality isn't as bad as a woman committing sex outside of marriage. A woman isn't just representing herself as a person; she is representing the whole family, the whole tribe. If my sister's reputation is bad, my reputation is bad." When one of Zuhra's sisters broke off an engagement, the whole family suffered the condemnation of their community. Zuhra fears what her family would say if they knew of her secret love. Because her father is dead, Zuhra needs permission from her brothers and uncles in order to marry. Or to travel. Or to do so many things.

☪

ON MY RECOMMENDATION, Zuhra has applied to the Columbia University Graduate School of Journalism, my alma mater. She is the one person on my staff with what my Columbia professors liked to call the "fire in the belly" necessary to become a brilliant journalist. So I think she would thrive there. I'd especially like her to be admitted because she plans to return to Yemen afterward and eventually launch her own newspaper. Then, in a way, she can carry on my work after I leave. As part of the application process, she is required to take a news-writing test, which I proctor on the last day before the deadline. It must be postmarked that day, but because it's the end of the month, no one has enough money to pay for postage with DHL, one of the only reliable mail services to the United States. I give Zuhra my last YR1,000, which isn't even close to enough. We have to take up an office collection. Manel, Hassan, Jabr, and Jelena all contribute their last *riyals*. We send Hassan off to fax a copy to New York, and Manel runs to DHL to mail it. It's inspiring to see that even the poorest among us empties her pockets.

To my great disappointment, Zuhra's improved English is not quite good enough to get her into Columbia. A professor on the admissions committee calls me personally to tell me that although the committee absolutely loves her application, they have reservations about her English. Zuhra takes the news like someone accustomed to disappointment and vows to try next year.

"We will find another way to get you to the U.S.," I say. "I promise." She needs to perfect her English abroad, as there is little chance of doing so in Yemen. Diligently, Zuhra begins applying for every fellowship abroad she can find. So many, in fact, that if a fellowship were offered for applying for the most fellowships, Zuhra would definitely win it.

It is Zuhra, and the rest of my women, I am most desperate to help. The men will be all right. They will always find work in Yemen; they will always have society's approval. My women I worry about. What will become of them when I am gone?

☪

ONE DAY, I am editing a health story with Najma when she says, "Jennifer, I need to tell you something."

"Okay," I say, looking up from my computer screen. "What is it?"

"Are you really leaving in September?" She sits on the very edge of her chair, leaning toward me, her dark eyes serious.

"Well, that's my plan."

"Jennifer, this is a very big problem for us. A very big problem. Noor and I were talking. No one else will read our stories so closely; no one else will help us like you do."

"Najma," I say, tears pricking the back of my eyes, "my goal in coming here is not to help you for a year and then abandon you. My goal is to train you, and train a person to take my place, so that you won't need me as much."

I am suddenly panicked about my reporters' future. No matter how good Zaid is—and he has his flaws—he is not a woman, and Najma is right; he won't care as much about their work. This, unfortunately, will be truer than I could ever guess.

The men resent the attention I pay the women. "You like the women better," they say accusingly.

"I like all of you the same," I lie. "But the women happen to always show up for work on time. They don't take cigarette breaks. They don't chew *qat*. They turn their work in on time. If you want to be treated like the women, try following their example."

This makes them grumpy. They believe it is their God-given right to smoke cigarettes and chew *qat*! It is their God-given right to take a nap for several hours after lunch! They should be considered better reporters simply because they are *men!*

One day I am joking around with Bashir, who has written a story about a group that works for women's rights and to preserve culture. "Well, what if the culture they want to preserve doesn't grant women rights; then what?" I tease. "Then they have a conflict. They can either preserve the women's rights or the culture, but not both."

This is said in jest, and he laughs. But then I make a reference to women not being free in Yemen, and he looks shocked and retorts that women are *totally* free in Yemen.

"Women can do whatever they *want* here," he says. "Noor doesn't have to wear her *abaya* if she doesn't want to."

While it may be true that Yemeni women are legally freer than most women in the region—they can drive cars and the dress code is not enforced by law—they can hardly be said to be unfettered.

"Bashir," I say, "do you have any idea what it is like to be a woman here and walk around *without* an *abaya*? She would be harassed constantly. *I* get harassed constantly, even dressed as I am, and it is much worse for Yemeni women."

Zuhra once put it like this: "A woman in Yemen would get harassed even if she were wrapped in an *abaya,* shut in a cardboard box, and on the outside of the box was written 'THIS IS NOT A WOMAN.'"

My dark-skinned foreign friends who could pass for Yemeni get hassled even more on the streets because they appear to be fallen Muslims rather than heretical foreigners. My Dutch-Indonesian friend Jilles had acid thrown at her and was handed a slip of paper with an illustration of how women ought to dress.

When I tell Bashir what kind of harassment women would face on the street here if they went without an *abaya* or *hijab,* Noor turns around in her chair. "It's true," she says.

Thus begins a debate on the status of women in Yemen. Noor claims that Islam does not require the *hijab,* culture does. This is news to Bashir, who argues that the Qur'an orders the *hijab.* The conversation gets heated, with more reporters joining in, but I have so much editing to do that I retreat to my office. When I return to the newsroom a half hour later, they are still locked in combat. I have to break up the discussion three times before they settle down and focus on their stories. "I know this is my fault!" I tell them. "But could you please go back to work?"

They dutifully turn back to their computers. But the second I leave the room, I hear the battle resume.

(☾

MY WOMEN ARE TEACHING ME at least as much as I teach them. Radia and Zuhra and occasionally the others take turns helping me with my Arabic, delighted to be able to correct *me* for a change. Every time I get something right, Zuhra claps her hands and says, "You're so smart!" I feel embarrassingly like I am five, learning how to talk all over again.

My Arabic lessons are a source of entertainment for the entire office. On the day I learned negatives—"I am not your mother, you are not a baker, he is not the president"—I rushed into the newsroom to practice on my staff. "I am not bread!" I announced proudly. It was the first word that came to mind. My reporters dissolved into giggles.

But it's not just Arabic they give me. They patiently explain to me bits of Yemeni history and culture, telling me about wedding rituals, Yemeni foods I haven't tried, and tribal honor. They bring in cakes for me to taste, such as *kubana,* a crumbly cornbread. They introduce me to their families at weddings and other celebrations. It's an enormous comfort to have such an enthusiastic pack of guides to help me navigate this multilayered world.

☪

IT TAKES A LONG TIME for me to get to know Najma and Noor more personally. They are both shy and seem to find me intimidating despite my best efforts. My relationship with Zuhra may also be a barrier. She has a sense of ownership of me, and the other women thus defer to her and stay respectfully at a distance. (Whenever someone else makes me tea or helps me with something, Zuhra asks why I didn't let her do it. "It's just, I think of you as *mine,*" she tells me. "You're *my* Jennifer.")

By mid-January, I still haven't seen Najma's or Noor's face, although Radia, Zuhra, and Enass all flip their veils back the second they cross my threshold. It takes another medical emergency for things to change.

It happens like this. One night we close the paper early. Manel and I are so pleased with ourselves that we head to his home in Hadda for a celebratory drink. Alex, Manel's roommate, has just returned from England with a bottle of duty-free green-apple vodka. It is sweet and synthetic and awful. But this is Yemen, and you drink what is available.

I hadn't thought I had had that much to drink, but I wake close to dawn feeling intensely nauseated. Thinking perhaps it hadn't been a good idea to skip dinner, I go downstairs and eat a yogurt. Then I remember that I have little green pills from an earlier Yemeni illness. They had worked wonders on nausea! I rummage through my drawers, find the green pills, and take two.

Half an hour later I wake again feeling worse. I take two more pills and crawl downstairs to make coffee. But I am too sick to drink it. When Aisha arrives to clean my house, she finds me sitting at my kitchen table, staring mournfully at my full cup. "Hospital?" she says, looking concerned. I shake my head. I'm just hungover, I think. I will get better. Going to the pool will probably help. I take two Advil and two more green pills and go for a swim.

My first flip-turn nearly makes me vomit, and I wonder if I will have to get out. But lap by lap I begin to feel better. After forty-five minutes, I climb out, shivering, and head to the sauna to warm up. But I can't seem to sweat; I just dry out and my fingers, oddly, stay cold.

The nausea worsens. I take two more green pills. After all, if I remember correctly, they can be taken every hour. I manage to keep from vomiting in the taxi and go home to collapse on my bed. I can't eat. I can't even get down water. I am exhausted but too ill to sleep. Zuhra calls me to find out why I'm not at work. She is worried.

"You should not be alone," she says. "You need a hospital."

"I'll be okay. I just need to rest."

I am still trying to sleep a half hour later when Noor rings me. "We are at your door," she says. "We have come to take you to the hospital."

Given my experiences with Yemeni hospitals, I'm not sure I want to go. But perhaps the doctors could give me some antinausea drugs, which might allow me to finally sleep.

I find Noor and Najma waiting at the bottom of my stairs. After removing their shoes, they stand to pull back their veils.

"This is the first time you have seen our faces," says Noor.

"Yes!" I stare from one to the other. Noor is much as I imagined her, very pretty, though with a rounder face and smaller chin than I had expected. Najma is also pretty, with a sparkly smile, despite crooked bottom teeth that bend inward.

"It is very sweet of you to come," I say. It is difficult for me to speak through the nausea.

They've been looking around my house curiously. "You don't live here *alone,* do you?" says Noor.

I nod. "Yes. It's just me."

They look at each other and then back at me.

"That is *terrible,*" says Najma. "You have no one?"

"We don't think you should be here alone," says Noor. "Not when you are sick."

"I'm okay."

They look deeply skeptical.

Outside, Salem is waiting in the van. I dread the ride, nauseated as I am, but Salem is as good a driver as there is in Sana'a. We head for the Yemeni-German Hospital, because it is the closest. This is the same hospital where I had the incompetent X-rays, but I don't know where else to go.

Najma and Noor tell the clerk at the front desk what kind of doctor I want, and he gives me a file. I pay him several thousand *riyals* and take the file to a main waiting room.

Several doors open off of the main waiting room, each for a different specialist. We wait for at least a half hour to see the internist, sitting mostly in silence, as I am too ill to talk. Men with their arms in casts come out of the orthopedist's office. Old women in *setarrhs,* traditional Sana'ani dresses of red and blue cloth, limp from the internist's office. Men sitting next to me cough and spit. I begin to wish I hadn't come, feeling that I am more likely to pick up an illness here than to cure one.

Finally, we see the doctor. He speaks English, so I tell Najma and Noor they can leave me. I explain to him the problem and say I hope he can give me something to ease the nausea. Then I show him the packet of little green pills I have been taking.

He pales. "Stop taking these immediately," he says. "These are for pain! Not for nausea."

I immediately realize my mistake. I have been taking the prescription painkillers I was given for my ribs, which are to be taken once every twenty-four hours, rather than the nausea pills, which are to be taken two every hour. Frantically, I try to remember how many I have taken. Six. Maybe eight. Will I be okay? Oh god, and I took two Advils!

The doctor assures me I will live, though I probably won't feel much better for twenty-four hours. I don't think I can survive feeling like this for that long and am grateful when he writes me a prescription for anti-nausea medication.

At the pharmacy, though, I am given an enormous bag of liquid, a needle, and a packet of powders. "To inject," he says. I stare at him in horror. He actually seems to expect me to mix up the powders with the liquid and inject the solution into myself. After what I have seen of the hygiene of Yemeni hospitals, I refuse to allow another needle into my arm.

We return to the doctor to argue about this. He says that I need the injection. I reiterate that I don't. Finally, clearly annoyed, he writes me a prescription for antinausea pills, which cost the rest of the *riyals* I have.

At home, I ring a friend in New York, who looks up the specific painkiller on the Internet to double-check whether I will die from the overdose. He also checks to make sure the antinausea medication they gave me is actually antinausea medication. It is, *al-hamdulillah*. But the list of warning signs he reads off to me about the painkiller makes me feel panicky.

"If you throw up something that looks like coffee grounds—"

"I don't have that."

"Or have pain and nausea in your stomach—"

"I have that!"

"Or you lose feeling in one side—"

"Nope."

"Headache—"

"Yes." My head is in searing pain.

He makes me promise that if I feel worse at all I will ring Nabeel and get someone at the embassy to help me.

In my journal, I make a list of lessons learned:

1. Never, ever, drink vodka selected by a twenty-four-year-old.
2. Never drink flavored alcohol, particularly green apple.
3. Never let a British person refill your glass while you aren't watching.
4. When you wake up nauseated three hours before your alarm, do not take little green pills for nausea without reading the packaging.
5. When you continue to feel nauseated, do not continue to take little green pills without reading the packaging.
6. When you purchase little green pills, try to make sure the packaging insert is in English.
7. Remember that lots of different kinds of drugs come in little green pills.

Seeing me weak and helpless has made me less imposing to Noor and Najma. They invite me to their relatives' weddings and talk to me about things outside of work. My illness has humanized me.

In February, Noor invites me to my first Yemeni wedding. She ducks into my office one day, aflutter with excitement, and shyly presents me with a beribboned card. I'm flattered to be asked and dying of curiosity about the ritual.

I have no idea what to wear. Everyone has told me that Yemeni women wear scandalously little to weddings, where there are no men to ogle them. All weddings are sex segregated. While the bride and groom do meet earlier in the day (or even earlier in the month) to sign the marriage contract, it astonishes me that the celebration of their union does not involve any actual union.

The men have big lunches followed by long *qat* chews, with music and maybe dancing, whereas women gather in wedding halls to sip tea, dance, and admire each other's outfits. Some more modern families allow the groom to pick the bride up at the end of the wedding, when almost all of the guests are gone, but this is not common.

While I've been told that it doesn't matter how much flesh I show at a wedding, I cannot bring myself to dress provocatively in this environment. I settle on a knee-length, blue silk dress with a fitted waist and spaghetti straps and wrap myself up in an *abaya*.

In the corridors of the wedding hall, swarms of women are shedding *abayas* to reveal spangled, candy-colored dresses and heavily made-up faces. The dresses resemble the most shameless of prom gowns or things a stripper might wear for the first thirty seconds of her act. There are women in see-through lace, women in black rubber miniskirts, women with trains ten feet long. It is impossible to overdress (or underdress) for a Yemeni wedding. Yards and yards of black hair, painstakingly straightened or curled, are sprayed into sticky towers or hang loose down girlish backs, a few strands tucked into a glittering butterfly barrette. In Yemen, my waist-length hair is merely average. The women's faces are painted with thick black eyeliner and colorful eye shadow, regardless of age. It looks as though they are all wearing masks by the same designer.

The married women wear small, round decorative caps and sit on cushions around the edge of the room, smoking *shisha* and chewing *qat*.

Feeling conspicuously modest and plain in my simple dress and bare face (save for lipstick), I wander down an aisle searching for familiar faces. Zuhra finds me first. She is encased in floor-length pink polyester with a sequined camisole top. Her thick black hair hangs in loose curls to her waist, and she wears tiny pink feathers as earrings. She looks *gorgeous*. She twirls in front of me, smiling, showing off a little. "Come," she says, taking my arm and leading me to a table near the front.

We sit and talk while Somali women circle the room with trays of milky sweet tea. Clad in a short, spangled dress, Noor hurries to greet me and introduce me to a dozen other cousins. Her mother comes over to introduce herself. "You are all Noor talks about," she says. "It's Jennifer *tammam,* Jennifer *tammam*!" ("Jennifer good!") I am enormously grateful. I had never been sure what Noor thinks of me.

Then the dancing begins. The whole outing is totally worth it just to see little Zuhra dance. One of the first to take the stage, she lifts her thin arms, gray from lack of sun, her hair swirling about her waist, lips curved into a sly smile, eyes downcast, hips a-shimmy. No Western woman in a disco could be more sultry a temptress than this candied mermaid, Zuhra, brushing back long strands of hair from her dark eyes and laughing.

Soon a flock of women converge upon the dance floor, a field of undulating butterflies. No two are wearing the same color. One fat woman has even squeezed herself into something that looks like a Hefty bag or an S and M outfit. Women form a circle on the stage, taking turns dancing in the middle to whoops of appreciation.

The dance is mostly in the hips. The upper body is still, arms carving slow arcs through the air. But what surprises me more than anything is the slackness and abundance of flesh. I had thought Yemeni women were all tiny, thin little things, but the fifteen hundred women on display are anything but. Their flesh is loose from lack of exercise, their backs utterly without tone, their arms jiggling when they wave. The physical consequences of their confinement. Their skin is mottled and pale, the result of being denied even a glimpse of sunlight through their *abayas*. When Zuhra returns, I look at my arm next to hers on the table and notice mine is browner.

When the bride finally arrives, she proceeds slowly down the raised stage running through the center of the room. Cameras flash and a black rayon wave ripples across the room as the women cover themselves with scarves to keep from getting caught on film. Only professionals take photographs; the rest of us had to leave our cameras at the door.

The bride is petite and dressed in a mass of Princess Diana–style white satin. I suspect her face is pretty, but it is obscured by thick layers of foundation, blush, eyeliner, and lipstick. I try to guess how she feels about her impending wedding night from her smile. It looks forced; she is posing for the cameras. But she doesn't look unhappy. She gazes down at the crowd with a sort of haughty triumph, as if lording her union over the poor, unfortunate spinsters around her.

"Tell me she is marrying someone nice," I whisper to Noor.

She nods. "She is," she assures me.

While I am pleased finally to experience a Yemeni wedding, the festivities ultimately make me restless. The music is so loud that we cannot talk, we can only dance or watch. After a while, women perch on the edge of the stage, dangling their feet and looking suffused with ennui.

So as soon as the bride is safely down the aisle and surrounded by women ululating and cheering her, I slip out with Zuhra. There is not much left of the ceremony, Zuhra tells me. The bride will hold court for a while and dance with the women. Eventually, she will either meet her groom at their new home later that night or return to her home and wait to meet him the next morning, when they are both fresh.

In the hallway, we pull on our long robes before heading out into the night. The streets are full of loitering men waiting for their painted women to emerge, once more swathed in anonymous black.

FOURTEEN

tropical depression

One day, the usually gentlemanly al-Matari marches into my office midmorning and announces, without preamble, "Then I will quit!"

"What?" I say, looking up from my computer.

"They have not given me my whole pay, so I will quit."

"Why didn't they give you your whole pay?"

"I don't know."

I march upstairs to the accountant's office with him. It turns out that al-Matari has forgotten that he recently borrowed money from work to buy a blender. Once he realizes where the money has gone, al-Matari tells me everything is okay and goes back to work. I hope it's a good blender.

Then when the accountants dole out my own February salary, they give me only $50. "That's all we have now," they say. *Right.* Still, this is plenty for the moment, and it is more important that the rest of my staff gets paid, which they haven't been this month. It's several days after payday, and they lack the various safety nets I have in times of crisis, like credit cards (which exist in Yemen but are not widely used).

My reporters don't just live month-to-month, they live in the future. They spend every paycheck before it arrives, so delays are always harrowing. A week before the end of the month, everyone starts coming to me to borrow money for dinner or *qat* or their aunt's hospital bill, which quickly drains my own pockets. By the second day of the month, every one of us—myself included—is flat broke.

I've been lending the little I have quite a bit. Now that my debts are paid off and my lifestyle costs very little, I have a few dollars to play with. I've loaned Zuhra $200 this week, though she has already paid me back. And I had to buy Samir dinner last night because he hadn't eaten. This is the first time in my life I have been able to do this, and it makes me happy. In New York, I could never buy anyone dinner.

I ask the Doctor to pay my whole staff, especially Manel, because he is leaving for Senegal, as well as my phone bill. I've made several international calls to report a story for *Arabia Felix*, and my phone bill is an unprecedented YR 30,000 ($150). The Doctor refuses.

"But I only use this phone for work," I say. "I made those long-distance calls for *Arabia Felix*, which didn't pay me a single *riyal* for that feature story. If I have to fork out for the reporting that I did, you are essentially asking me to *pay* for the privilege of writing for *Arabia Felix*."

The Doctor is unpersuadable. He tells me that the paper hasn't been making money (of course it hasn't—it hasn't turned a profit since it launched, according to Faris) and thus there is no money to pay my staff. Manel will have to wait for his salary. Which is a whopping $300.

"Manel is leaving the country *tomorrow*," I say. "You will pay him *today*!"

The Doctor tells me that I should stay out of financial matters, because they are none of my business.

"When my staff threatens to quit because they have not been paid, it *is* my business," I say. "I do not expect anyone to work for free."

Desperate to get Manel paid before he gets on a plane, I finally ring Faris.

Within minutes, he e-mails me back with one word: "Done." Which is generally what he says when I ask him for something he thinks is reasonable. Sometimes this means he will immediately do what I want, and sometimes it doesn't. Sometimes it means he just wants me to shut up.

But ten minutes later, Mas comes in to tell me my phone bill has been settled. An hour later, Manel has been paid. I guess the Doctor found some money. Now all I have to worry about is editing a paper.

☪

I AM WEARY. I'm still not sleeping enough, and I wish that getting even basic things done around the paper didn't require a full-scale battle. I'm also lonely. I'm without a roommate again and my nonstop schedule hasn't allowed many social excursions. So when the cowboy Marvin (who had first stopped by my office months ago and has since become a friend) and his wife, Pearl, invite me to join them for a week in Soqotra later in the month, I accept immediately. It will still be work; Marvin wants me to write about his livestock program, and I imagine Soqotra will have other stories to offer. But I will get a break from Sana'a.

"Just make sure you arrange for everything to run smoothly while you are gone," Faris says. Right. Like that has *ever* happened.

Jabr and Bashir try to hug me good-bye, but I won't let them. *"Why?"* they complain.

"Because you're Yemeni. And it's not the sort of thing Yemenis ought to do."

Really, it's that Yemeni men interpret casual physical contact much differently than Western men do. Western men don't think twice about being embraced by a woman, but a Yemeni man might immediately assume my morals were coming loose and that he could take advantage of this. I also refuse to hug my male reporters because I am scrupulous about leaving no room for misinterpretation of my relationship with them. Nothing is more important to me than maintaining this boundary and being taken seriously as a boss and a woman. I cannot bear the thought of them thinking of me sexually.

It already makes me uncomfortable that Jabr constantly proposes articles related to sex. He writes me reports on the increasing use of Viagra and other sexual stimulants, the rising popularity of pornography, the sexual side effects of Red Bull, and how young men and women are beginning to hook up via Bluetooth technology, which leads to all sorts of *haram* behavior. Though the tone of these articles is always condemning, a little too much glee goes into the writing of them.

When I hug Luke good-bye, the Yemeni men protest the inequity. "He's Californian!" I say. "It's an essential part of his culture."

☪

I HAVE A FIT of anxiety about leaving the paper and fuss at Luke and Zuhra, leaving them lists and making sure they know which pages are due when.

"Just go," says Luke. "We'll be fine."

"Okay. Just remember the Health page should be done the first day of the cycle. And try to keep on schedule." I pick up my suitcase. "Oh! I feel like a mother leaving her child with a babysitter for the first time."

"*Yalla*," says Luke. "We'll try to keep the kid alive."

☾

MARVIN, PEARL, AND I catch the Yemenia flight to Soqotra, leaving in the middle of the night. None of us sleeps on the plane. Despite my exhaustion and anxiety over abandoning the office for a week, I am excited. I remember my neighbor Mohammed telling me that people who haven't seen Soqotra have only lived half a life. Yemenis speak rapturously about the tropical desert island, as one might speak of paradise. Even those who have never been there extol its charms. I prepare myself to enter a fairy-tale world.

We arrive at eight a.m. and emerge into oppressive heat—the kind difficult to imagine until it flattens you. The Soqotra "international airport" is one tiny building, thronged with people. Herds of foreigners from our plane mingle with crowds of Soqotri people hoping to get some work. The first thing I notice about Soqotris is their teeth. On the mainland, I am constantly confronted with rotting brown teeth. But Soqotris must not chew as much *qat* or smoke as much tobacco. Or perhaps they have been blessed with good genes. Their teeth are beautiful and white, dramatically so against their dark skin. A mix of Asian and African, Soqotris have very black skin and sculpted faces. I find them *gorgeous*.

Pearl and I go outside to find Rasheed, a Soqotri man who works with them and drives their company car, a monstrous white SUV. Rasheed is slim and handsome, with sparkling black eyes and a rascal's smile. With all the windows open, we cruise along a coast so spectacular I almost forget the heat. The ocean glitters in the morning sun to our left, and mountains rise precipitously to our right. The lower slopes are peppered with fat, fleshy trees topped with pink flowers—the Soqotri desert rose. The coastline scallops in and out, creating pretty little lagoons. It only takes about fifteen minutes to reach the wee village—excuse me, the hopping capital city—of Hadibo. At first I don't recognize it as even a town. It looks more like the ruins of something. Low stone walls, which apparently are buildings, crawl across the dust everywhere. At least, they're buildings according to the Soqotri definition of the word, which doesn't necessarily include a roof. This is the most populous area of the eighty-mile island. No exact census exists, but the population is estimated to be between forty thousand and a hundred thousand.

As we rumble down what passes for the main street, Pearl points out the Soqotra Women's Development Association, which sells local handicrafts and offers opportunities for female tourists to meet with local Soqotri women; the Soqotri honey store, run by a French man and Lebanese woman who have been training the Soqotris to manage hives; a tiny grocery store selling soft drinks, tinned beans, and candy; and plain, boxy hotels without signs.

On the other side of town (the foreigners' area, the Soqotri version of Hadda), we come to the house Pearl and Marvin rent from Rasheed. A metal door painted with red and blue diamonds opens into a pebbled courtyard. On our left is a raised, tiled area about the size of a large room, with only three walls. Just past that is an enclosed room. Across the courtyard is a kitchen containing only a sink, and opposite is a small, pink-tiled Yemeni bathroom with a squat toilet and a cold-water shower. (Cold being relative; the water in Soqotra is never less than warm.)

Pearl and Marvin insist I take the one closed room and string up their mosquito net on the tiles. I drag my things into my room and cover the tiny, thin mattress with my sheet. The small bed, adrift in a desert of linoleum, depresses me, making me feel acutely single. I lie down for a nap. It is stifling, nearly too hot to sleep, but I manage to slip into a tropical torpor for a bit before waking around noon. We all take quick showers to cool off and walk into town for lunch. It's so hot I have trouble making my legs move. The dusty main street is deserted. It feels like the American Wild West at high noon.

We find a restaurant at the other end of town. Lunch is cold slices of fish, rice, and tea. This is all there ever will be for lunch on Soqotra, unless you want meat, rice, and tea. There is almost no agriculture on the island, so fruits and vegetables don't appear in restaurants. But as it is my first meal, I enjoy it. We sit and talk and swelter. Marvin tells me more about the livestock project.

After lunch, we walk (slowly, as the sun is still burning down) to the small *souq*, where we peer into the shops. Goats are everywhere. They are not happy or healthy goats. Their fur is matted, their bellies bloated, and their tails coated with excrement. In the *souq*, several are tied under tables, ready for slaughter. In one of the small shops, I buy a light cotton dress for $3; everything I brought feels too warm. I wash it as soon as we get home and hang it on a line in the courtyard. A half hour later, it is dry.

Desperate for a swim, we all pile into the SUV and head to a beach on a protected little peninsula with two pointed rocks at the end called Di Hamri. A few camping shelters have been set up here, with an open-air shower.

The men wander off, to preserve our modesty, and Pearl and I drop our things on a sheltered stretch of rocky beach. After waiting for the men to disappear from view, I strip to my swimsuit and hurl myself into the water. It's crystal clear. I put my goggles on and am awestruck. Coral mushrooms up from the ocean floor, fanciful kinds of coral I could not have dreamed up—my previous encounters with coral being limited to jewelry shops. There is bloated round coral, branchlike coral, brain-shaped coral, and hundreds of kinds of fish. There are black-and-white-striped fish with yellow tails, black fish, long blue fish, and tiny little fish too small to eat. I have never been scuba diving or snorkeling and have never swum in water so clear. I am deliriously happy. I swim out and out, until men on the shore begin waving their kerchiefs at me to come back. But I can't stop, luxuriating in my newfound floatiness.

The sun begins to set around the corner on the cliffs, and I stay in the water until it dissolves. When I emerge, I feel near-human. On the beach, I shower in a little palm-frond-shaded booth on the rocks and talk to Pearl while I comb out my hair and pin it back up with chopsticks. It seems that last year, a couple of tourists swam out a bit too far and were caught in a riptide. Their bodies washed up the next morning.

"That is why those men were waving you in," she says.

The only thing missing from the afternoon is a stop at a roadside ice cream stand. In this climate, ice cream feels critical. But there is no ice cream on Soqotra. There is hardly any refrigeration, and what little exists is usually on only after dark, when the island's few generators are turned on.

We drive back past tiny villages of stone walls and palm-thatched roofs. Once we've changed, we eat dinner at the same restaurant where we had lunch. None of the restaurants have names; even the Soqotri can't tell you what they're called. They simply say "the restaurant of the Taj Hotel" or "the restaurant across the street from the Taj."

Dinner is *ful* and *fasooleah* with bread, and some sheep for the sheep eaters. Afterward, Pearl and I walk over to the Taj Hotel so she can show me where "all the cool people hang out." Most of the expats and tourists eat at this one restaurant, though all of the restaurants serve exactly the same thing: beans for breakfast, meat and rice for lunch, and beans for dinner. There are no menus.

The next morning, I head out for a walk before the heat becomes insufferable. In my new cotton shift, I trek up into the shrub-covered mountains. From a distance, the area looks bare and unpopulated. But every few minutes, I am surprised to stumble upon a house that blends so closely into the rocks around it that I haven't seen it. Every time I think I am alone, a child bursts from a bush and runs across my path.

I hurry back to shower because I'm going to a workshop conducted by U.S. veterinarians, here to teach Soqotri women how to care for their livestock. When we arrive at the training, held at the small, filthy local hospital, we are quizzed by Jennifer, a testy woman working for the U.S. embassy. She won't let men into the training, because it's full of Soqotri women, but says I may watch if I promise not to be disruptive.

In a small, airless room that reeks of feet, some thirty-five women, all in black *abayas, hijabs,* and *niqabs,* are gathered. A blond U.S. military veterinarian sits at her computer flipping through the slides of her Power-Point presentation, while a male Soqotri veterinarian reads them out loud. They have been translated into Arabic. Occasionally there are English subtitles, such as "Disease History," "Prophylaxis," "Defecation," "Urination," "Gait," and "Voice."

"The goal is to teach women basic care, not to make them vets," Jennifer says.

I ask why only women are being trained, and Jennifer explains that women do most of the work on the island, particularly the herding. The women come from villages all over the island, handpicked by their local councils for their ability to speak and read Arabic. Soqotris have their own language, the origin of which is still debated. The women are dressed in their fanciest *abayas,* with spangled sleeves and embroidered trim, their feet shod in high heels. It is difficult to imagine an outfit less suited to examining livestock. Their fingers are stained with henna and *naqsh.*

I struggle to breathe in the stale air, and sweat runs down my spine, soaking my cotton dress. The heat and the stench are overwhelming. The women flip through handouts of the presentation, without taking notes, while the Soqotri vet explains how to examine animals for disease.

During breaks, the staff and I race outside for a breath of fresh air, but the Soqotri women do not leave the room. They are encouraged several times to go outside, but evidently neither the heat nor the funk bothers them.

By the end of the second lecture, I am drooping and in need of escape. I sneak out into the relentless midday glare, heading for the Tourist Information Office, as Pearl has suggested it might help me find things to do here.

At the office there are posters on the wall but nothing else, save a few DVDs locked in a display case. I ask the young man there—in Arabic, mime, and English—if he has any brochures. He shakes his head.

"We have no information."

"No information?" I am incredulous.

"Mafeesh." (Nothing.)

Well, if the Tourist Information Office is out of information, I doubt I will find it anywhere else, so I head home.

We lunch at the same little restaurant with the friendly French/ Lebanese beekeepers. We laugh at the décor, as the walls are plastered with photos of luxury travel destinations, mostly featuring pools of deep blue water and palm trees—places landscaped within an inch of their lives that could not possibly be mistaken for wild Soqotra. Rasheed helps me draw up a list of things to do and see. He's far more informative than the Tourist Information Office.

After lunch, he drives me in his pickup truck to Wadi Ayeft while Marvin and Pearl stay behind to work. The *wadi* (valley) is about a forty-minute ride away, and only the first quarter is on pavement. The rest is on rocky trails so bumpy that I get blisters on my back from bouncing against the seat. There is a handle on my side of the car (and no seat belt, natch), so I pull myself forward with that, clinging to the truck for dear life as we bounce our way up mountain trails.

Finally, we abandon the truck and continue on foot into the valley. Cliffs of red rock rise up on either side, and jagged peaks appear before us, including the tallest mountain on the island. We pick our way across rocky ground, Rasheed pointing out frankincense trees and all manner of other exotic and storybook-looking species. He shows me a plant whose pointy spines contain an antibacterial sap, and another with tiny yellow fruits that resemble cherries but taste woody, like mealy apple-apricots. He throws rocks at the tree until the fruits shower down, and we eat them. These are the first fruits I have seen here.

We pass some locals. The *wadi* dwellers herd goats up and down the cliffs, and many, including Rasheed's uncle, live in caves.

I notice that Rasheed greets other men by touching noses with them once or twice and making hand gestures. I ask about this. He tells me that the number of nose touches is important: If Soqotri men have not seen each other in more than a week, they must touch noses three times. "Otherwise, there is trouble." There are variations on the greeting for encounters with people one's own age and with older people.

We continue along a dried-up riverbed for nearly half an hour before it opens into a pristine pool of freshwater, next to a small cascade that stretches across its far end. Tiny red crabs cling to the sides. Rasheed walks a few yards from me, keeping passing men away while I change and slip into the water. It is delicious to paddle around in its silky coolness. When I climb out, Rasheed joins me, and we sit on the rocks at the edge and talk.

There, a rare feeling of relaxation spreads through me. I am cool, I still have energy, and there is nowhere else I need to be. It is a whole, perfect moment and the first glimmer of pure happiness I've felt in weeks.

Rasheed tells me endless stories, first about his deep friendship with the French ambassador. On the ambassador's first trip to Soqotra, Rasheed had welcomed him to Hadibo by joking, "Welcome to Paris."

"Have you ever been to Paris?" the ambassador asked.

"No. Just the Paris of Soqotra."

"Would you like to go?"

"You must be joking."

But the ambassador wasn't. A few weeks later, Rasheed had a visa, plane tickets, and hotel reservations in Paris. He was instructed to leave his Soqotri *mahwaz* behind and dress as Parisians do.

So Rasheed went to Paris. The girl who was to meet him there rang to ask what airport he was coming into. This was his first shock. "There is more than one?" As the girl tried to explain to him how enormous and overwhelming French airports are, Rasheed assured her that he had been to an international airport, as Soqotra had one. We both laugh when he says this.

In Paris, he was immediately confronted with confounding things, such as an escalator, which he had never seen. He told me he had been afraid to step onto it and had called back to the only other Yemeni on the plane to ask him if it was safe to get on.

Then the girl who met him at the airport had kissed him on both cheeks! He was mortified. "This made me very shy," he said. "And she said to me, 'You are in Paris now, you must leave your Soqotri self in Soqotra.'" She made him take her arm (another shock) as they left the airport. He had yet another jolt when they got on an elevator, which he had never seen. "What was that?" he said in alarm when it began to move.

The French girl instructed him how to use silverware. "And then after three days of practicing with silverware, she took me to a Chinese restaurant!"

"And you had to use chopsticks!"

"Yes!"

We collapse in giggles.

Rasheed's stories get more personal as the sun slides down the sky. He is the sole male supporter of fourteen women. His wife and two children are currently in Sana'a. He doesn't sound too fond of his wife. "There are problems," he says. "But my family likes her."

Rasheed has only ever truly loved one woman. They were childhood sweethearts, always competing with each other in school for first place in their class—so fiercely that she once stole his books right before an exam to try to keep him from studying. Before unification with the more conservative North, boys and girls went to school together, and girls didn't cover their faces. When Rasheed was later sent to the mainland to study, he mourned this girl. Something was missing from his life, he tells me. He missed her so much he called his mother and said he was coming home. But his mother chastised him, reminding him of the money spent on his education. So he called another relative and came home.

He told the girl that he loved her and wanted to marry her. Neither family was happy. Soqotris are not supposed to choose whom they marry. But the girl said she would wait for him while he studied abroad for three years. He set off once more.

While abroad, he heard that her mother had married her off to a wealthy man from the United Arab Emirates. The girl had refused to marry the man, but her family had forced her. She is now living in the Emirates and has children, but it is obvious that Rasheed still loves her.

"I will not make trouble for her life," he says. "But I hate people from Emirates now."

I murmur sympathetic things and try to distract him from his evident sadness by asking him to describe local weddings. Soqotri mountain and coastal dwellers have very different ways of celebrating weddings. People on the coast, he says, have music and drums and dancing, because they are more African. But people in the mountains instead have fierce poetry contests, usually among five groups of people, each group reciting a poem. "It's a very *hard* competition," says Rasheed. "Until around four in the morning. They argue by poetry, one guy saying something like 'You don't have enough *qat*,' or 'You are not serving enough meat at your wedding.'"

Mountain weddings also apparently involve jumping contests, during which men leap up and down while the crowd makes "jumping noises" to accompany them.

The sun turns the cliffs above us red and darkens the palm trees around the pool of water into silhouettes. We continue to sit by the pool until the rocks become too sharp against our bottoms, and we have just a half hour of daylight left to get back.

Something about the air of camping and summer vacations and days at the beach here makes me feel nostalgic and melancholy. I find myself dwelling on happy summers of my past, appreciating them anew. In the car on the way home, Rasheed and I both fall silent as we watch the sky darken.

"I like this time of night," I say.

"It is the time when each person is alone with his thoughts, thinking about things," he answers. Exactly so. Our silence is companionable after our long afternoon of talking. I drift off into memories of other vacations in wild lands—happy times bicycling through the mountains, climbing peaks, rock climbing, running through rain, eating meals of fresh corn and blackberry pie, drinking by campfires, and basking in warm compan ionship.

I don't think I took these things for granted then, but they are even more precious to me now. Here on Soqotra, away from the distractions of work, my solitude feels acute. I feel a sudden longing for a lover, someone with whom I could share this. It occurs to me that this is the longest time I have been alone since I was a teenager; I have always been romantically involved with someone. I want to climb a mountain again with someone I adore, pick blueberries, tell each other stories as we clamber our way through rocks and trees before sunset. Though I have long avoided life- time commitment, I now think that maybe it would be nice to stay with someone for a while. A long while.

Chances are I won't find this person in Yemen. Not with my work schedule and the dearth of romantic prospects. I resign myself to months more of solitary nights and wonder if it would help if I made some more friends.

I'm jolted out of my reverie as Rasheed pulls the truck up by our house. He smiles at me. "I'll come find you tomorrow."

☾

FOR THE REST OF MY WEEK on Soqotra, I rise at five A.M., when the roos- ter goes off. This is the only time the heat is bearable. Still, when I climb the hills near town, there is no cover, no shade, no relief from the sun. When I return from a two-hour walk my second or third morning, I am dizzy and on the verge of vomiting. Pearl is anxious that I have sunstroke. I strip and get into the shower. I soak my hair in the hopes that it will keep me cool.

Pearl disappears and comes back with a straw hat for me. "Are you going to make it?" she asks. "There's a plane out on Monday."

I am appalled that my discomfort is so apparent.

"I'll be okay," I reassure Pearl. I'm determined to stick this out.

In the late afternoon, Rasheed comes to fetch me for another adventure. Our second trip is to Diksam, a cooler, mountainous region in the center of the island. The mountains are barer than I had expected, save for the fantastical dragon's blood trees, which look like giant stalks of broccoli standing on end. Rasheed shows me the red resin in the trunk that Soqotri women use for makeup.

On our way up into the mountains, we pick up several men, including one of his uncles. There are always men on the road needing a ride, and Rasheed always picks them up. They stand in the back of the truck or crouch low. Occasionally, one shouts at Rasheed to slow down. Because Soqotra has had a road for only a few years, every driver on the island is a novice.

When we reach the top of one mountain, we pull over next to two tiny stone huts, to have tea at Rasheed's uncle's home. The inside of the house is cool and welcoming. We sit on the floor, which is covered with thin woven mats and uncluttered by any furnishings. A woman brings us sweet tea made with goat milk and fresh flatbread that we dip into our mugs. Children, dirty and half-dressed, with enormous brown eyes, gather around me to stare.

The women question me, wanting to know (of course) if I am married and have children. In my lonely, travel-weary state, it makes me sadder to have to lie about having a husband and to tell the truth about the absence of a child. A young woman, in her early twenties and newly married, is the most interested in me and aggressive in her questioning. She wants me to stay the night. But we peel ourselves away close to sunset and drive home mostly in silence, picking up men along the way.

☪

I LOOK FORWARD MOST to my afternoons with Rasheed. It is fun to travel with him, to listen to his stories and not have to talk. The next afternoon, he drives me to a protected lagoon near Qalansiyah. It takes an hour or so to get there. As we approach the rocky cliffs above the sea, he slows down and tells me to close my eyes. The truck lurches forward.

"Now open."

Framed between two walls of rock is a vast expanse of pristine white sand and a lagoon of clear, aquamarine water, sparkling in the sun.

"*Jamil,*" I say. *Beautiful.*

Our last and best adventure is the Hoq cave. I've been dying to see it, but Rasheed initially resists, saying that it is too late to set out. "It's an hour-and-a-half hike," he says. "To tell you the truth, I am feeling lazy about hiking."

Well, I am not feeling lazy about hiking, so I put my foot down. We drive along the northeastern shore until we come to the fishing village closest to the cave. Soqotri law holds that cave visitors must take a guide, so that locals benefit from the tourism. We pick up a man who says he is afraid to go into the cave himself, but he can show us the way. He doesn't have a flashlight but assures us that a group has gone up before us and that they will have one.

The three of us set off up the mountain. It is a steep, difficult climb, and our guide sets a breakneck pace, which is all the more impressive given that he does it in purple plastic flip-flops. Still, I manage to keep up. I am happy to be getting some real exercise. I even have to prod Rasheed along at one point. "I'm stepping on your heels," I tease him. "Pick up the pace."

We make our way past dozens of the pulpy fat-trunked desert rose trees. They are so adorable that every time we pass a good one, I cry aloud, "Fat tree!" and throw my arms around it. Rasheed finds this so entertaining he begins pointing them out. "There's one over there," he says. "Hug that one too!"

Our guide becomes noticeably nervous as we near the top and falls behind. You can't see the black maw of the cave until you are right upon it. Then it opens before you, a wide dark gash in the mountain's side. I pause, panting, and turn to look down at the sea below. The mountainside falls away dramatically, and the sky is just turning pink over the water. Rasheed catches up with me and we stand gazing down.

"I'll wait outside," the guide says in Soqotri. "There are *jinn*."

Jinn are mentioned in the Qur'an. As my friend and Arabic teacher Hamoudi explains: "Before the God made humans, he had only angels and *jinn*. Iblees was the king of the *jinn*, who were all made of fire. God made the *jinn* of fire and the angels of light. The God then said, 'I will make a human, Adam, from mud, and everyone should pray to him, just once.'

"Iblees, the king *jinni*, was the first person to say no to the God. He said, 'No, I will not worship humans, because they are mud and we are fire. We are better!'

"God said, 'Go away.'

"The *jinn* said to God, 'Then we will make humans do bad things.' . . . God said, 'Go, and try to make humans do bad things. But if they do, you and they will both be in hell.'"

Muslims believe the *jinn* can enter a person's blood and force him to commit terrible crimes. A human can either follow the *jinn* to hell or choose a higher path. A human possessed by a *jinni* often requires an exorcism, which involves an imam reading the Qur'an over the afflicted.

Not all *jinn* are evil, however. There are Muslim *jinn*, who have been convinced of the righteous way. But these are apparently not what our guide is worried about encountering in the cave.

There is no sign of any other tourists, and we have no flashlight. I fish around in my purse and find a lighter with a tiny bulb at the end. Rasheed and I step into the cave.

"Here, *jinni jinni!*" he calls, to torment the guide.

We pick our way across the uneven rock floor, skirting pools of water. "Look up," says Rasheed.

Stalagmites of astonishing length hang everywhere, like Stone Age chandeliers. A thousand dripping daggers of stone hang over my head. I've never seen anything like them. Around us crowd accidental statues and gargoyles in a Gothic sculpture garden. Pools of water form in bizarrely symmetrical basins. Cathedral ceilings stretch away into blackness. It is the Notre Dame of caves. It catches up all of my breath. Silently, Rasheed and I pick our way as deep into the cave as is possible with our tiny light.

When I stop again to gaze up at the magnificent stalagmites, Rasheed whispers, "Turn out the light."

We stand in the total darkness, listening to the drip of the water and the silence in between and our breathing and the rustle of—bats?

I want to go all the way to the back of the cave, but we do not have enough light or time. It is nearly dusk, and we still have a long climb down the mountain. "I promise, the next time you come, we will go to every cave on Soqotra," says Rasheed. "We will do the all-cave tour."

Our guide is pacing anxiously outside. We join him and hustle down the path. I take the lead, full of renewed vigor. We race the sun down the mountain and emerge from the scrub at the bottom just as the sky turns deep blue and the first few stars wink on.

After dropping our guide at his village, we stop to visit a friend of Rasheed's mother's. The sky is heavily salted with stars when we arrive at the little stone hut by the sea. A woman comes out to greet us and ushers us into a small courtyard. As we settle ourselves on mats laid on the ground, the family gathers around us, friendly and inquisitive. A pot of a reddish fish stew is set before us, and we dig in. It is delicious, the fish falling apart in our fingers. It must have been caught just hours before. We follow this with fresh flatbread and the usual milky sweet tea. Afterward, I am offered a bowl of sour milk. I expect it to resemble yogurt, but it tastes like rotten milk. I gag and pass it to Rasheed. I politely decline the dates fermented in goat skin.

As we sit there, eating and talking with the family, a wave of tranquility washes over me. For a moment, I feel a second flash of pure happiness, to be outside on a cool, starry night, with warmhearted friends, and eating simple food. I could sit there for hours.

Travel is always like this, I remind myself. Uneven, with stretches of loneliness and anxiety followed by unparalleled moments of bliss and discovery. In the droughts, I have to learn to trust that the joy will come.

FIFTEEN

the artificial man

Six months into my tenure, the paper is on a regular schedule, I'm sleeping more, and I've started to do some of my own reporting. Most significant is a whirlwind trip to the Kharaz refugee camp, home to some ten thousand refugees, mostly Somali. I go with officials from the United Nations High Commission for Refugees. We fly to Riyan in the South and drive west along the coast to Shabwa and the Maifa'a Reception Center, where the Somalis who wash up on Yemen's shores are processed—if they survive the journey. My cleaning woman Aisha probably landed here.

It's much hotter than in Sana'a, and our driver blasts the air-conditioning. Red cliffs that remind me of the Grand Canyon rise on our right. To our left, the sea is dotted with colorful fishing boats. I'm squished in the backseat next to a Yemeni UNHCR official and Amal, a tiny woman reporter for the *Yemen Times*.

No matter where they come ashore, Somalis either find their way to the Maifa'a Reception Center, or villagers who see the refugees on the beach alert UNHCR, which sends transport, says Aouad Baobaid, a field specialist who travels with us.

"When we can't get to people—we can't find everyone—the villagers take care of them," he says. "They feed them and put them up for the night, women with women, and men with men. They even bury the dead."

There are plenty of dead. In 2006, UNHCR reported that some twenty-seven thousand people made the perilous voyage, with three hundred and thirty dying on the way and another three hundred still missing.

Maifa'a, a cluster of whitewashed cinder-block shelters baking in the southern sun, was established in 1996 to register the refugees. They are asked when they left Somalia, how their journey was, why they fled, and where they arrived. We wander around, asking questions, examining food stores, and interviewing workers. Afterward, we visit several other spots along the coast where refugees often wash ashore.

In the morning, we fly to Aden and drive two and a half hours inland to the camp. Kharaz sprawls on an isolated expanse of steaming-hot desert, many miles from towns, roads, water, and work. It was the only land on offer, say the UNHCR officials leading us around. There are no walls around the vast complex of look-alike cinder-block shelters mingled with a cluster of tents for new arrivals, and refugees come and go as they wish.

Only about 5 percent of refugees stay at the camp. The rest head for urban areas, where they hope to find jobs washing cars, cleaning houses, or doing other sorts of menial labor. The lives of camp refugees consist primarily of waiting—waiting for Somalia to calm down enough so that they can return, waiting for job opportunities, waiting for better food, better shelter, better health care, waiting for something miraculous to lift them out of their misery.

For this reason, any visitor to the camp is instantly surrounded by scores of anxious Somalis who hope that this person is the miracle they have awaited, that help has arrived at last. Many carry handwritten or mimeographed letters that they press into the hands of visitors. Most are addressed to the UNHCR and request all manner of aid.

A woman named Asli Abdullahi Hasson hands me a letter describing the bombing of her home in 1991, the death of her relatives, and her flight from Somalia. On her way to Yemen, men "tried to rape [her] in front of [her] husband," she writes. "He defended me unfortunately he was fired bullets. He was not dead but had a bad wound." She ends her tale with a simple plea. "Please," she writes. "Assist me to look for a better future." There are countless stories like hers, and as many letters.

In February, the air already feels stifling, and my clothing is quickly drenched in sweat. By summer, the heat grows deadly, and many refugees fall ill, says Dr. Fawzia Abdul Naji, the gynecologist/obstetrician in residence at the camp. She is one of three doctors working full-time at Kharaz.

We visit refugees in the cinder-block homes and the cluster of tents. In one of the homemade tents lives Khadija Mohammed Farah, who shares three tiny rooms with six people. Inside, the air reeks of excrement, and flies coat every surface. A woman lies motionless on a thin mattress. "She is very ill," says Khadija. In another room is a rudimentary kitchen with a camp stove and kerosene lamp. Khadija has been at the camp for two years and is still awaiting a more permanent shelter. Her four children cling to her while she complains about the conditions. Twenty-five or so Somalis crowd around us to add their own laments.

"Many journalists come here, and nothing ever changes," cries one.

Khadija says that she wants to return to Somalia, when it is safe. But until then, she feels trapped.

"Look," she says, pulling down the front of her colorful dress. "I was burned horribly."

Her entire chest is a mass of scar tissue, caused when a lamp accidentally ignited a fire in the camp.

A man pushes to the front of a crowd. "Won't you help me!" he cries, pulling down the front of his own shirt to reveal a crater-shaped scar. "Help me, I am all alone with four kids."

The psychological scars many bear from witnessing unthinkable brutality are even worse. Issa Sultan, fifty, originally of Mogadishu, tells me he was forced to flee to Yemen with his wife and three children in 1995 because of the terror of the wars between Somali clans.

I interview scores of Somalis, scribbling furiously in my notebook. Working keeps me from becoming overwhelmed by the sheer misery of the place. I cannot get my mind around desolation on such a mass scale. I will never complain about my life again.

By the end of the day we are exhausted, overheated, emotionally drained. Yet we are lucky. We have the luxury of climbing back into our refrigerated Land Cruiser and driving away. So much of what I see in Yemen is a constant reminder of my good fortune. Every day I witness scenes of poverty and deprivation, yet my American passport allows me to walk away at any time. After living here, I can never again take any of my privileges for granted.

(⁕

I AM WORKING on the Somali story at my desk in Sana'a the next day when I get a phone call from customs.

"You have a package," the man says.

"Great." I am expecting a box with a replacement battery for my computer, a power cord, chewing gum, and medicine from a friend in New York. It's been taking ages to arrive. But I can't imagine why this man is calling me; usually packages are delivered without preamble. "Well, bring it on over then."

There is a silence on the line. Then, "Ah . . . Well, you see, there's a problem. It contains something offensive to the Muslim faith."

"*What?*" I stop looking at my computer screen and turn my attention to the call. "What is it?"

"Ah . . ." The man clears his throat. "It's . . . It's some sort of . . ." The customs officer stumbles over his words. "It's—an *artificial man!*"

Suddenly I know what it is. A friend in Manhattan has joked about sending me a vibrator to keep me company in this lonely place. Oh dear.

"I'm not sure I know what you are talking about," I say carefully. "Could you describe it to me?"

"It's—!" The man is deeply uncomfortable. "It's—! It's *purple!*"

I suppress a wave of hysterical laughter. "I see." I twist the phone cord around my finger and wonder how much trouble I am in. "A purple artificial man."

"Yes!"

I don't know what I am supposed to say. "Well, I don't think I know what you are talking about," I tell him. "But if it's offensive to you, why don't you just throw it out and bring me the rest of the package?"

"It will be destroyed."

"Great, destroy it! That's fine. But you can bring me the rest of the things, right? All the rest of it is legal? Because I am expecting some very important computer parts and medicine." I am desperate for the rest of that package. My battery has been recalled, and Luke and I have been sharing a power cord for weeks.

"I don't know," says the customs man.

"Look, there is no reason why you can't bring me things it is legal for me to receive. I want the rest of that package, okay?"

The man mumbles something and I hang up. I have a story to write after all, and I am on deadline. I push aside the unsettling conversation and go back to work.

Haleema Mohammed, 45, of Galkayo realized that staying in Somalia was no longer an option one unforgettable night in 1991, when she was forced to watch as her brothers were slaughtered in front of her eyes.

"Forty people were killed that night in Galkayo," she said. "Five were my brothers."

Mohammed, sitting in a tent at the al-Kharaz refugee camp in Yemen's Lahej Governorate, speaks with calm stoicism, her gaze defiant and unwavering. Her eyes, which she says were black in Somalia, are now blue. They were bleached by Yemen's merciless desert sun, she says. . . .

I am deeply engrossed in my writing when Radia comes into my office and hands me a DHL slip. "Where is the package?" I say.

"No package."

"No package?"

"No. At customs."

Now I'm worried. Why would they drop off a package slip but no package? What are the customs agents planning to do with my things? What am I supposed to do?

"Radia," I say, "I have to find that package." I explain to her that something that was in the package offended the customs agents and that I told them to throw out that item and bring me the rest of it. I cannot see why this would be a problem.

"I will send a driver," says Radia. "Salem can get it for you."

But a few minutes later she is back in my office. "The Doctor won't let us have a driver," she says. "He says you should go."

"I can't go! I'm on deadline!" Not only do I have to finish writing my refugee story, I still have to edit the rest of the paper. Work on my story has already slowed me down.

Radia shrugs. "He says you have to go."

The Doctor has been sulky and resentful ever since I forced him to pay my employees, which I must say I don't think was an unreasonable request. "It's a closing day! Tell him that if I have to go to the airport myself, the paper will close four hours later." The Doctor hates it when we close late.

She disappears again.

When she leaves another reporter comes in to tell me that my phone bill is overdue. Sabafon has changed the amount of my bill four times in the past month, by wildly varying amounts. I have no idea how to tell which total is accurate.

I'm stewing over this when a series of reporters come into my office asking for my camera, which we use for almost every story now because the photographers rarely can be bothered to work. But I can't give it to them, because I have two hundred photos of refugees in my camera. I can't download them because my computer has no memory or battery left. "Go tell one of the photographers to do his job," I say crossly.

Zuhra comes into my office, anxious to help, but I am so distraught I am almost inconsolable. "You need someone to do things for you," she says. "Faris should hire someone just for you, so you don't have to cope with all of these things."

I manage a weak smile. "That is unlikely," I say. "I can't even get him to pay for business cards for my staff; forget an extra employee."

Still, I run upstairs to ask Faris for help. I explain to him why I need a driver to go to the airport and fetch this package, which contains computer parts we need for work. The entire paper runs on my computer, after all. I don't mention the vibrator. Faris promptly sends Salem off to the airport.

An hour later, Zuhra comes into my office looking anxious. "Salem is calling from customs. They need to know, the power cord that is in your package, is it a . . . a *sexual* power cord?"

I stare at her. "No," I say. "It is the power cord that goes to this computer." I tap my Apple.

"Oh. Okay." She hurries out of the room.

A few minutes later, she is back. "Um, they have to know, is the battery in the package, is it a *sexual* battery?"

"Zuhra. It's *square*."

She looks at me quizzically.

"I mean, I just can't imagine how it could be used sexually. Look, the battery has a serial number and an Apple logo. They can look it up online if they want. It's a standard Apple battery."

She nods and heads off again but is back a few minutes later.

"Sorry! But they want to know if the chewing gum is *sexual* chewing gum."

I despair. "Zuhra! How on earth could chewing gum be sexual? Are these men completely out of their minds?"

"I don't know!" Zuhra twists her hands together.

She looks extremely distressed to have to ask me these awkward questions. I feel sorry for having put her in this position.

"No," I finally say. "The chewing gum is absolutely not sexual."

I feel compelled to explain to her why the police are asking such interesting questions. Mortified, I say that my friend has included this one verboten item but that the rest of the package was completely innocent.

She listens calmly and goes back to the telephone. Moments later, she returns to tell me that customs has determined that everything in the package is sexual. They will not give it to Salem.

I nearly lose it. "Are these men *stupid*?" I say. "The battery is obviously a computer battery!" I am trembling, despite my dim awareness of the humor of the situation. I cannot believe that the customs officers are about to get away with stealing hundreds of dollars of things from me. No matter how offended they are by the vibrator, there is no reason they cannot deliver my medicine and computer parts.

I start to cry from sheer frustration but quickly dry my eyes when Faris comes in and hesitates in front of my desk. "Jennifer, if you want to receive things like this, you should tell me. I could have had it routed through the embassy. Salem almost got arrested at the airport. I just had to talk to the police to get them to release him."

I want to dissolve into my carpet. I cannot remember ever feeling so completely humiliated.

"I didn't know what he was sending," I say. "All I want is the computer battery and the cord and the medicines that are in that package. I had no idea they would try to arrest Salem. I'm really sorry."

He says he will try to get those things for me but chastises me for not talking to him earlier, so things could be done "a different way."

Now everyone in the entire office knows what was in my package. I am ashamed to face them, but I have no choice but to brazen it out. I go about my work as normally as possible, and no one says a word. I don't even catch anyone smirking. Zuhra comes in my office later that afternoon to tell me that her family supports me. "My sister says it's unfair, that it's personal and what they have done is wrong."

I am embarrassed that she has told her sister but grateful for her compassion. I never would have expected such a response from a conservative Muslim, but my Yemeni reporters are always surprising me.

When I have calmed down a bit, I finish my refugee story. My staff is still being kind, particularly Hadi, who invites me outside to eat with him. He shares his pan of *ful* and his bread. I am not hungry but I eat anyway, thankful for his gesture of friendship.

☪

A WEEK LATER, I go to Faris to ask if he has made any progress in obtaining my package. He avoids looking me in the eyes, fiddling with a pen on his desk.

"You see," he says, "the problem is that customs doesn't have your package anymore."

"It doesn't?"

"No. Ah, security has it."

"*Security?*"

"Well, apparently your package is now considered a national security threat. And, ah, they are testing the chewing gum."

"They are *testing the chewing gum?* For what?"

"For, you know, Viagra or something. Like a sexual stimulant."

What on earth would I do with a sexual stimulant in this country? I want to say. I am completely alone.

"Faris, it's *Trident*. It's a famous brand. They can look it up on the Web!"

"These are not educated men, Jennifer."

"Apparently not."

"They don't know how to look anything up. They might not be able to read."

I sit in silence for a moment. "I bet they took it all home," I say. "I bet they just want it for themselves."

Faris nods slowly. "They probably do."

We sit in silence. "I guess I wouldn't want it back now anyway then." I look up at him.

He nods gravely. "You probably wouldn't."

SIXTEEN

the power of peanut butter cups

There are moments, even whole days, when everything falls into place. Reporters give me coherent stories, photographs come in on time, and the men actually return from lunch at a decent hour. Progress is irrefutable. But just when I am feeling most hopeful, I run up against obstacles that it is not in my power to remove. I can edit poorly written stories. I can assist shoddy reporting. I can enforce deadlines. But some things, only Faris can remedy.

Staffing is one of these. Every time I feel I have enough reporters, somebody quits. They all leave for the same reasons: They are not paid enough, they receive no health insurance or other benefits, and the administration treats them shabbily.

My reporters are attractive to international employers, who constantly poach them, because they are educated and speak English. When the Red Cross offers Hassan a job with decent pay and benefits, he has no choice but to accept, though he loves being a reporter. He and his Yemeni wife have just had a baby, he's having expensive medical problems, and he's just taken a Canadian second wife. But he also leaves because of the Doctor. For months, the Doctor has been harassing Hassan, withholding his salary until I march into his office to remonstrate. This happens with monotonous regularity. The Doctor claims that Hassan isn't working. I tell the

Doctor that Hassan certainly *is* working, and that if he weren't, I would be the first to know. Hassan has no idea why he is singled out for abuse, and the Doctor gives me no reason other than Hassan's alleged laziness— which is laughable. He is one of my most reliable men.

I am heartbroken to lose Hassan. He is a passionate journalist, dedicated to improvement, and without a disagreeable bone in his body. Unlike the other men, he relishes criticism of his work so he can learn. But Faris refuses to invest in his staff. Every time I tell him how important this is, that without decent reporters the entire enterprise is worthless, he tells me he pays them a livable wage. While it may be true that $200 a month is relative riches in Sana'a, it is obviously not enough to support a family or to keep reporters from looking for other jobs.

"It takes me *months* to train a reporter," I tell him. "When they quit I have to start all over again with someone new. The paper is constantly losing its most valuable people."

Faris shrugs. "So you can feel you are doing some good in the world," he says. "You train them so well they get other jobs and succeed."

I didn't come here to train journalists so that they could leave the profession, I say. "I came here to make this a better paper and to help the staff to become more professional. I cannot do this when everyone keeps quitting."

☪

NOT LONG AFTER HASSAN GOES, Bashir gives notice. For once, his chubby face isn't smiling. His wife is pregnant, and he has been offered a well-paid job with a telecommunications company. I've spent six months training him. Now all of my careful cultivation has been rendered meaningless. Again, Sisyphus springs to mind. I can't help tearing up when he tells me. Bashir is sad too. "I don't want to go," he says. "But I have no choice. I don't make enough here to support a family."

Whenever I tell Faris that low wages and lack of benefits are losing us valuable employees, he reminds me that the paper isn't making money. He seems to think that if only we wrote better stories, we'd all be rich. I remind him that it is not the mission of the editorial staff to make money; it is our mission to create a brilliant product. It is the job of marketing and advertising to *sell* that product. Faris has no idea what marketing means. I try to explain a few of the things that the marketing department of *The Week* did while I was there. It hosted lunches with famous speakers; it held film nights with celebrities; it gave copies of the magazine to colleges and schools. It did demographic surveys and sent direct mail to the likeliest readers. Not all of these are possible in Yemen, but they could be adapted.

Faris is reluctant to take the publisher's responsibility for marketing and advertising problems. After all, he is working full-time for the president. So he wants me to find someone who can market. He's already paying five men to do marketing, he says, but they have no impact. I have no idea where to start. I want to help him, because I want people to read the product I work so hard to edit. But I only stretch so thin. I cannot be both editor and marketer, even if that were ethical.

It's clear that Faris's loyalties are to the regime, not to reporting. And he mistakes public relations for journalism. In that case, why does he even have a paper? He has given me his reasons: to encourage tourism and development by writing about Yemen's attractions. By writing about Yemen in English, he believes he can communicate Yemen's charms to a broad international audience.

But this still fails to explain Faris's lack of interest in quality. Even if he wants the *Yemen Observer* to be no more than a cheerleader for the country, I would expect him to care about how well it is written and reported. I would expect staff retention to *matter*.

Zuhra offers an explanation. "In Yemen there is no such thing as bad paper and good paper. The quality of journalism overall is bad." Because all newspapers in Yemen—both Arabic and English—contain legions of mistakes, expectations are low. Quality doesn't matter. Publishing a paper in English is prestigious enough, she says. Who's going to complain about quality, other than me and a few ambassadors? And why should Faris invest in quality when he can expect such low returns for it?

Owning a paper also gives Faris power, she says. He can protect himself through media, using it to further his own goals. Publishing in English also allows him access to the international community. If the paper lands in trouble with the government, the case gets international attention.

Zuhra respects Faris, who has been generous and kind to her. But she thinks him too pragmatic to produce brilliant journalism. He cares more about selling ads than he does about printing stories that could change the country.

☪

COME APRIL, Faris is chronically absent. Even if he does manage to slip upstairs to his desk while I am in the building, he avoids me. Never once does he poke his head in to see how things are going. Never once does he tell me I am doing a good job. Or a bad job, for that matter. Sometimes I wonder if he remembers I am here.

This is not the relationship I've dreamed of having with my employer. After his effusive warmth during my first trip, I had hoped to be invited to dinner at his home, introduced to important Yemenis, confided in about national affairs. I had imagined us meeting over coffee or lunch to brainstorm new ideas for the paper and to discuss our progress. I had thought he would be someone I could turn to for guidance, or at the very least information about Yemen's inner workings. It would have made all the difference.

These dreams have vaporized. Not only is Faris physically not present most of the time I am in the office, but when we do meet, our conversations average forty-five seconds. I can always sense his impatience to finish with me and get back to his Really Serious Work for the President. Talking with him makes me so anxious that I nearly always decide that several of the urgent matters I needed to discuss with him are not so urgent after all. Maybe Hassan can wait another week to get paid. Maybe I don't need that plane ticket back to New York. Maybe I can do without a copy editor. I begin to come to him with a list. Otherwise, his snapping fingers and persistent "Next?" drive all of my carefully considered concerns from my head.

I'm busy editing one evening in April when Faris is spotted in the office and someone races to tell me. Back when Manel was around, he'd run to my office and say, "Porsche parked outside. World's handsomest Yemeni spotted upstairs. Hurry."

But tonight when I run upstairs to ask him for five minutes—just five minutes!—he tells me he must speak with Jelena of *Arabia Felix* first. He, Jelena, and al-Matari then have a screaming fight in his conference room for an hour. It seems unwise to interrupt. I've finished my work, but I loiter downstairs, waiting for my five minutes.

Because I'm in my office, I don't see Faris slip out the front door. Only when I emerge to ask Enass if he's free yet do I find out he has escaped once again.

In the hope that Yemenis understand Faris better than I do, I consult my reporters. They have no suggestions. To them, Faris is a godlike, mythic presence. Zuhra aside, most would never dare question anything he does. Even al-Asaadi is cowed by him. Ibrahim takes me out to dinner one night, and I spill my woes over fried fish, hummus, and chewy flatbread. He is mystified. "You've done *wonderful* things for the paper," he says as I glumly tear off strips of the bread and stuff them into my mouth. "He should be grateful to you."

"I'm not sure Faris ever *looks* at the paper," I say. "And I definitely haven't sensed any gratitude."

On April 13 (oh, notable day!), for the first time in months, I spy Faris's silver Porsche in the street. I toss my purse and books in my office and take the stairs two at a time. The door to Faris's office is open, and when I peek in I can see him sitting in the yellow light of a lamp, staring meditatively at his computer screen.

"May I come in?"

He nods, without enthusiasm and without looking at me.

"Faris," I say, perching on the edge of a chair opposite his desk, "I have been trying to get in touch with you for weeks. I am very concerned that you are not answering my phone calls or my e-mails. Did you read my e-mail?"

He glances at his screen. "Frankly? No." He touches his mouse nervously, glances again at the computer screen, and shrugs. "It was too long."

I look at him in disbelief. My e-mail was a paragraph long. A short paragraph.

"Just tell me what you want."

This is hardly encouraging. "Well, first of all, I want a better relationship with you. It feels terrible when you ignore my calls and e-mails. I don't like being avoided. I mean, I *am* running your newspaper. There are many things I would really like to discuss with you."

"To tell you the truth, I have been avoiding you because it makes me feel bad to see you," he says. "I cringe inside myself when I see you."

His words are a dozen *jambiyas* hurled through the air and pinning me to my chair. Everything I've struggled for, and he hates me. "Why?" I look at him with helpless bewilderment. "What have I done?"

He pauses, fiddling with his pen. "You are doing an excellent job with the paper," he says. This is the first positive feedback I have gotten since I arrived back. "But you don't seem to want to work with the advertising and marketing guys. If they ask you to do something, I want you to help them. Not tell them, 'Stay away from my reporters.'"

"But, Faris, I—"

"I want you to help them. The paper doesn't make any money."

That argument again. "Faris, may I explain something?"

"Yes."

"You brought me here to make the paper more professional, right? And to increase its credibility."

He nods.

"The key to doing that is keeping a firm wall between advertising and editorial. If our readers see that we are writing about our advertisers, if they see that we write about people who give us money, they will think that every story we print we only write because someone paid us to run it. It destroys our credibility."

Faris nods as if he might understand.

"I don't want them using my reporters for that reason—it teaches them the wrong ideas about journalism. Also, I am short-staffed as it is. I can't spare news reporters to do advertising."

"I know you need people."

"So we should hire advertising their own people. Qasim obviously needs a staff."

I have become so fed up with Qasim stealing my reporters that I ran a help-wanted classified seeking an advertising intern. But when a man showed up who was eager to help, Qasim sent him away.

Faris has no suggestions. He just reiterates how much he needs me to help the advertising people. But he isn't done with me yet.

"Regarding al-Huthi," he says. "Tone it down. Do you hear me?"

"Tone it *down*? It's the biggest story in the country!" The Huthis are conservative Shiites in the North who have been periodically battling the government since 2004. Their specific demands are unclear, but they seek the restoration of Zaydi Shia dominance in Yemen and denounce Saleh's close relationship with the West.

In January, fighting between Huthis and the government resumed, and hundreds are rumored to have died. We are not allowed to send a reporter to Sa'dah, the northern province where the fighting is centered, because the roads are blocked and there is a complete media blackout. So Ibrahim has been reporting the story based on phone calls to the governor of the region and other sources.

"I am telling you: Do not run it on the front page of every issue. Do you hear me? *Tone. It. Down.*"

"I hear you, but—"

"There were errors in the last story."

"If the government doesn't want us to make mistakes, then it should let us into Sa'dah so we can see what's going on for ourselves."

"You want to go to Sa'dah?"

"*Yes,* I want to go to Sa'dah!" How thrilling it would be to be able to do some real reporting on this story. I am certain that the information we get from the government is far from accurate.

"Fine. I will see if I can get you in. I would love it if I could send you to Sa'dah."

"Why? Anxious to get rid of me, Faris?" Small smile.

"No—we'd have an exclusive."

"And possibly some real information."

Ignoring this, Faris comes to what seems to be an even bigger problem: I've fired our photographer Mas. I explain again why I dismissed him: He did no work. He sat around listening to music on his laptop and complaining about being bored, but the minute I needed him to photograph something, he was nowhere to be found. After months passed without Mas producing a photo, I fired him.

Yet some people in the office seem to think I should have kept him, largely because he is the Doctor's son and a favorite of Faris's.

They may be right. It has hurt my standing with my staff and it has upset Faris deeply.

"When Mas was young and had leukemia, I paid for his treatment,"

Faris says. "Mas is like a son to me. I like to see him around the office." His eyes glisten with tears. I am consumed with self-loathing. How could I be such a beast? I knew about Mas's cancer. He had told me after doing a photo essay on a little boy in a Sana'ani cancer ward. "If you don't want to work with him, couldn't you still have kept him around the office?" says Faris.

I'd love to work with him, if he would actually *work,* I think. Instead I say, "Faris, I am sorry."

I feel terrible that I have failed to understand the intricacies of Faris's relationship with Mas, and also the difficulties of firing someone in an office controlled by nepotism. I might have avoided this pitfall had Faris spent a little more time with me, helping me to understand how things work here. Now I find out these things too late.

I apologize abjectly, saying that I will do anything to make things right. Faris says he hasn't told me this before because he didn't want to cry in front of me. And on cue, he sheds two tears. I feel sick.

Before I leave the office, we go quickly through the other things on my list. For example, I need the plane fare to the United States for my two-week break, as my salary is not enough to cover it.

Without a word, Faris pulls a wad of $100 bills the size of a grapefruit out of his pocket. I stare wide-eyed, never having seen that much cash in my life. He peels off thirteen bills and hands them to me. Feeling that I am being paid to go away, I crumple the bills in my fist and slink out of the office.

☪

A FEW DAYS LATER, I am scrambling to finish an issue early enough to attend a Dutch friend's farewell *qat* chew before meeting a Jordanian friend for dinner when Faris rings.

"This is really important. There's this British guy here, head of Middle East security or something. We need an interview with him. Set something up immediately and get back to me."

"Great," I say. "We can interview him Saturday." It's a Thursday, and I am looking forward to having a night off and a free day Friday to pack for my trip home.

"Saturday is too late, he'll be gone. Arrange it for before then."

So much for my evening plans. But I need to get back into Faris's good favor. "I'll talk with him tonight," I say. "What did you say his name was? And his title?"

"I don't know," says Faris. "Something to do with the Middle East. Find out."

I ring the British Embassy, but because it is the weekend for the rest of the Yemeni world, it is closed. There's an emergency number on the recording. I hesitate. This isn't exactly an emergency. But I really need to make Faris like me. I think about his disappointment if I fail to get this interview, and my fingers start to dial the emergency number all by themselves.

The woman on duty says she'll pass on my message, and five minutes later, Ambassador Mike Gifford calls me back.

"Look," he says, "I am having a dinner at my house tonight for Peter Gooderham," (my target, the director for the Middle East and North Africa in the British Foreign and Commonwealth Office). "Why don't you join us? We have plenty of room. And you can interview him there."

"If you're sure it won't be a problem. I hate to intrude on his dinner."

"No problem at all. We would be delighted to have you."

So relieved I'm bordering on happy, I ring Faris and give him the good news.

Mike Gifford's wife, Patricia, welcomes me warmly and introduces me to a few others, including a chatty man named Khalid who works for Islamic Relief and has been to Sa'dah. I question him furiously about the situation there. I also talk with a reporter from *26 September,* also there to interview Peter; a British man working with the Yemeni Coast Guard; and a member of the British House of Commons. I drink a gin and tonic and enjoy myself immensely. There are worse jobs.

Peter Gooderham is seated near me and is quite charming, quizzing me about my work. He finishes eating before I do, so I regretfully abandon my third helping of fish and brussels sprouts to interview him in the living room. He talks for nearly an hour, and I fill my notebook. I hardly have to ask any questions. He just rattles on until the other journalist gets impatient.

I stay until close to eleven P.M., heading out with the last stragglers. At home, I kick off my boots and write the entire interview by twelve thirty A.M. The photo is e-mailed to Faris by one A.M. I fall asleep feeling very pleased with myself indeed.

☪

I RETURN from a brief holiday in New York in early May with renewed determination to work on my relationship with Faris. There are urgent reasons for this. Al-Asaadi and Zaid are both due back in Yemen in June, and I need to figure out whom I am training to be my successor. It seems obvious to me that it won't be al-Asaadi, because he hasn't shown any interest in learning from me or in perpetuating my reforms at the paper. Zaid, on the other hand, has been eager to learn and seems ripe for training. One of my main reasons for doing this job is to create reforms that outlast me.

My first discussion with Faris on this topic is not inspiring.

"Al-Asaadi will be editor in chief and Zaid will be managing editor," he says when I ask him what will happen in June.

My heart sinks. This will never work. Al-Asaadi and Zaid cannot stand each other. When they both come back, I expect nothing short of total catastrophe.

"Faris," I say, "you know those two do not get along."

"I need everyone to work as a team," he says.

"Of course. But I need al-Asaadi not to disrupt what I have done. We have a terrific schedule now, but when he was here before, he constantly tried to sabotage me. We do get along as people, you know. We've even been e-mailing each other since he's been gone. But I do not want all of my work undone." Faris seems to have the wild idea that he can just throw us all together, establish no clear hierarchy, and let us fight it out. I don't know what to do. My reporters need a clear hierarchy. I need a clear hierarchy. Zaid and al-Asaadi will definitely need a clear hierarchy. I dread June.

☪

I ALSO RETURN from New York with a secret Faris-softening weapon. His two older sons have advised me to use, in times of crisis, Reese's Peanut Butter Cups as a way to get their father to pay attention to me.

"He'll give you anything you want if you bring peanut butter cups," they tell me.

You cannot find peanut butter cups in Yemen, so it isn't until April that I can get my hands on a good supply. I've brought back five bags.

So when Faris comes into my office one day to ask me to cover a story, I tell him I would really like to sit down and have a leisurely talk about my successor and the future of the paper.

"Sure, yeah, okay, but not now, I have a meeting," he mutters while backing toward my door. It is clear that he has no intention of having a talk with me, leisurely or otherwise.

"Faris," I say, "I have peanut butter cups."

He stops in his tracks, turns to look at me, and walks back toward my desk. His eyes dart around my office. "Where?"

"I'll tell you," I say, "when you sit down and talk with me. Not before."

"Ah," he says, looking crestfallen. "I'll get back to you." And with one last wistful look at my desk drawers, he turns and walks slowly out my door.

A few days later, he waylays me at a party at Nabeel Khoury's. I'm standing in the courtyard, halfway through a gin and tonic, being bored rigid by a series of earnest young men from the American Embassy, when Faris grabs my arm. "You wanted to talk?" he says, pulling me up the stairs to the house.

Yes, I think, though this wasn't exactly the venue I had in mind. Still, Faris wanting to talk with me is so novel that not for anything would I miss this opportunity. I let him lead me into the empty living room, where we settle on the sofa.

"Now we can have that leisurely chat you've been wanting," he says as he reclines.

Grateful for the gin in my hand, I explain how I would like to see things unfold. I would like Zaid to work under me, shadowing me until I leave, and then to take over the paper. "Al-Asaadi has *had* his chance to be the editor, and he is not a good manager," I say. "He could be a great reporter, or maybe do something else—you mentioned the magazine—but I really feel that it is time to let Zaid have a chance to run things." I need someone with Zaid's passion, someone open to my ideas.

Faris nods and listens attentively, not interrupting or rushing me. I am beside myself with delight. He says that he will talk to al-Asaadi (I am not to attempt this myself) and work things around the way that I want them. "Just keep in mind," he says, "Zaid is not a marathon runner, he's a sprinter. He'll go all out and then give up suddenly."

"I'll keep a close watch on Zaid," I promise. "I will keep him in line."

We then discuss several story ideas Faris has from his sources at the top. He tells me about the panic going around that cell phones are mysteriously killing people. I've heard this rumor from my staff, who have all become frightened of their phones. "There are some people who are afraid to take my calls," Faris says. "They say they can't answer something that says 'private number,' because it might kill them."

He gives me several other ideas. I am thrilled. This is the most productive talk I have ever had with Faris. I tell him so. After forty-five minutes, I actually feel satisfied, and we stand to rejoin the party outside. A rain shower has released a cool, starry night.

"So," says Faris, looking at me expectantly as we walk toward the door, "do I get my peanut butter cups now?"

☪

IN EARLY JUNE, I screw up again. The first Thursday of the month, I am having a bad closing day. Hadi has taken off just before deadline to attend a wedding, leaving me with no designer. Samir is enlisted to help us finish the issue, but he is slower than Hadi, and I get impatient and storm around the office.

Things are going much better overall, so why do I still have fits of temper? I think about my former editors. I remember Jim McGarvey at the Morris County *Daily Record,* who would scream that I was the most disastrous reporter on the planet one minute and then shower me with praise the next. Yet he was a brilliant editor. I think about all of the other editors I have known. Few of them were particularly stable, with the possible exception of my editor at *The Week,* but the pressures there were not the pressures of a daily. Maybe these fits of impatience on deadline simply come with the job.

Feeling better, I write the final captions and pack up my bags. At seven thirty, just as I am grabbing a bottle of French wine from my house and heading for dinner with a new neighbor, my phone rings. It's a private number. Faris.

"*Salaam aleikum,*" I say.

"I need you to go back to the office," he says. "Did you put something on the front page about the Huthis being behind the explosions at the armory?"

It takes me a minute to remember. My brain erases each issue from its data banks as soon as it's put to bed. The Huthi rebels in the north of Yemen were rumored to have caused explosions in a cave near Sana'a.

"Yes," I say. "But we quoted someone from the Ministry of the Interior."

"The minister is denying it," says Faris. "Get back to the office and change the front page or the paper will be closed down and we will be taken to court. And I want you to fire whoever wrote that story."

"Farouq and Radia wrote it," I say. I presume Farouq did the interview, because he is the one with the contacts.

"People have to double-check their facts," says Faris. "Radia should have—"

"Don't blame Radia for this!" I'm incensed. Why is Faris jumping to the conclusion that Radia is at fault? Didn't I just say Farouq *and* Radia wrote it? "Farouq worked with her, and he was the one who gave me the story." He also has several more years of experience as a reporter, I want to point out. He is the one responsible for overseeing Radia's work.

Yemeni men immediately blame the women for anything that goes wrong. If the accountant makes a mistake, he blames Radia. If an administrator makes a mistake, he blames Enass. God forbid the men ever take responsibility for their own mistakes.

A male Yemeni friend explains the phenomenon to me this way: "They cannot admit a mistake because they are afraid of the punishment. We're used to being punished every time we make a mistake."

I am immediately abashed that this had not occurred to me; it makes sense in a culture in which children are beaten for not having the right answers. Plus, Yemen is a country in which the government crackdown on any misstep can be severe. No *wonder* they don't want to admit mistakes.

But Faris is hell-bent on punishing someone. "Well, when I find out who wrote it . . . !" he says.

"Faris, I just *told* you who wrote it." He doesn't want to have to fire Farouq, I think. Farouq is a man and therefore less dispensable. "Anyway, have you told the designers to hold the paper?"

"I have."

"How did the ministry know about the story?"

"Apparently Enass posted it online and someone saw it and called the ministry."

Well, that was fast! We finished the story five minutes before I left the office.

"Is Luke still in the office? I was on my way to meet people . . . ," I say lamely, knowing there is no way I can get out of going back to work. Yet a dinner date is such a rarity that I hate to miss it.

"Jennifer, this is the news business and in the news business—"

"You don't need to tell *me* about the news business. I've been in it for twelve years." Which, I want to point out, is longer than the *Yemen Observer* has been in print. I am also tempted to point out that no *real* newspaper would let the people in power tell us what we can write. "Anyway, I am on my way."

I race back to the office. By the time I arrive, I have calmed down. Luke is still there, chewing *qat* with the guys. Faris had phoned and made Luke read him the story. It wasn't even anonymously sourced—we used the name of the director of the interior minister's office. Enass actually heard Radia interview the man, so there is a witness to the conversation. Of course, women aren't taken seriously as witnesses. Luke and I figure that the director must have spoken out of turn, and then, when the story was posted, he got in trouble and was forced to deny his statement.

Luke has already found some additional photos for the front page, and together we reconfigure it. It all goes smoothly. We are just finishing when Faris calls to check in.

"What story did you put on the front page?" he says.

"A cheerful little story about Yemeni expatriates getting surveyed so that they can be provided with new services," I say. "Do you want to know what is on the rest of the front page?"

"No," he says. "I trust you."

He trusts me?

I tell Faris our theory that someone at the ministry had spoken out of turn, got in trouble, and then retracted.

"But he's denying it," says Faris.

"Yes, I *know*. But I am quite certain that Radia would never lie." On this point, I will not budge.

Faris has calmed down and seems almost willing to accept that Radia hasn't committed a crime. He asks me to promise that I will call him if we run anything else on the Huthis. Saleh is very touchy about any story about these rebels. God forbid we actually find out what the government is doing up there in the North.

Later that night, after a glass of wine with my neighbor, it all seems funny. We laugh about it until after midnight, when I reluctantly head home to bed.

☪

THE STORY ABRUPTLY CEASES to be humorous the following Wednesday, when Faris summons me to his office.

"I need to speak with you," he says. Faris never needs to speak with me if things are going well. Heart racing, I leap up the stairs to his office.

"We're in trouble," he says. "The minister of the interior is suing us. What do you think we should do?"

"But we never printed the story!"

"About twenty Arabic papers managed to pick it up from the Web before we took it down."

"Christ."

"He denies that he said anything. He is denying that he even spoke to a reporter. That anyone in his office spoke to a reporter."

"But Radia did speak to someone in his office."

"He's saying she didn't."

"I really don't think Radia would lie."

"Well, either he is lying or she is lying."

"He has a motive to lie; she doesn't."

"Look. . . ." Faris clicks through a few Web pages. "He put it on the Web. That he is denying everything."

"Hmmm."

"So what should we do?"

"Well . . ." I think for a minute. I am glad that Faris is asking my advice and has not just called me to his office to chastise me. "In the States what we would do is write another article, with the minister's reaction to the previous story. Set the record straight." I still think the minister is lying, but we have no way to prove that anyone spoke with Radia because we have no way to record phone calls. And Faris is basically asking me how to cover our asses and not get the paper closed.

"That won't work."

"But then it would be on record that we wrote the 'correct' version."

"That would just make everything worse. Things aren't done like that here."

"Okay, so what are our other options?"

"I don't know." He fidgets with his mouse, clicking on and off websites and twirling in his chair. "Jennifer, the minister of the interior refused to shake my hand yesterday at the Italian embassy. I have never been snubbed like that. Do you know what that is like?"

"No . . ."

"I have a lot of enemies here. There are a lot of people who are after me, and I want to keep them from getting at me through the *Yemen Observer*. You understand? So the next time we have a story like this, just print the official government press release and that is *all,* okay?"

I nod. So much for holding power accountable.

We sit quietly for a few minutes.

"I mean, who is going to take responsibility for this?" he says. "They could put someone in jail."

"I will." I am not going to let Radia—or any of my reporters—go to jail. But they will never send me to jail. It would be political suicide. Besides, it would be far too embarrassing for Faris; he simply would not let it happen.

By the time I'm dismissed, I have the feeling that Faris didn't really want my advice after all. What upset him most was that the minister had refused to shake his hand. People in power were irked with him. And he wanted to make it clear to me that this was my fault and unacceptable. I could do anything I wanted to with the paper—so long as I didn't lose him any friends in power. One more false step, I think, and even peanut butter cups won't be able to save me.

Slowly, it dawns on me that this is not going to change. There will always be limits to what we can write. Faris will never allow me to hire the staff we need. Salaries are not going to rise. My reporters won't all stick around, and those who do are not going to become paragons of the profession in one year. This is what I have to work with. These are the parameters within which I will have to find new ways to define success.

SEVENTEEN

a world beyond work

Now that my reporters are submitting almost all of their stories promptly on deadline, I'm spending more time with them than ever before. It's immensely gratifying to have the luxury of explaining all of my edits to them and chatting with them about their lives. I've even changed my routine; I go to the gym before work, so I can lunch with my staff.

My favorite lunches are at the fish *souq,* where al-Matari or one of the other men picks out a large fish or two and we take it to a restaurant to be roasted and served with squishy, buttery bread called *ratib.* I am always the only woman there, and men stare at me the entire time. But surrounded and protected by my male staff, I don't mind. Some afternoons we go for *saltah,* a Yemeni meat stew with a bubbling broth of fenugreek, in Baab al-Sabah, the market street near my house. The men spread strips of cardboard on the stones for me to sit on and run off in different directions to buy *saltah* and bread and tangy raisin juice. They even order me my own little pot of vegetarian *saltah,* which tastes like a spicy potato stew. We squat in a circle while passing men stare at the oddity of a woman eating in public. It makes all the difference that I now have time to do this; my relationships with my reporters become easier as we spend more non-work time together.

The mere act of getting the paper on schedule has transformed my life.

Not only can I spend more time with staff, but for the first time in six months, I have time to go out with friends after work. Of course, I first need to find friends. I have some, but I've spent so much time in my newsroom that I've hardly met anyone outside of work other than Shaima, Marvin, and Pearl. My solitary times on Soqotra musing on distant loved ones reminded me of how critical my friendships are. The e-mails I get from faraway friends are a comfort, but I need people *here*.

Anne is the first to step into the void. I'd met her a couple of months earlier at my first diplomatic party, but now I finally have time to see her. An intern at the Dutch Embassy, Anne is twenty-two, but age has ceased to mean anything to me. In New York, most of my friends were close to my age or older. But in Yemen, I collect friends from ages twenty-two to sixty-seven. There are so few expats in Yemen that just living here gives us a strong common bond. Besides, Anne is precocious. She grew up in Saudi Arabia and has traveled extensively. A voracious reader, she often whips through a book a day, speaks perfect English and decent Arabic, makes friends easily, and is consistently sunny and cheerful. I am a little bit in awe of Anne. Our mutual love of books initially brings us together; there are few books in English available in Yemen, so we trade our stocks. In the evenings, she is often the person who drags me from the office after a long day. We make dinners together at my house or go out to eat, and she introduces me to her legions of friends.

In early spring, she invites me on a trip to Kamaran Island with a group of mostly Dutch friends. I've gotten bolder about taking time off, and so without even telling Faris, I leave the paper in Luke's hands on a closing day and head for the Red Sea. I don't want to miss a chance to meet people away from work.

The occasion is Floor's birthday. Floor is Ali's new girlfriend; they began dating while he was working for me (much to the dismay of my women). When we go to Kamaran, Ali is temporarily away in the United States. Floor is slender and blond, easygoing, and drives her own car, a massive army-green jeep. With her is her best friend, Serena, an Australian doctoral student in political science, and Matt and Nina, a couple from New York.

Xander, a tall, dark-haired Dutch development worker, drives the second car, with Anne and her new Dutch boyfriend Florens. I am squeezed into the last car with Yahya, a Yemeni; Lama, a tiny, wild, married Yemeni woman; and Zana, a vastly fat Albanian with short-clipped blond hair and watermelon breasts.

Zana is from Kosovo and works for the National Democratic Institute with Floor and Lama. We pass the time asking Lama how to say various things in Arabic, focusing on phrases to make men leave us alone. Zana asks how to say "It is nothing that would interest you."

"There is no Arabic translation for that," says Lama, "because here, everyone is interested in everything."

We drive up over the jagged peaks of the Haraz Mountains, majestic and misty. It is cool in the mountains, and I am astonished at their greenness. The color comes from the crops planted in diminishing terraces rising up the slopes all around us. On one peak, our three cars meet up at a bootleg alcohol shop. I am amused to find the tiny, unmarked shed plastered with enormous photographs of Saddam Hussein and stocked with bottles of Glen's gin, Bell's whiskey, and Heineken. When I ask what other contraband is available, Serena says, "Anything you want." Several of the Dutch buy hashish, and we all chip in for cases of beer.

As we descend from the mountains toward Hodeida, the air grows softer and warmer, and the valley alongside the road greens with banana trees. Soon, it is so hot that we have to roll our windows all the way down.

We arrive at the boat launch in Selim just after dark. The air is thick, warm, and sticky. The police at the docks make a big fuss over our papers, delaying us while they hold conferences among themselves. The man who seems to be in charge is very confused about how many of us there are. Serena tells him there are fourteen of us, but he doesn't understand. "Five and five and four," she says, pointing out our three groups. He cannot add, and she shows him on her fingers. He frowns and scribbles and counts us again.

Finally, we are allowed to board three rickety fishing boats, our bags of contraband clanking as we heave them over the sides. Even then, the boat drivers are in no hurry to set off. They busily compare cell phone features while we grow impatient. We have already been traveling for seven hours.

After sitting for ages breathing exhaust fumes from the boat, little Lama finally loses patience. *"Mumkin,"* ("Can we . . . ?") she says, tapping the driver. And we all join in with the *"YALLA!"* (Let's go!)

With a sudden push, we are speeding across the water. I look up. The stars are bright and the moon fuzzy with humidity. There are no lights anywhere. Our boats themselves lack headlights and the water is dark around us. The enchantment hits us all in a rush. Our boats fly, faster than our cars had on land, through the dark. Our wake and the waves around us glow white in the moonlight.

"Wow," we say in one awestruck voice. I trail my fingers in the water.

"This is my first time on the Red Sea," says Nina.

I'm suddenly excited. "Me too!"

Our driver asks Nina for her flashlight, and she hands it over. It strikes me as odd that he doesn't have his own. He flashes the light skyward and then toward the other boats. They flash back, directing us.

It takes us twenty minutes to cross the water. As our boats push up against the rocks of Kamaran, which is still invisible in the dark, a voice booms from above.

"Welcome to Kamaran!" It is a Yemeni voice speaking warmly in English. As I clamber across the other boats and up the rocks, a strong hand grips mine and hauls me to the top. Mohammed al-Zubairy's round brown face appears in the dark, glistening. He introduces himself and turns to the next guest. "Zana! You made it!" He remembers the name of everyone who has been there before, particularly the women.

From the top of the cliff, I see the modest buildings of the Two Moon Tourist Resort silhouetted in the moonlight. Those on land are already scurrying to pick out their round, pointy-roofed, thatched Tihama huts. These are scattered across the sandy plain around a circular, stone main building that houses the dining room, kitchen, and bathrooms.

I follow the group slowly, wondering who might let me share their hut. All the seventh-grade anxieties about not fitting in with the popular crowd surge up from my unconsciousness. Everyone else already knows each other. Anne is the only person I really know, and she is sharing a hut with Florens.

"Jennifer!" calls Floor. "Do you want to be in our hut?"

Rescued from social rejection! Floor is the ringleader of this group, and I am grateful for her warmth. I hurry to join her and Serena.

By the time we've dropped our things and run into the main building, everyone is lounging in wood and rope chairs, sipping their first cold beers. Floor announces that she is going for a swim, followed by Anne. I waver long enough that they head out without me. (Alcohol or swimming? It's a tough call.) But I finally decide I want nothing more than to be underwater, and Mohammed leads me across the sand in the dark.

He remembers having seen me before, somewhere in Sana'a.

"I was attracted to your face," he says. "And here you are, on my island!" I am flattered.

We walk across a dune, passing the dripping Floor and Anne on their return trip, to a small square building. Not until we get there can I make out the outline of the shore. I start for my swimsuit, but Mohammed tells me I don't need it here. "Just swim! Be free!" he says. "It is night. There is no one to care."

These are magic words to a girl who has been swaddled from head to toe for months. Euphorically, I strip off my long skirts and walk naked across the sand. Mohammed has gone discreetly ahead and is already out in the water, wearing his boxers, far from me.

The water is deliciously cool. We swim out, Mohammed (staying a respectful distance ahead) guiding me away from underwater hazards. I flip onto my back to see how the moon looks from the Red Sea. It looks fuzzy. My worries about the paper dissolve and float out to sea. I follow Mohammed's instructions and feel free. I am tempted to float out here all night, but I remind myself that I didn't come here to be alone.

I join the others for a beer before dinner. We've all shucked our Yemeni drapery—even Yemeni Lama has stripped down to a tiny pair of shorts. It feels like the first day of summer vacation. Mohammed and his staff have whipped up a vast feast of seafood and salads, which we boisterously inhale before heading outside to relax under the stars and fuzzy moon. Nina passes me a joint, and I take a couple of hits. I never smoke hashish, and the drug immediately blows me sideways. I fall asleep in my chair, and when I open my eyes Anne is watching me. "You look tired," she laughs. I stumble over to our hut, curl up on my rope cot, and am instantly asleep.

We wake early to find crepes and mango juice already waiting for us. After breakfast, everyone heads in different directions—some to swim, some to take a boat to a nearby island, some to read in the shade. I linger in the main lodge with Mohammed, curious to know more about his resort. "I wanted to create a place where people could be free," he says. "This is why I came here." He opened the resort in 1997, after President Saleh gave him the land to open the island to tourism investment.

"I like the sea," he says. "I grew up close to the sea. I wanted to protect the environment in some way, in my way."

Using only natural, local materials, he followed the traditional building methods of the Tihama region, the western coastal area, to build the huts. The resort is isolated from the rest of the island, where some thirty-five hundred Yemenis make their living from the sea.

There are two reasons the island is called Kamaran, says Mohammed. First, if you sit at the very tip of this spit of land, just as the full moon rises in the sky, you can see its reflection on either side of you. *Qamaran* is a transliteration of the Arabic word for "two moons." Second, for two weeks a month it is possible to see the moon shining in one side of the sky while the sun is shining in the other.

The forty-two-square-mile desert island is fringed with white sand beaches and surrounded by coral reefs. I'm eager to see these reefs but have never snorkeled, so Mohammed teaches me. I have seen coral before only off Soqotra. In flippers and masks, we drift over what looks like heads of cabbage. Tiny silver fish dart in and out of them. Beside these are the labyrinthine shapes of coral folded in upon itself to resemble the cerebellum of a sea monster. Spiky sea urchins abound. Branch coral reaches purple-tipped fingers toward the sky. A rainbow-colored fish swims by, flapping tiny wings, and an enormous mussel (which Mohammed calls a "murder shell") opens and closes its rippled blue lips. A shoal of long, cylindrical fish—the kind served for dinner the night before— dashes quickly away as if suspecting the fate of their missing brethren.

As we swim, Mohammed silently points to things and I gurgle my awe. After an hour of exploring, I head to shore and trek across the dunes, thick with crushed white shells, to join the others on a distant beach.

It is early evening when we all return. I take some photos of the sunset and join the others for a riotous cocktail hour. Florens and Xander amuse us by covering their sunburned bodies with yogurt. We trade our Yemeni adventure stories and laugh and then eat another fish and vegetable feast.

Afterward, we move outside to celebrate Floor's birthday with more drinks, dancing, and even a fireworks display. We crank up the stereo. I lift my arms to the starry desert sky, relishing the tickle of my loose hair across my spine, and feel happier than I have felt in months. Festivity, food, and, finally, some nonwork *friends*.

Close to midnight, boats arrive to take us to the mangroves. We climb into two fishing boats, clutching bottles of whiskey and beer, and zoom off into the dark sea, the moon our only light. Drenched by the sea spray, we toss beers from boat to boat, teasing each other. At a spit of sand near the entrance to the mangroves, we all strip down for a moonlight swim.

When we grow chilly, we climb into the boats and race each other back, drinking and egging each other on. By the time we get to sleep, there are no moons left on Kamaran Island.

The trip to Kamaran throws open doors to the outside world. I return with a host of new friends, who will introduce me to still more new friends, and at long last, a social whirl begins. I still have to work six days a week. I am still the first to leave parties on Wednesday nights, because my staff and I are among the few people in Sana'a who work Thursdays. I still have moments of impatience and exhaustion. But now, I have learned to walk out the door in time for dinner. I have learned to leave things undone on my desk. After all, as I am always telling my reporters, the great thing about the news business is that there is always a next issue.

EIGHTEEN

dragging designers from the qat shed and other drug problems

*Whenever I leave the newsroom for too long in the afternoon, my men dis-*appear. Initially, I have no idea where they go and send other reporters to find them. But it doesn't take long for me to discover their hideout: the *qat* shed. This is a grimy little room tucked just inside the *Observer's* gates. Dirty *mafraj* cushions are squeezed against the walls, and boxes of news-papers are stacked in the corners. Here, the men smoke cigarettes, stuff their cheeks with leaves, and try to hide from me. I stand in the doorway of the *qat* shed calling, *"Amal!"* (Work!) until they reluctantly hoist them-selves from the cushions and follow me inside. Of course, this doesn't happen right away. They first try to convince me to join them. "Chew, Jen-nifer!" they urge. "It's nice!" Farouq holds up an alluring branch of green leaves and waves it at me. "It will relax you." On occasion, I give in and chew a little with them, though I can't say it makes me any calmer.

My male reporters chew every day, often late into the night. Most Yemeni men chew, though not all make a daily habit of it. The nationwide dependence on *qat* is perhaps Yemen's greatest development hurdle. The thirsty plant drinks the country's aquifers dry, sucks nutrients from the soil, steals hours of productivity from workers, and causes a wide range of health and social problems.

I don't need scientific reports to know the adverse effects of *qat;* I see them every day. My men constantly complain of insomnia and lack of appetite. Many of them are painfully thin, the result of skipping supper in favor of a cheekful of greenery. Their teeth are brown with decay. Several have complained to me about the depression that follows a good chew, which I've experienced myself. "But that's when you just chew some more!" say my reporters.

Qat also keeps journalists from meeting deadlines, which causes *me* health and social problems. When the typical Yemeni workday ends, at two P.M. (not ours, alas!), many men rush from work to stuff themselves with stews and breads to line their stomach in preparation for a five-hour *qat*-chewing session. Because my reporters work evenings, they chew in the office (or the shed). On closing days, the drivers bring us rice and chicken for lunch so we don't need to leave the newsroom—but the men still manage to sneak out to buy *qat*. Often, we will be ten minutes from finishing an issue, and all of my male reporters will simultaneously vanish. They cannot fathom getting through an afternoon without their fix.

Qat has been cultivated in Yemen for centuries—some evidence suggests it grew here as early as the thirteenth century. Ethiopia and Yemen are the two biggest producers, although it also grows in Kenya, Uganda, Tanzania, Rwanda, Zimbabwe, Turkmenistan, and Afghanistan. There is some disagreement as to whether the plant originated in Ethiopia and spread to Yemen or vice versa. An Ethiopian legend holds that a goatherd was the first person to chew *qat*. One night he noticed that his goats were particularly wakeful and frolicsome. So the next day, he followed them and found them munching green *qat* leaves. The herder tried some for himself, and a habit was born.

Until the 1960s, *qat* chewing in Yemen was mostly an occasional leisure activity for the rich. But in the 1970s and '80s, rising household incomes and increased profitability for farmers contributed to the spread of the practice. Now, about three-quarters of men and a third of women chew *qat,* according to a 2007 World Bank report. Other studies have found chewing even more prevalent. Most *qat* chewers are habitual users; more than half of those who chew do so daily.

☪

MUCH OF WORK LIFE in Yemen revolves around *qat* chews. Friends working as consultants for government ministries report that decision making often happens in the *qat* chews that precede official meetings, rather than in the meetings themselves. "Which means that Yemeni policies are often made by men who are high as a kite," says one consultant.

It's easy to see how *qat* became so prevalent. For farmers, *qat* is lucrative—ten to twenty times more profitable than other crops. Its contribution to the economy is equivalent to two-thirds of the contribution that oil makes (oil revenues make up 75 percent of Yemen's budget), according to the Ministry of Planning. Thus, farmers are understandably in no hurry to switch to alternatives—even when rising global food prices threaten to starve the country and increasing cultivation has led to a serious water crisis.

Qat production and distribution also employ about one in seven Yemenis. But while it may supply jobs, the drug bleeds money from Yemeni families. A tenth of the typical Yemeni household income is spent on *qat*, and some poor households spend more than a quarter of their income on it. Money spent on *qat* is money that isn't spent on food, medicine, or other necessities—hitting children hardest.

My male reporters, who are always out of grocery money weeks before payday, somehow still manage to buy *qat*. So it doesn't surprise me to learn that 94 percent of nonchewers and 77 percent of chewers admit that *qat* has a deleterious effect on the family budget. Just under a fifth of Yemenis are forced into debt to finance their drug habit. It's not unusual for a reporter to stand in front of my desk with a cheek full of *qat* asking to borrow money for dinner.

Qat eats up hours as fast as it eats money—hours that might be spent on more productive pursuits. More than a third of *qat* chewers indulge their habit for four to six hours a day and nearly a quarter chew for more than six hours a day. When men joke that *qat* is Yemeni whiskey, I say, "Yes, but we don't tend to drink whiskey for six hours a day, seven days a week."

One of the most entertaining bits of information I found in the World Bank report was that men dramatically underestimate how much *qat* their wives are tearing through. Fourteen percent of husbands said that their wives chew, but 33 percent of their wives reported chewing. This may be because there is more of a stigma attached to *qat* for women than for men. Or it could be that men are just out of touch with what their wives are doing, given that they spend little time together.

Because men and women chew separately, the practice contributes to sex segregation as well. Primarily, it keeps men away from their families. My reporters, for example, would rather spend all night chewing with their male friends than go home to their wives and children.

Before coming to Yemen, I was very curious about *qat,* and I have chewed my fair share in my efforts to assimilate. It's nearly impossible to avoid *qat* chews, as almost all social life revolves around them. Even the expat community has adopted the tradition. Whenever someone leaves the country—and there is always someone whose contract has just ended or whose diplomatic term is up—there is a farewell *qat* chew. There are also housewarming *qat* chews, birthday *qat* chews, and just-because-it's-Friday *qat* chews. The main difference between Yemeni chews and expat chews is that at a certain hour, the expat *qat* chews turn into cocktail parties when everyone spits out their leaves and picks up a glass of wine.

Overall, I probably wouldn't mind the whole *qat* phenomenon were it not for its interference with work. I don't try to ban the practice; it would trigger mutiny (though the *Yemen Times,* I find out later, bans chewing at work). But I do try to keep the men from running out to buy it while we are closing an issue. It's a losing battle but one, for some reason, I don't seem able to abandon.

"This has got to be the only country in the world where reporters are allowed to run out and buy drugs when on deadline," I say to Luke.

"It's not *drugs,*" says Farouq. This is a regular argument. Yemenis do not consider *qat* to be a drug.

"It's a mood-altering stimulant. What else could it be?"

"It's just *qat,*" says Farouq.

Hadi sides with him. Hadi, Farouq, and al-Matari are my most devout chewers, though Jabr often chews with them. He has trouble talking with his mouth full and sometimes spits bits of leaf at me when trying to explain a story. I try to imagine the reaction of my editor at *The Week* if I did this to him.

At least Luke admits it's a drug. One day he comes to my office to report a conversation with Hadi.

"Hadi just came in and said, 'The *qat,* it is killing me. I can't sleep at night. I am spending all of my money on it. It is making my wife mad at me. It takes away my appetite!'"

"That's because *it's a drug,*" he told Hadi. "When the negative consequences outweigh the benefits, and you still continue to do it, then that means *it's a drug.*"

Hadi just shook his head sadly and stuck another leaf in his mouth.

Another reason I don't try to ban *qat* is that I am not sure that my men could do their jobs without it. They might fall asleep on their keyboards. Or go home for a nap. Journalists on *qat,* I figure, are better than journalists suffering from *qat* withdrawal.

In contrast, my women are almost universally opposed to *qat.* Najma constantly writes health stories about its deleterious effects as a passive swipe at the men. Here is an excerpt from one of her masterpieces: "The *qat* chewer is prone to a lot of bad effects after taking *qat.* He becomes unable to sleep and he feels lazy and worried. He is also prone to be weak in sexual performance, focusing on things or information and to lose control on sperm. His appetite is badly affected by chewing *qat* and he tends to sit alone. He also suffers from some difficulties in urinating."

But there's some evidence that my men are coming to grips with what *qat* really is. One day in May, Farouq pops into my office as I am finishing editing a front page.

"Do you need me?" he says.

"Why?" I ask warily. "Where do you need to go?"

"I need to take your permission to go buy some drugs," he says, grinning broadly.

I laugh. "Well, since you put it that way, you have my permission to go buy drugs."

"*Shukrahn!*" And he's off like a shot.

I don't complain. Farouq has been inordinately kind and respectful lately and receptive to my thoughts and criticisms. We've just finished going over a story he wrote about a graduation project that two Sana'a University students did on religious conflict. Islam is vastly misunderstood, both by "bad" Muslims (who use Islam to justify terrorism) and non-Muslims, the students say. To address this, they wrote a booklet and held a workshop to increase the understanding of Islam in a post–September 11 world. A few parts of the story made me cross, particularly the sections that referred to the Western media as a homogenous entity, as if every newspaper and magazine in the Western world were conspiring together and speaking with one voice, when, in my experience, the Western media is a multiheaded beast encompassing an infinite number of voices. Doesn't it include both *Mother Jones* and the *New Republic*? *Playboy* and the *Wall Street Journal*? While it's true that some voices are louder than others, I've personally found the "Western media" to be pretty free and various.

When I try to explain this to Farouq, he responds, "But don't the Jews control all the media?"

"Farouq," I say, "tell me what percentage of Americans you think are Jews."

"I don't know."

"Just guess. I am curious what you think."

He considers for a moment. "Twenty percent?"

I hold up two fingers. "*Ithnayn.* Two percent. Tops."

He is shocked. He had assumed that the entire United States was ruled by a Zionist cabal.

I sigh. "Farouq. I have been in the media for twelve years and I don't recall ever having been controlled by Jews." In fact, I reflect, my last three bosses were Catholic. "And while there are certainly plenty of biases evident in newspapers and magazines, I've read quite a few pro-Muslim stories. Even in the *New York Times.* Which is, in fact, owned by a Jew. The U.S. media is not one big anti-Muslim block."

The United States was founded on the idea of religious freedom, I add. "It's illegal to persecute anyone for his or her religion."

It's strange to hear myself sounding so patriotic. I've spent a great deal of time agitating *against* the U.S. government—going to anti-Bush demonstrations, signing petitions, marching for peace, and supporting gay rights. Yet in Yemen, I find myself defending the government I have done nothing but complain about for years. And it's true that in comparison with the corrupt and inefficient Yemeni government, mine is beginning to rise—just a bit—in my esteem.

Farouq is surprised that it is illegal to persecute Muslims in the United States and surprised that any paper has written anything pro-Muslim.

Even more, he seems surprised that the United States encompasses diverse viewpoints.

In his story about the students' Islam project, a source claims that the reason the United States is so afraid of Islam is that it is worried that its entire population will convert.

"I don't think that's *quite* it," I tell Farouq. "The reason some people in the U.S. worry about Islam is that terrorists have used it as an excuse to attack our country." But I leave the quotation in anyway.

Farouq doesn't argue with me. He listens. This alone is progress. He has begun to ask me more questions and seems to be trying harder to impress me. Last week he redesigned the front page. He does this fairly often now, coming into my office to show me the two pages side by side in the hopes I will choose his. Sometimes he is right; I am the first to admit I have little design sense. But in this issue I have been quite firm about where I wanted which stories, and when I express this to Farouq, he just shrugs. "You're the boss," he says. "It's your call."

His deference makes me feel so warm and fuzzy that when he tells me he needs to leave just before deadline to go buy drugs, I don't try to stop him.

NINETEEN

bright days before the deluge

I have stopped fantasizing about going back to New York. I have stopped think-
ing of anywhere as home other than my own lovely gingerbread house in
Sana'a. I sleep through the night more often than not. I eat meals. When I
return to the Old City at sunset and see the gold and rose evening light
setting the houses aglow against a darkening sky, I feel like the luckiest
person on earth. The paper has never run more smoothly; we're on such a
predictable schedule now that I can make plans with friends even on closing days.

This is how it happens. My canny reporters figure out that meeting
deadlines means getting out of work earlier. Getting out of work earlier
means spending more time napping, chewing *qat,* or, in rare cases, with
their families. In other words, all it takes is for them to realize that they
are not just making me happy—there is something in it for *them.*

It sounds so simple. I suppose every manager realizes this at some
point: that you must convince your staff that they themselves will benefit
from doing what you want them to do. There's a big difference, however,
between reading this seemingly simple philosophy in a management self-
help book and trying to implement it at a newspaper in a foreign culture.
Not that I've ever read a management book. Or—until now—been a
manager in a foreign culture. I just fumbled in the dark until one day, light

dawned, the paper closed at three P.M., and we all sat around marveling at ourselves and wondering how it happened.

Almost everything I learn in Yemen happens through improvisation, through feeling my way over each hurdle, each newsroom battle, and—after 1,001 mistakes—actually hitting upon a successful strategy. For example, one closing day in June, I discover that it isn't just Faris who can be manipulated with peanut butter cups.

I arrive at work that morning feeling cheerful and excited about social plans I have later. "I don't feel like dawdling around here today," I announce to the newsroom. "How about we have the earliest close ever?"

My reporters look up from their computers. *"Insha'allah,"* they say, looking dubious.

I have three front-page stories edited before eleven thirty A.M., which gives me plenty of time to hustle my staff. It is then I am struck with genius.

"The first person to get me his or her front-page story gets five peanut butter cups," I say. "The second person gets four, the third person gets three, et cetera. Now, go!"

I cannot believe how well this works. Noor gets her story in first, followed by Jabr and Radia. Soon, the men all have chocolate-swollen cheeks, and the women's hands keep disappearing under their *niqabs.*

As I am in the middle of designing a page with Samir, who is filling in for a tardy Hadi; ringing Sharabi to demand that he come in and give us photos; and ordering my reporters about, Luke swings away from his computer to look at me.

"When you leave here, you really ought to think about joining the circus," he says. "You have all the skills to be a ringmaster."

My stomach tightens. *When I leave here?* The phrase fills me with panic.

It is a frenetic day, but we do indeed close early. Farouq turns in a decent story about two brand-new X-ray machines that were intended to screen containers entering Yemen's ports but that failed embarrassingly in a public demonstration. When the officials put a machine gun through one of the machines, it failed to detect it.

Ibrahim files a story about three officials in Dhamar who were fired on corruption allegations. Zuhra writes another story about Anisa al-Shuaibi, whose rape case goes to trial this week. Luke and I joke that Zuhra is on the sodomy beat after she turns in a series of stories on abused prisoners, raped women, and sodomized men. Every story she reports seems to involve some kind of bodily violation. My little human rights crusader.

Najma gives us a story about how an overabundance of fluoride in the water of some villages is turning children's teeth brown, and Noor writes a piece about a march through Sana'a to demand funding for children's programs.

All of our pages are done by two P.M., though I stick around a bit to prod my staff along, proof pages, and make sure all of the captions are written and grammatical. "Do you need me?" I ask Hadi before making my escape.

"No," he says without hesitation. "Go home."

"Yes," says Luke, turning to me. "*Please* go home."

☪

EVEN WHEN DAYS don't go this smoothly, I now find my reporters' mistakes more entertaining than exasperating. Take Bashir's translation of Farouq's story about the Huthis: "The minister of endowment and giddiness Hamoud al-Hitar said, 'We will try to convince the rebels to surrender and lay down arms and stop the war against the camps of the State.' He adds, 'Last Saturday, the scholarship committee arrived to Sa'ada to transfer massage from the scholarship to the rebels about the war there.'"

I am sure that a massage by the minister of endowment and giddiness could play a productive part in conflict resolution. But it seems unlikely to happen.

Jabr turns in another of my favorite leads, for a story about a fundraiser for a charity that helps children with cleft palates. "One thousand and seven hundreds dollars for work of Yemeni smile that provide operations for children who have genital problems and who can not smile, said Nerys Loveridge, the Principle of the school. The money delivered to the ambassador of British during the open day that held in Sana'a British School on Wednesday."

It's common for Arabic speakers to mix up the P and B sounds. There is no P in Arabic. Thus I often get sentences like this: "There are some teams of masked soldiers called IRF (Instant Response Force). 'They enter the cell and beat the crab out of the prisoners,' he said."

Zuhra pulls her weight in the malapropism department too. When she is assigned to write a story on the celebration of Passover by fifty Yemeni Jews who live in the North and are under government protection in Sana'a after threats were made against them, she describes their food restrictions as such: "Jews are not allowed to eat inflated bread during this time." In a story about a group of people protesting shoddy medical treatment, she refers to them as "people who have had kidney plantations."

But perhaps my favorite is this paragraph from a health story she wrote on fertility treatments, which—alarmingly, given the country's already astronomical birth rate—are increasing. "Women must take medicines that stimulates the ovaries to produce eggs, and the men must stimulate their male liquid. Then, the mother will be in stupefaction in order to take out the eggs. Laser peels the chosen egg from the surrounding cells to guarantee that it will be fertilized appropriately."

I relish having time to discuss these errors with my reporters. The macro structure of our paper has fallen into place, allowing me to focus on the micro structure of my staff's stories. Now, instead of hurriedly rewriting everything alone in my drab office, I have reporters come sit with me while I edit their stories. This allows me to explain every change I make.

It's good that I now have time for these editorial tête-à-têtes, because in the spring I acquire Zaki, who replaces Hassan as the Business page editor. Charming to the point of obsequiousness, pudgy, bespectacled Zaki has a mere passing acquaintance with the English language. I spend hours coaching him and trying to break his habit of using meaningless business jargon sure to befuddle our readers. His stories are full of sentences like this: "Professor, Mohammed Muammar al-Shamiri, Supervisor of Group Insurance, said awareness on the importance of securing is very important either individuals or institutions on the all economic fields in Yemen." Decipher if you dare.

Zaki is eager to learn and gets me his page before deadline, so I don't complain. Besides, by now my standards for staff run something along the lines of "Must type with at least two fingers and sometimes show up."

Zaki is also a source of intriguing cultural information. One afternoon, he bursts into my office, wildly excited.

"Jennifer," he says, settling into the chair next to my desk and leaning toward me. "I met with the *jinni* yesterday!"

"Oh, great!" I say, thinking he has met my journalist friend Ginny. "I had dinner with her just last night!"

Zaki looks at me in horror. "You *did*?"

"Yeah," I say. "At the Indian restaurant."

"At the *Indian restaurant*?" Zaki looks very confused. I suddenly realize that Zaki means *jinni* as in *jinn*—the oft-evil spirits made of fire and capable of possessing people. It turns out that Zaki was recently called in to help with the exorcism of a possessed woman. And this may not surprise anyone, but it turns out that the bad *jinni,* in this case, spoke English, with an American accent. This is why the sheikh who was reading the Qur'an over the possessed woman needed Zaki to translate.

"Her face changed shape!" he says. "And she turned colors!"

"You saw this?" I say, eyebrow arched.

"Yes!"

"And you really believe in the *jinn*?"

He looks offended. "Every Muslim believes in the *jinn*!"

"Ah," I say. This was all before I actually read about the *jinn* in the Qur'an some months later. Not only do all Muslims believe in the *jinn,* they find it inconceivable that there are countries without *jinn*. I tell my Yemeni friends that the closest thing I can think of are ghosts, but they are the leftover energy or spirits of dead people, whereas the *jinn* were never human. I suppose the evil spirits or demons that possess evangelicals in the South and make them speak in tongues are the best Western version of the *jinn,* but with a different backstory.

Zaki describes how the woman writhed and moaned in American English before he returns to the newsroom. I've told him that he can write about the *jinn,* but I would like to see if scientists and doctors have any possible alternative explanations for the physical changes in the woman. Perhaps this is too secular a demand, but I am curious to hear what they might say.

I sit mulling this all over and then walk to the newsroom. Something is bothering me.

"Zaki," I say. "Did this woman know English?"

"No!" he says. "She is completely illiterate!"

"Hmmm."

"I know a woman like that too," says Bashir (who often stops in to help, despite having quit months ago). "She was completely illiterate, but when the *jinni* possessed her, she spoke perfect English with an American accent."

It turns out that pretty much everyone in Yemen knows a woman like this. At a loss for words, I turn back toward my office.

"You had better watch out," says Najma. "Since the *jinni* is American!"

"If the *jinni* is American," I say, smiling, "then I don't think I have to worry."

I AM GROWING CLOSER to all of my reporters. It's easy to spend time with my men outside of the office, because they can go where they want whenever they want. But my women all have curfews. They can't be out after dark, and I can't take them to dinner at a restaurant. Most women don't go to restaurants. (It's nearly impossible to eat while wearing a *niqab*.) Also, when I invite my women to lunch, they often decline because they are fasting. My women are frequently fasting, sometimes just because they want a little spiritual extra credit. Still, many afternoons I eat with Zuhra at al-Mankal, the nearby Jordanian restaurant where I now have lunch most days and where the manager brings us a wooden screen to hide her from view. Other days, I buy falafel sandwiches for me and Radia, who never goes home for lunch, and we sit eating them at her desk. None of the men are around then, so she flips up her veil while she eats and helps me with my Arabic homework.

My women are, however, more likely than the men to invite me home. It's easier for them; they don't have to worry about jealous wives. The first time I have lunch at Zuhra's house, I am struck by how joyful a place it is. She and her three sisters drag me to their bedroom after we eat, and we lie on the bed looking at scores of photos and a series of home movies. One stars Zuhra and Shetha (her sister now married and living in Dubai) playing old village women wrapped in the traditional Sana'ani *setarrh* (a red and blue cloth now worn only by the elderly). Ghazal, Zuhra's youngest sister, dances toward them in a skimpy dress. She doesn't cover her face or glittering eyes and exudes self-confidence. "Put something on!" Zuhra says in the film. Aping the old gossips who sit around judging the younger generation, they ask Ghazal if maybe she is *American*. Are you *praying* in America? Who is your father? (Two questions Zuhra says are often asked of young girls.) We all roll around on the bed laughing and poking each other.

"This is what we are like all the time," Zuhra says. I have a pang of envy. When I was a child I fantasized about having a big, noisy family. Zuhra and her sisters and mother are as close as I can imagine any family being. "We're like *Little Women*!" Zuhra says. I am surprised she knows the book. And I think they might have a bit more fun than those March sisters.

☪

IBRAHIM IS ONE OF THE FEW MEN who dares to invite me home. I go to his house, some forty minutes outside of Sana'a, for lunch one Friday afternoon. Ibrahim and his wife, Sabah, live with a passel of relatives and children. Upstairs, I take off my shoes and settle in a large carpeted room, where the curious eyes of little people soon surround me. A plastic sheet is spread on the ground, and platters of fish, salads, breads, rice, chicken, radishes, and *zahawek* (the spicy Yemeni salsa I love) are piled in front of me. Because I am the only non–family member present, men and women eat together. If I were a man, I could eat only with the men. Sabah is very pretty and asks me the usual questions. Am I married? Yes, of course. Do I have children. I hesitate. No, I say, waiting for the usual cry of dismay. But to my surprise, she brightens. "Like me!" she says. "You are like me." I hadn't realized that Ibrahim had no children. He and his wife are both in their thirties and have been married since they were around twelve. Such early marriages are common in Yemen, though there is a growing movement to increase the minimum matrimonial age. I constantly hear reports, from both Yemenis and westerners, of young girls forced into marriage before their bodies and psyches are prepared. These appall me, and I find it horrifying that it is acceptable for grown men to find twelve-year-olds sexually appealing.

But Ibrahim and Sabah share a genuine affection that isn't often obvious between husbands and wives here. It is unusual for a Yemeni man to stay with a woman who hasn't given him children. Yet Ibrahim and Sabah occupy themselves with caring for their herd of nieces and nephews and appear happy.

☾

ALL THIS PROGRESS with the rest of my staff leaves me with just two people to worry about: al-Asaadi and Zaid. Faris has promised to keep al-Asaadi out of my hair by making him the editor of a new magazine he's launching and has approved my choice of Zaid as my successor. While I am dismayed that I only have a couple of months to get Zaid up to speed when he returns from London, I have high hopes that his journalism studies abroad have molded him into something resembling an editor. All I will have to do, I hope, is polish his edges. Yet I am plagued by anxieties. I have no idea what Zaid will be like as a manager. I have no idea how al-Asaadi will take to his new job.

My relationship with al-Asaadi has improved with distance. He calls and writes me enthusiastic e-mails from upstate New York, where he is studying and working as an intern at a newspaper, congratulating me on what I have done with the *Observer* (which he reads online). "Only now can I appreciate what you did for us," he says. "I am so grateful for all I have learned from you." I am astonished. Who is this man, and what has he done with my belligerent little fellow editor? Yet this doesn't quell my fears that our old battles will resume once we are face-to-face again.

Al-Asaadi arrives in Yemen a week before Zaid. He demonstrates his Americanization by kissing me once on each cheek, a first. We have lunch together soon after his return, at al-Mankal, my favorite haunt. We chatter easily about his time in the United States and about work. Jamal Hindi, the Jordanian owner of al-Mankal, comes over to tell us that he is going organic. He spent eight years living in Hong Kong and the Philippines, where he learned about macrobiotics and became interested in organic food. Once he began eating organic, he says, he lost seventy-five pounds. Now, Mr. Hindi is still a very large man, so it's a bit alarming to imagine what he looked like before.

The first organic restaurant in Sana'a! I pull out a notebook and interview him. I also interview the manager and several people eating nearby. In between, al-Asaadi tells me his plans for the new magazine, called *Yemen Today*. I look at his list of proposed sections and story lineup and am very impressed. *Newsweek,* look out! We discuss stories and timelines, and I'm amazed at how well al-Asaadi and I get along when we aren't battling for supremacy. A huge burden has been lifted from my shoulders; now all I have to worry about is Zaid.

☾

ZAID ARRIVES FROM LONDON about a week later, and I take him to the same restaurant. Like al-Asaadi, he greets me with a kiss on each cheek. Yemeni men who have been abroad are particularly fond of this Western custom. Frankly, I prefer not to be kissed. I've become incredibly protective of my physical space here; every touch begins to feel like a violation after a while in a country where most men and women never even speak to each other.

We have a fantastic lunch. He tells me about his studies in London, although he spends more time talking about all of the women he got to hug and all the whiskey he drank. He also tells me about the scandal he created when he arrived at Sana'a airport. "When I was in London, people asked me what was the first thing that I wanted to do when I got back to Yemen," he says, "and I said that the first thing I wanted to do was to kiss my wife. I missed this woman like you would not *believe.*"

So when his wife met him at the airport, he lifted her veil and he kissed her. "She was angry at me for about twenty seconds," he says. "Then she kissed me back."

Her relatives are less forgiving. His wife's father and brothers are still furious with him. Heaven forbid a man demonstrate his love for his wife in public.

I update Zaid on life at the paper, give him an outline of our schedule, and talk with him about how I would like our relationship to work. Until I leave, I am in charge. To present a unified front, I want him to run anything he says to the reporters by me first. Zaid concurs.

He then announces that he has given up *qat* entirely. I find this hard to believe, as I have rarely seen Zaid in the newsroom without a massively swollen cheek.

"You should ban it from the newsroom," he says.

"There would be mutiny!"

"No, the men would thank you for it in the end."

Oh really?

This lunch leaves me feeling even more relaxed. At last, I have someone willing to help me! At last, I can begin to shift a bit of my burden and begin to think about the future.

☾

AT HOME, I've started building a family. My new Scottish housemate, Carolyn, whom I met at the Soqotra airport and who had originally planned to stay for just a month, moves in for the rest of my time in Yemen. This delights me, as I'm not eager to evict someone who does my laundry, occasionally cooks, and entertains me endlessly with her adventures following in the footsteps of Ibn Battuta and leading tour groups through Iran, Saudi Arabia, and Tashkent.

Just when I've settled into domestic life with Carolyn, my Dutch friend Koosje rings one morning while I am making coffee.

"Remember how you said that maybe I could live with you if I had to move out of my house?" she says.

"Yeees . . ."

"Well, I *do* actually have to move out. So, would it still be possible?"

"When?" I stir my coffee.

"Twenty minutes? I'm already packed."

What can I do? I can't leave a pretty blond Dutch girl to the streets. So half an hour later, I have a second housemate. They bookend me agewise; Carolyn is forty-nine and Koosje twenty-two. Koosje is an intern at UNHCR.

It surprises me to find that I love living with other people. For years I have thought I could only live alone. After all, I have lived alone quite happily for the better part of twelve years. Now I find I am a communal creature after all. I love coming home and sprawling in my *mafraj* with Carolyn or Koosje. I love the flurry of their comings and goings. I love that there are always other people around to help, say, fix the washing machine. Funny how you can get to thirty-eight and still find out so many new things about yourself.

We all get on famously, spending our free evenings lounging in our *mafraj*, talking over drinks. My friends are more diverse than ever before: Dutch students, German development workers, Ethiopian housecleaners, Kenyan consultants, and Yemeni economists. It occurs to me how insular my world was in the cosmopolitan city of New York. I could not have anticipated, for example, that it would be a Republican oil company executive from Texas, a man named Don, who would become one of my most loyal friends in Yemen.

☾

OF COURSE, my life is never quite trouble free. Just when my reputation is beginning to recover from my little run-in with customs, it suffers a new insult. One Thursday afternoon, Floor rings. She has the alcohol left over from Kamaran; may she drop it off for the party we are throwing at my house that night? No problem, I say. Swing by the office. There are three bottles of whiskey and two of vodka, which clank suspiciously as I trot from Floor's jeep back to my desk. I stuff them into my gym bag, which is sitting on a chair by the door, and go back to editing a front-page story.

A few minutes later, I hear a sharp clang, followed by the shattering of glass. My gym bag has thrown itself from its chair, as if offended at being asked to carry the contraband. I look up, horrified to see the spreading pool on my carpet. Immediately, my office smells like an Irish bar at closing time. I panic. I've wasted alcohol, in a dry country! I should be taken out back and shot. Worse, my door is open and any minute a reporter is going to walk in and step into a puddle of vodka. Just one bottle has broken, thank god. I vault over my desk and begin to frantically pick up the pieces of glass. I am grateful it wasn't the whiskey.

I am still on the floor, my knees soaked in booze, when Qasim walks in. *"Dageega!"* (One minute!), I say. *"Law samaht, ureedo dageega."* (Please, I need one minute.) I wave my hand at him, trying to send him away, but he just walks all the way in and looks over my shoulder at the three bottles of whiskey I have just rescued from certain ruin.

"Oh!" he says.

I curse my ineptitude. Qasim leaves my office, probably to go tell Faris

I'm a mad dipsomaniac bent on destroying the remaining morals of my staff. First vibrating artificial men, now this!

I open all my windows and stash the other bottles under my desk, but my office still reeks like a tavern.

Luke strolls in, stares at my carpet, and sniffs the air. "Well," he says. "There goes the rest of your reputation."

"Hey," I say with false cheer. "At least vodka doesn't stain. My carpet has never been so sterile."

Our stalwart receptionist, Enass, without saying a word, walks in and hands me a bottle of carpet cleaner.

I have another special delivery that day. Abdurahman, Ali's dad, calls to say he's bringing me a bag of organic avocados, which cannot be found in Sana'a. I am so ecstatic I briefly forget the vodka. That evening, in my taxi home, I stroke them, just to feel their firm roundness under my palms. I can't remember the last time I was so excited to put something in my mouth. Anne and Florens come over to help me mash the avocados into a dip for the party. Which turns out to be a roaring success, in that few people can remember the details of it the next day. I've never had such a crowded house. My *mafraj* overflows with people, several of whom I've never met. Everyone from Kamaran is there, plus Marvin, Pearl, and Ginny. I wear a short, sleeveless dress and savor the feel of it sliding up my thighs as I raise my arms to dance. It's springtime, and it feels like it.

After we've all been dancing for a while, Marvin requests cowboy music. I put on a country song and he and Pearl actually two-step around the room, knocking over several drinks as they swish around. It feels like a real party. (Yemenis of course have parties too, but they are always sex segregated and usually revolve around *qat* and sugary tea.) The only thing missing tonight, I think, is romance.

C

IT ISN'T LONG, HOWEVER, before this last void in my life is delightfully filled by a twenty-six-year-old German water researcher for the Dutch Embassy. Tobias is intelligent and attractive, tall, with oversized feet and hands, like a puppy that hasn't quite grown into his extremities. His square Germanic face is softened by floppy dark hair, large blue eyes, and an infectious grin. I meet him through Kamaran Island friends, and when he moves into a house nearby he begins inviting me over to parties and *qat* chews. Our mutual attraction is increasingly obvious, but weeks pass before we admit it to each other.

It happens on a weeknight. I'm exhausted from work but when Tobias asks if he may come over, I perk up. It's the first time we've been alone together. We make drinks and curl up in the *mafraj*. After a while, he suggests watching a movie. I put on *Half Nelson,* and we press close together in front of my twelve-inch computer screen. Tobias moves his arm around me and I slide into his embrace. I have no idea how *Half Nelson* ends. I'm not even sure if we turned it off or just left it running as we made love, first in the *mafraj* and again, moments later, in my bed.

He wakes me at dawn. After we say good morning properly, he sneaks home and I get ready for work, feeling more cheerful than I have since I got to this country.

I skip the gym and walk to work. The spring is back in my step, the kind of spring that makes men on the street pay twice as much attention to me as usual. I dare not meet anyone's eyes, I feel so incandescent with sensuality. When Luke walks into my office, he says, "Okay, what happened to you? Why the Cheshire cat smile?"

I say nothing at all.

☪

TOBIAS SPENDS ALMOST EVERY NIGHT with me that week, and on Friday, we don't leave my house. We spend about twenty-one of twenty-four hours naked and entwined, until hunger drives us finally out of bed, and Tobias cooks us pasta, which we wash down with a bottle of wine in my *mafraj*. The *muezzins* keep calling out Friday prayers, the wail of the preachers prompting Tobias to cry out, "You people don't know what you are missing!" But we are praying, in our own way, to our own decadent gods.

As the sun slides down over the rooftops around us, filling my *mafraj* with gold, Tobias falls asleep in my lap, looking angelic and terribly young. I stroke his hair and run my fingers over the decorative curl in his earlobes, his dark eyelashes, his flushed cheeks, his pale, flat stomach. I like him. The age gap between us and his return to Germany in a few months makes a future unlikely, but for the first time all year, a simple glow of well-being makes worry feel impossible.

I dream that night that I have a good fairy who has been watching out for me. She looks like a middle-aged housewife, plump, with short dark hair, and she seems slightly annoyed.

"Well, it looks like things are now going exceptionally well for you," she says, a touch resentfully. "So I am going to go find someone else to help, someone with *real* problems."

☪

THERE ARE PEOPLE in this world who can go for years without being touched. I am not one of them. I can't survive more than a month of physical loneliness without wanting to crawl out of my skin. Which means that I've been wanting to crawl out of my skin almost since I got to Yemen. I am deeply physically needy, and I refuse to be ashamed of this. So when one of my closest Yemeni friends, a virgin, confesses to me that she also thinks constantly about sex, I try to reassure her that she is not an immoral freak. Don't you think Allah gave us these desires for a reason? I say. That he gave us these bodies for a reason? This does not shock my Yemeni friend. In fact, she seems quite heartened. "This is true," she says happily. "Why *would* we be given bodies like this?"

Shaima, on the other hand, simply buries her desires. One night as she drives me home from dinner, we chat about men and relationships.

"I have never kissed a man, Jennifer," she confesses.

"Never?" Shaima is over thirty years old. I kissed my first boy in fifth grade. No, wait—first grade! I still remember his name. Bobby Woodward. Audacious tyke.

"Never."

"So how do you . . ." I want to say, how do you survive never being touched? How can you bear the loneliness? But I swallow the words.

"Jennifer, I just ignore my body," she says in answer to my unasked question. "I try to forget it is there."

☪

MY RESEARCH for our next health page gives me a little more insight into Yemeni sexuality. While searching for interesting new studies, I stumble across a piece in *New Scientist* on how oral sex causes cancer. Apparently anyone who has had five or more partners is about a trillion times more likely to develop throat cancer. While I am spiraling into despair about this, Jabr comes into my office. He is my only reporter not working on something.

"Jabr," I begin cautiously, "do you think we could get away with a story on oral sex?"

He looks at me blankly. "What is oral sex?" he says. From the awkward way he forms the words, it is clear that he has never heard the phrase.

I am shocked. Most of my male reporters (according to Luke) are surfing porn sites every time I turn my back, so I thought they had a pretty graphic image of what oral sex is.

I start to explain, but for the first time in my life, I find myself too embarrassed to describe a sex act.

"Don't be shy," says Jabr encouragingly.

My stomach twists. "I'm not! It's just . . ." It's just that I don't want to accidentally excite you, I think to myself.

Instead, I pick up the dictionary from my desk and read him the definition. Neither of us cracks a smile.

"Um, so, what I am wondering is, are we going to get in trouble for writing about this? Is it okay according to Islam? Between married people, of course!"

"Let me check," says Jabr gravely. "I will read the study."

A half hour later, I stop in the newsroom to find Jabr reading through everything Google has turned up on oral sex. He has consulted with Noor and Najma, neither of whom has heard of oral sex. All three reporters are single, so perhaps this is not surprising.

Noor turns to me and says, "We don't have such a thing in Yemen as oral sex."

"You don't?" This cannot be true.

"No," Jabr agrees.

"We are a conservative country," says Noor. "We don't do this."

"Not even married people?"

All three shake their heads.

"But it's . . ." A thousand inappropriate explanations of why it's healthy and necessary threaten to burst out of my mouth. I bite my tongue. "Let's drop it then. We'll run the iPod story instead."

This is absurd, given that the iPod story is about the effect of iPods on pacemakers, and hardly any Yemenis own either gizmo. But at least it won't scandalize anyone.

Curious to find out the truth, I report the conversation to Luke. "They claim there is no such thing as oral sex in Yemen."

"Oh yes there *is!*" he says, laughing.

"I figured you would know."

I guess the gay men have all the luck. Once you're engaged in one illegal activity, you might as well go all out.

Later, married Yemeni women tell me that oral sex *does* exist but that many people consider it shameful. "Women are not honest with each other," says one Yemeni woman. If a woman admits that her husband "kisses her vagina," others disparage the act as disgusting. Some think that a man who performs oral sex is being too servile to his wife and unmanly. "It's just how we are trained, to think our bodies are disgusting," says my friend. "Some women don't feel husbands should witness birth because they will be disgusted. Women think organs are a disgusting place. Women internalize these sexist ideas. In Islam, you should take a shower after sex."

☾

IT MAKES ALL THE DIFFERENCE to have Tobias waiting for me after work. Someone to whom I can pour out the frustrations of my day, someone to hand me a drink and sit with me looking out over the boxy brown houses of Old Sana'a glowing in the dark, holding my hand. Someone with interesting stories of his own. My reporters sense a new lightness in me. The women tell me I look pretty twice as much as usual, looking slightly suspicious. How do they get through their lives? I wonder. How can they bear sleeping alone every night? They must have passions of their own, but what do they do with them? Offer them to God? Perhaps that is it. Perhaps if I had God, I could be happier alone. I could be happier without fingers brushing against my skin, without a warm body curled around me. But I do not have God. All I have is a persistent and not necessarily wise openness to love, and a relentless desire to be loved in return.

Despite how well things are going, I've been looking forward to a break from my six-day week, from my twelve-hour days. But the thought of returning to a job in New York, the thought of once again climbing onto the endless treadmill of work and rent paying and rushing from place to place in anonymous crowds, fills me with dread.

I have no idea what I will do at the end of this year. I've scarcely had time to look up from my desk. But now that I have become human again and made room for joy and leisure in between manic workdays, my brain finds itself with time to look up at the horizon. There is nothing there.

TWENTY
the deluge

Just when I am at my happiest personally and most optimistic about my paper's future, harbingers of doom appear. It takes less than a week for me to realize that Zaid's English has failed to improve one iota during his ten months in London. How he managed this is beyond me, but I struggle to edit his stories and it becomes clear that he is not remotely capable of editing anyone else's work. After fighting so hard to sell Faris on Zaid, now I am going to have to do some rethinking.

Zaid already seems to have lost his resolve to give up *qat*. The day after our lunch, I walk into the office to find him stuffing a leaf into his mouth. I raise an eyebrow.

"It was a gift!" he says. "I couldn't refuse it! It would be rude!"

I have also begun to have trouble with Hadi, who has always been the most reliable and devoted of designers. He has been coming in later every day, sometimes not appearing until noon. This mystifies me. One morning, desperate to lay out a page, I collar Luke.

"Hadi hardly ever gets here on time anymore! What is going on?"

"Did you know he got a car?"

"He got a car?"

"So that's why he's been coming in late."

I don't get it. Shouldn't a car get him here even earlier?

"He's been working as a taxi driver in the mornings."

Ah. This is not unusual. Many Yemenis string together several jobs to make ends meet. If Faris raised staff salaries, it might keep them from taking side jobs that distract them from their work. Even al-Asaadi worked for UNICEF while editor in chief of the paper. This not only took him away from the office too often but was entirely unethical, as the newspaper regularly covers UNICEF's activities.

Some reporters make it difficult for me to agitate for higher pay. When the men want a raise, they begin doing less and less work, if they bother to show up at all. I try to explain to Hadi—who just asked for a raise—that if he wants to be paid more, he should prove that he is worth it. He should be showing up *early* and getting an exceptional amount of work done. That is what would make me want to help you get more money, I say. This baffles him.

The Missing Link does the same thing. A day after asking for a raise, Jabr doesn't show up at work or even call in with an excuse. When I finally get him on the phone, he says he is napping.

"Jabr, if you're hoping for a raise, it's not terribly wise to start skipping work. You should be demonstrating how much you deserve it, not what a shirker you are."

My frustration with Hadi builds until one morning in late June. Hadi, who was the happiest with our new schedule, has begun to drag our closes.

"You cannot keep coming in this late!" I say, accosting him as he walks in the door one closing day at noon.

"Do you have any pages?" he says belligerently.

"Yes, I have pages! But that isn't the point. You are supposed to be here in the morning. You have a *job!*"

Things escalate until we are shouting at each other in the hallway. I ask Zaid for help, saying I have to get Hadi to the office earlier. He goes outside to talk with Hadi, and I retreat to my office.

A few minutes later, Zaid appears in my door.

"Hadi has a big problem," he says.

"I know, he can't get to work on time," I say crossly.

"No, he has a big problem at home. He said he wants to sleep in the office and never go home. It has to be serious for him to say that. He was crying just now."

I feel guilty for yelling at him. "If he has a reason he can't get here on time, he should tell me."

"I think you should talk with him."

I go outside and find Hadi on the front steps, leaning against the building. I touch his arm.

"Hadi, I am sorry I yelled at you. I don't like yelling at you. I love working with you, and I want things to be good between us," I begin.

His anger is gone. He smiles at me, his long black lashes still damp with tears.

"If you have a problem, some reason you can't come in, you can tell me," I say. "You can talk to me."

"Thank you," he says, reaching out to pat my arm, an unusual gesture. "Thank you." He's short of money for things he needs at home, he says. He's also been having bitter arguments with his wife. It's unclear if the two problems are related. I promise to try to get him a little more money from Faris and he promises to try to get to work earlier.

☪

ON JUNE 26, I must somehow sense what the day has in store, because I wake too depressed to eat and cry all the way to the gym. It all builds up, my worry about Zaid, my fear about leaving the paper, my anxiety over the future, and the floodgates open. Thank god I'm wearing dark glasses. I run five miles on the treadmill and bike half an hour, as if I can somehow get away from myself. I head out afterward to find that none of the hotel taxi drivers will give me a ride, because they are all curled up in the trunks of their cars, green leaves sticking out of their mouths.

Irritated, I stride out to the main road and hail a cab. The driver argues about the price, but I get weary of fighting and climb in. I just want to get to work.

I am staring out the window for the first half of the ride, watching the storefronts and child salesmen and pyramids of tomatoes and watermelons spin by, so I don't notice my driver's activities. Then a frenzied movement in my peripheral vision arrests my attention. I look over to see that my driver has his grubby hand around his penis and is vigorously and quite openly jerking off.

At first I refuse to believe it. But then I look again. I am *not* imagining it.

In horror, I pull some *riyals* out of my purse and throw them at him, leaping from the car in the middle of a major intersection. "You *disgust* me!" I yell. Dodging cars, I run panting and nauseated across the street, my bags banging against my back. I cannot get over his complete lack of shame. Did he think he could get away with that, just because I was a foreigner? I wish I hadn't paid him. I wish I had remembered the Arabic word for "shame." I wish I had hit him. I stop and look around. I have no idea where I am. I am probably only halfway to work. But I have been on this route so many times, I figure if I just keep walking I will see something I recognize. It's hot, and the sun and dust press down on me. Once again I am grateful for my dark sunglasses as I stumble crying down the street, trying to stifle my sobs as I pass groups of construction workers. I walk and weep all the way to the office. My women are gathered at the gate, as if expecting me. It is lunchtime, and the men are gone.

"Do you have a cold?" says Zuhra, looking anxious.

"No, I just . . ." I start crying again, and Zuhra and Radia follow me to my office. I tell them the whole story, but they don't look impressed.

"This happens to all of us," Zuhra says. "It is normal."

Radia concurs. They are harassed constantly, both by taxi drivers and men on the streets. Even fully covered, fully disguised.

"One time a man even offered me money to go to a hotel with him," says Radia. "But what can we do? This is what men are like."

This is what men are like.

"You should not be subjected to this!" I cry. "It is *not* normal. I can't bear the fact that you think of this as normal! You should not have to suffer these horrible men."

They concur. "But what can we do?"

☾

AT THE END of the month, the rains come with a vengeance. While the mornings are still sunny and clear, by the afternoons dark clouds have filled the sky. It's unwise to start walking anywhere between lunch and dinner; that's when the deep purple bellies of the clouds tear open, flooding the city.

It's nearly rain time one closing day when al-Asaadi rings to tell me he has a front-page story. A group of Belgian tourists was barred by the Tourism Police from traveling to the picturesque village of Kawkaban and are outraged. They complained that they had read in our paper that Yemen was inviting and safe, and now the minister of tourism is holding them captive in Sana'a. Al-Asaadi wants the headline to be GOVERNMENT KIDNAPPED US, SAYS TOURISTS.

I politely suggest that the word "kidnapped" may be slightly loaded, and al-Asaadi concurs. We change it to TOURISTS BLOCKED FROM TRAVEL. I'm trying to explain how I want things laid out to Hadi, but both al-Asaadi and Zaid are hovering, blocking my way.

"Three editors in one place is two too many," I say in frustration. "Could I please have some space to finish telling Hadi about this paragraph?" No one moves, and I throw the pages I'm editing to the floor. It's a bit melodramatic, but experience has taught me that my reporters don't respond to subtlety.

This jolts the men into action. Al-Asaadi slips back upstairs to his new office, and Zaid storms off in an adolescent funk.

"Do whatever you want with the paper. I'm leaving," he flings at me before toddling huffily off down the road, despite the fact that I have invited him to chew *qat* at my house after work.

This is the first of several dozen times that Zaid will "quit." He'll tell me he's done with the paper, storm off in a sulk, and then the next morning at the office he'll be back in front of his customary computer. "Funny," I'll say, "I could have sworn you quit yesterday." It gets so the day doesn't feel quite complete if I haven't driven Zaid to quit.

With Zaid gone, I quickly finish my edits and find Ali, who has come back from the United States to work for me again. Luke has been moved upstairs to edit *Arabia Felix,* so Ali temporarily fills his shoes. Rain spatters my hair as we walk to his antique powder-blue car. By the time we are on the road, the rain is coming down in blinding sheets. It's the hardest rain I have ever seen here. Knowing the Sayilah—the moat-like road around the Old City—will be flooded, we turn off Zubairi Street to wind our way through the back alleys. But the windows have fogged so badly we cannot see out the back or side. I pull Kleenexes out of my purse and daub at the windshield, but it refogs as fast as I wipe. The streets are flooding with fast water, and I am genuinely afraid that we will be swept along into the Say-ilah and go under the rushing muddy river. At last, unable to see and un-able to find a passable street, Ali stops the car on a hill. We sit, waiting out the storm.

"Too bad we don't have a flask," I say, fiddling with the broken radio.

"I was just thinking that."

While we are waiting, I get a text from Zaid.

"I thought u'll show me more respect, but girls and Ibrahim are your favorite and me at the end of your list. U made me feel empty and noth-ing. Thanks and sorry can't understand u anymore."

What am I going to do with him? I myself am no model of comport-ment, but I can at least say with a clear conscience that I have never once threatened to walk out on my job. At least the girls never fling themselves out of the office in a funk or threaten to quit.

"Ali, help me," I say. "Couldn't *you* take over the paper?" He is half-Yemeni, after all. His English is flawless. He's ideal.

"No *way*," he says without pausing for reflection. "I just don't care about it enough—not like you do."

Maybe I care about it too much. I want to control what happens to it after I leave; I want to shape Zaid into a model editor; I want my reforms to be immortal. I want better conditions for my reporters and a better reputation for the paper. I want the *Observer* to be *effective,* to influence public thought. But I'm starting to realize that no matter how hard I work, no matter what kind of plans I make, these things are beyond me. I cannot single-handedly save this paper. I'm still pondering this when Carolyn rings. "Now don't panic," she says. "But I thought I should warn you. . . ."

As if it had absorbed the full weight of my hopes and dreams for the *Ob-server,* a large chunk of the roof of my 350-year-old gingerbread house has collapsed. A massive pile of ceiling, dirt, and rubble has tumbled to the hallway of our top floor, just outside the room where a houseguest was sleeping. And the rain is pouring in.

I panic, picturing a massive river of water cascading down my stairs, sweeping away our shoes from the landings. "I should get home," I tell Ali.

The rain has eased a bit, so Ali and I park and pick our way through ankle-deep water to my ruined home. Outside, crowds line the flooded Sayilah and its series of bridges. A carnival atmosphere prevails, adults as excited as the children to see the sudden river circling the city. I've never seen the water so high; it must be more than ten feet deep. Children slither down the stone embankments and splash into the muddy brew. A taxi floats by. A large truck is semisubmerged under the bridge. Forgetting my roof for a moment, I pull out my camera and begin snapping photos. Men walk by with their white *thobes* pulled up, revealing their undershorts. When they do this, they wrap their robes around their *jambiyas,* so it looks like they are all walking around with enormous erections. Sometimes men even hold on to each other's *jambiyas* as they walk, with no apparent thought for the overt eroticism of the gesture.

Fifty photos later, we tear ourselves away from the spectacle and splash down the street to my house. When I unlock the gate, Ali and I race to the top floor. An avalanche of mud, straw, plaster and rock litters the last staircase. I stop short of the landing, because there is nowhere left to stand. A waist-high pile of roof fills the hallway. A few drops of water hit my hair and I look up. Sure enough, above us is only a jagged chunk of Arabian sky.

My home, the paper, this city—always falling apart, always needing to be rebuilt. This is the ride I am on.

TWENTY-ONE

bombs, breakups, and bastille day

On the first Monday in July, an unlikely event restores my faith in my staff— a bombing. That afternoon, I put the paper to bed early and go home to try to nap. Sleep refuses the invitation, and I get up to check my e-mail, to find messages from Fox News, CBS, and Global Radio Network asking if I am still in Yemen and if I have any more information about the terrorist bombing in Ma'rib, a city a hundred miles east of Sana'a that is popular with tourists for its spectacular dam and ancient ruins. Why hasn't anyone on my staff called me?

I'm dialing the office before I even finish reading the e-mails. Al-Asaadi is still there, *al-hamdulillah,* working on *Yemen Today.*

"Don't let them send the paper to the printer!" I say. "We have to add the Ma'rib story." Al-Asaadi has only just heard the news himself. This is, I think, as close to a "Stop the presses!" moment as I am ever likely to have. In a flurry of excitement, I ring Farouq and Ibrahim and ask them to report the story pronto and file it directly to me. I can edit it from home and send it to Zaid at the office for layout.

While waiting for them, I ring the spokesmen at the Ministry of the Interior and the Ministry of Information. I don't get anywhere. They just keep giving me each other's phone number and don't seem to know anything. If I were in the United States, I think, I would just get in a car and go to the scene of the bombing. But this kind of on-the-ground reporting is nearly impossible here. Getting to Ma'rib would mean not only finding a car, but crossing some thirty military checkpoints. For non-Yemenis, getting through those requires a sheaf of travel permissions: sheets of paper containing the name of the traveler's organization, vehicle number, and dates of travel, authorized by the Tourism Police. Who has time for that on deadline?

If you are one of the rare foreigners who track Yemeni news, you notice after a while that there are almost never witnesses to newsworthy events. You never get the story from the guy who lives near the site of the car bomb, who heard it go off and watched the car go up in flames while bystanders raced for shelter. This is partly because journalists are rarely allowed anywhere near a crime scene and partly because witnesses would never speak to a journalist. They're too afraid of getting into trouble. Of course, it also doesn't often occur to Yemeni reporters to interview anyone but official sources. When I ask my reporters to find out what regular people on the street think of a proposed law, for example, their typical response is, "Who cares about regular people?"

The dearth of eyewitnesses and other nonofficial sources makes for dull and often misleading stories. I don't trust the Ministry of the Interior to feed me anything but fraudulent pap, the aim of which is to make the government look good and anyone in conflict with them look bad.

I hound Ibrahim and Farouq until they e-mail me their stories, and I weave them together. Nine people are believed dead, seven Spanish tourists and two Yemeni drivers. They were ambushed by a suicide bomber who drove a truck full of explosives through their convoy at the site of the Ba'ran Temple, also called Arsh Bilqis (the Queen of Sheba's Throne) in Ma'rib.

I e-mail the finished story to Zaid, tell him which photo to use, and send a copy to al-Asaadi to put on the Web. It's a little exciting. Despite the tragedy, and the sorrow and fear it evokes, I can't help but feel that familiar guilty journalistic thrill at a major news story breaking.

The story requires weeks of follow-up. This has never been the paper's strong suit, but my reporters amaze me. They interview a surviving Yemeni driver who still has shrapnel in his right eye and left ear. They write about the financial hardship facing the families of the two dead and two injured Yemenis, who have no way to support themselves now that their sons and cars are gone. They write about the decline in tourism.

The bombing, we report, has all the hallmarks of an al-Qaeda attack. Yet some sources suggest that it is the work of a new al-Qaeda cell, not of the veterans who trained in Afghanistan. Zaid writes a piece exploring the differences between the old and new al-Qaeda and why young men might be drawn to careers in terrorism.

Yemen is a fertile breeding ground for terrorists for many reasons. It is one of the poorest countries in the world, with a corrupt government. This corruption results in major inequities between rich and poor, fostering a strong sense of injustice. Despite significant oil revenues over the past thirty years, the government has failed to provide effective education and health services, sustainable water supplies, and reliable power to its people. The regime gives land and commercial contracts to its supporters while neglecting areas controlled by its opponents. Rumors abound that the president's cronies profit from smuggling of arms, oil, and drugs; after all, little effort has been made to stop such smuggling. Exacerbating matters, a corrupt and incompetent judiciary makes it difficult to address grievances. No wonder people feel angry and impotent.

A weak government, poor intelligence services, and lax immigration procedures also mean that terrorists can operate more freely in Yemen than they can in stronger neighboring countries, such as Saudi Arabia. The Saudi government has attacked terrorism with will, determination, and resources not found in Yemen and made it very difficult for terrorists to operate there—so many have moved to Yemen.

My staff reports all of this. I am bursting with pride in my reporters for continuing to generate story after story in the wake of the attack. It's a huge reminder of how far we have all come.

☪

NOW THAT ALI has taken over as copy editor, we fly through pages. Closing is faster than it was with Luke, who was rather Yemeni in his approach to closing times. Ali doesn't loiter in the *qat* shed shooting the breeze with the guys, doesn't vanish for four hours at lunchtime, and doesn't chew at work. He even helps my other reporters with their writing, and they help him to conduct interviews in Arabic (which Ali speaks, but not confidently enough to interview government officials).

With the notable exception of Zaid, progress is all around. Sure, I still see atrocious stories. Editing itself doesn't get that much easier. But there's no denying the changes in every single one of my journalists. And that *matters*.

My grand delusion that I can spread democracy in the Arab world by loosening the stays of the Yemeni press has dwindled, as have my illusions that any story we write could have the smallest impact on government policy. But in the place of these lofty dreams are smaller, more stably built achievements. My reporters almost always use more than one source per story. They can integrate statistics into trend pieces. They've got a rudimentary grasp of ethics and journalistic integrity. Some of them even occasionally write a good lead. These modest achievements will outlive me. That is something.

Sometimes, when I look at my work at the newspaper and squint in just the right way, I can even see it as a microcosm of democracy itself. After all, every staff member participates in the creation of each issue. I solicit their ideas. I value the contributions of women and minorities. Of course, I wasn't democratically elected, but what newspaper chief ever was?

☪

ONLY AFTER THE ADRENALINE of writing about the bombing has worn off do I turn my thoughts to my own safety. Throughout all of my months in Yemen, all of my late-night walks through the Old City, never once have I felt in danger. Yes, men harass me constantly and everyone stares, but I haven't felt threatened with violence. The Ma'rib bombing suggests that perhaps I've become too complacent. Just a couple weeks before, Koosje and Tobias had traveled to Ma'rib, to the same temple where the Spanish tourists and Yemeni drivers were killed. It could have been them. For a few weeks, my friends and others in the expat community seem a bit edgier than usual, but eventually we all go back to worrying about our work and love lives. It is impossible to live on full alert all the time. I wonder why the bombing doesn't make me feel like fleeing the country, but then I think, September 11 didn't make me feel like fleeing New York, did it? There's danger everywhere, and attempts to predict the terrorists' actions in an effort to dodge it are a fool's game.

☾

NOW THAT I'M BACK to worrying about more personal things, my thoughts turn to Tobias. He will leave soon, before I do. We've only been together a couple of months, but we're about to be forced into some decisions. Either we go our separate ways and call this a summer fling, or we try to keep going. Staying together would involve either a long-distance relationship (which I don't want) or one of us moving. Tobias is heading back to graduate school, to work on a doctorate. And I am—well, I don't know yet. I guess I'm flexible. The truth is, neither of us is sure what we want. I genuinely adore Tobias. He's smart, he's sexy, and he makes me laugh. But I have no idea if we'd be a good match in the longer term. We're at different places in our lives; my student days are long past and his are not yet over.

During Tobias's last few weeks, we don't have time to see much of each other, which makes our parting less dramatic. Still, resigned though I am to the logical end of our romance, I'm sad to see him go. Maybe he isn't the perfect life partner for me, but a small part of me wishes we'd at least had time to let things run their natural course, whatever that might be. I never have an easy time saying good-bye. We set all of our concerns aside to spend one last night lying under my stained glass windows, in each other's arms. Then he is gone. A group of us walk him to the taxi, and I am the last to hug him. In full view of my neighbors, the driver, and our friends, I stand on my toes and kiss him. "You'll get in trouble," he whispers. "I don't care," I say. And I turn away, before anyone can see my tears.

In the morning, I listen to the new Wilco album, *Sky Blue Sky*. The first song reminds me of an empty summer day in a small New England town. The kind of day on which I had a lemonade stand to raise money to buy a water pistol, but no one passed by, and the air was still and quiet except for the occasional drone of a plane overhead or a passing fly. That feeling . . . like a pause in the middle of life, after which anything could happen.

☾

I ESCAPE LONELINESS by burying myself in work, spending even more time with my staff as our time together shortens. Zaid can't seem to make up his mind how he feels about me. One moment he's telling me that I taught him everything he knows and that he reveres me, and the next he's quitting again because I haven't been respectful. But I'm still trying with him, still hoping that somehow he will manage when I am gone.

One mid-July closing day, he's already quit once, so I'm surprised when he approaches me as Ali and I are finishing photo captions. "Are you going to the Bastille Day reception at the French ambassador's house Saturday night?" he asks. I want to go, but I don't have an invitation. Because I cannot legally be listed as the editor in chief on the masthead, all invitations now go to Zaid. Before he arrived, when they were still addressed to al-Asaadi, Enass passed everything to me.

"I have an invitation," Zaid says. "Wanna be my date?"

"Okay, I'll be your date." It's my peace offering. It is also a decision that will change the course of my entire life.

☪

ON BASTILLE DAY, the day of the French ambassador's party, I have an un-usually productive day. I edit all three health stories, including Adhara's piece on the danger of listening to headphones in a lightning storm. She mistakes thunder for lightning, however, and keeps referring to "thunder strikes." I also edit Jabr's surprisingly adequate report on the harassment of women by taxi drivers. Near and dear to my heart.

My male reporters are terribly excited about the French party (the women of course are not allowed to go) and arrive at the office decked out in smart Western suits, their hair neatly combed or slicked back. I feel slightly less spectacular in plain black pants and a long royal-blue embroidered Turkish tunic. Nothing to be done. Useless to worry about fashion in Yemen. I put on exceptionally bright red lipstick and hope that will spruce me up.

Zaid, Jabr, Bashir (who still drops by to help us on closing days), and I all pile into photographer Mohammed al-Sharabi's battered car, and away we go. Zaid makes me sit in the front, and the three men squish together in the backseat. Zaid rings someone on his cell. *"Feyn ant?"* he says. Where are you? Yemeni men begin every phone conversation like this. They cannot possibly talk to someone if they don't know exactly where that person is.

"Do you know what that means?" asks Bashir.

"Of course," I say, mildly insulted. "That's baby Arabic!"

"No one speak Arabic!" says Bashir. "She can understand us now!"

We arrive early at French Ambassador Gilles Gauthier's house and loiter outside the gates with a few other overeager invitees. At last, we are all admitted to the front garden, where we are subjected to a very thorough security check. My laptop, gym bag, and purse are taken away, and I am marched through a metal detector. In the wake of the Ma'rib bombing, everyone has tightened security.

A path of fairy lights leads us past a gauntlet of solemn French officials, who shake our hands and murmur, *"Bonsoir."* Beyond them, rows of bushes open into a large backyard sheltered by tents. At least a dozen banquet-sized tables are covered with food, and the bar stretches about a city block long. Waiters circulate with platters of juices, wine, and shrimp. I take a glass of wine and look around. No wonder security is so tight; the place is teeming with ambassadors. Just then, the new Deputy British Ambassador Chris Shute, who arrived recently and has become a friend, catches my elbow. "Come," he says. "I'll introduce you to the new British ambassador." I'm eager to meet him, since former Ambassador Gifford had been so helpful to me.

Chris leads me through the growing crowds to a tall, dark-haired man in a pinstriped suit, with the sparkliest blue eyes I have ever seen. I offer him my hand. "I'm Jennifer Steil, editor of the *Yemen Observer.*"

"Tim Torlot," he says, twinkling at me.

My heart trips over itself. *This is the man I want to marry.* The thought flashes through my mind only seconds after our hands meet. It's completely irrational. He's a stranger. Marriage is not on my agenda. But suddenly I'm more wide awake than I have been since I got to this country. I'm awash in joy and sorrow all at once. Steady now, Steil. Ambassadors are all married. I want to check his left hand, but I can't look away from his eyes. I wonder how old he is. There's no white in his hair, and his body is straight and slender.

Pulling myself together, I ask him how long he's been here and what he's seen of Yemen. He's only been here three days.

"Where were you posted before Yemen?"

"Iraq, most recently. Shorter stints in Afghanistan, Chad, and the Central African Republic . . ."

"So really this is the safest country you've been to in years."

"Yes. I'm beginning to wonder if the Foreign Office hasn't been trying to tell me something," he says, smiling. His eyelashes are curly and tipped with gold. Focus, Steil!

He asks how long I've been in Yemen.

"About a year. I'm leaving in a month and a half," I say. "My contract is up at the end of August."

He looks disappointed. Or am I projecting? I don't want to leave Yemen, I realize. I desperately do not want to leave Yemen.

"Everyone I meet seems to be about to leave."

"Yes," I say. "High turnover rate, I'm afraid."

We make small talk. What about the press in Yemen? he asks. Is it free? Which subjects are taboo? I talk about the *Observer* while he listens attentively. It must be something they teach diplomats: Never look away from the face of the person you are addressing.

Neither of us looks away, until I begin to worry I am monopolizing him. The line of dignitaries waiting to meet him has grown to unwieldy proportions.

"I'd love to talk longer," he whispers. "But I am supposed to be meeting all these people."

"Right. Sorry! I'll leave you to it then. I've got a few people to meet myself."

"I'm ever so pleased to meet you. Here—I've even got my cards already." He hands me one.

"How efficient. It took me three months to get mine. And now I'm out. But it's terrific to meet you." He takes my hand one last time, and I reluctantly release him to the queue.

Feeling slightly dizzy, I head to the bar. It takes forever to get there. Every person I have ever met in Yemen is at this party. There are close to a thousand guests. I feel like I end up talking to most of them.

But there is only one conversation I record in my journal.

TWENTY-TWO

pomegranate season

Zuhra comes flapping into my office one late spring day at twice her normal speed. "I got it!" she says, her smile so big I can see it through her *niqab.* "They gave it to me!"

"What?" I say. "Who gave what to you?"

"The embassy! The fellowship!"

"Which one?" Ever since Zuhra was rejected by Columbia, she has been madly applying for every fellowship that might take her out of the country.

"*Your* embassy!" Zuhra says. "They are sending me to America!"

"They are?" I hug her. She's too excited to stand still and is bouncing on her toes as if her grubby sneakers have grown springs. "Zuhra, that's fantastic news! Tell me about the program."

The Near East and South Asia Undergraduate Exchange Program is offering Zuhra full tuition and living expenses at an American university for one semester. Zuhra already has an undergraduate degree, but this does not disqualify her. Besides, given what I know of the Yemeni education system, a bonus semester couldn't hurt. The embassy won't tell her the exact dates of travel or where she will be placed until later.

I'm thrilled, and relieved that I will not be leaving her behind when I go. How could I walk out of the *Yemen Observer* while she was still there?

How could I leave her in the hands of Zaid, whose inability to fill my editorial shoes grows more apparent every day? We cross our fingers and hope she gets sent to New York, where I think I will be in autumn and where her oldest brother, Fahmi, lives. A friend of a friend has offered me a free apartment in Manhattan for two and a half months, which at least gives me somewhere to land and sort out my future. Zuhra and I talk about what she will need to take with her. "I need some long skirts and shirts!" she said. "Modest things."

I laugh, because the things Zuhra ends up buying to go to the United States are the same things that I bought to come here. Because Yemeni women wear *abayas* over their outfits every day, many hardly own any modest clothing. Underneath those polyester sacks are usually tight T-shirts and jeans, nothing they would want men to see.

Packing up to go is easier now that I know Zuhra will also be leaving. Not that I've done much packing—I'm still working the same schedule and haven't had time. Nothing about these last couple of months feels final. There is no gradual decline of workload, no slowing of pace. I work flat out until the day I walk out the door. Is there any other way to do it with a newspaper? Issues still have to be closed, on the same deadlines. There is little time for reflection and no easing of pressure. I feel a desperate need to experience as much as possible before I go.

Thus, when my friend Phil Boyle calls from the British Embassy to offer me an interview with Shahid Malik, parliamentary undersecretary of state for international development and Britain's first Muslim minister, I jump at the chance. Malik is in town for just a couple of days, and Phil is offering interviews to only the *Yemen Observer* and an Arabic paper. "I'll do it myself," I say. I suppose by now I should trust my staff to interview ministers, but I want this one. Editors shouldn't get too far away from reporting, I rationalize. I don't want to forget how to do it.

So a little before six P.M. one Wednesday afternoon in early August, I appear at the gates of the stately British ambassador's residence. I'm riding a wave of euphoria, happy with work, happy to see the guards who swing open the vast metal doors to admit me, and, I can't deny, excited to see the man whom all of this is arranged to protect.

Only a minute after I'm inside, standing between the vast lawn and the house, the gates swing open again and a forest-green Land Cruiser whips around the corner and into the driveway beside us. Several men with machine guns leap out and begin searching nearby rooftops with their eyes. Just behind them is Ambassador Tim Torlot, who springs from the backseat with the enthusiasm of a seven-year-old released from school.

"It's terrific to see you!" he says, having landed practically at my feet. "But I presume you're here for work and not pleasure?" He's all a-twinkle.

"Well, I don't believe I've been invited for *pleasure* yet." I can't believe I just said that out loud. Am I *flirting* with the ambassador?

But he laughs and flushes. "I'm afraid we haven't had time to organize a single event for pleasure yet."

We stand there talking for so long that he nearly makes me late for my appointment with the minister. At last, he ushers me into the house and parks me in his study while he goes to track down the minister. I examine the bookcases lined up against the wall. Books in English! Hundreds of them! It's been so long since I saw this many books in one place. I run my fingers along their spines with undisguised lust. Isabel Allende, Shakespeare, A. S. Byatt, Iain Banks, Tim Mackintosh-Smith, Freya Stark, Oscar Wilde, Philip Larkin, W. Somerset Maugham, a host of *reference* books! Every book on the shelf is something that I have either already read or am longing to read. I wonder whose books these are, Tim's or his wife's. (He is, of course, married.) Who is the reader? I want to ask Tim, but he has vanished.

A man from the embassy comes to fetch me. I have only fifteen minutes, so I get right to my questions. What does the minister see as the most pressing issue facing Yemen? (Population growth.) What are the most important aspects of the ten-year development plan the UK is signing with Yemen? (Population, education, water, the usual.) How does the UK plan to help Yemen integrate economically into the Gulf Cooperation Council? This one throws him. He stammers and gives me something vague. Phil commends me for that one as he ushers me out of the room. As usual, I've used up more than my allotted time. I'd been trying, unsuccessfully, to get him to say something that fizzed a bit, something not quite on script. When I walk out of the house, Tim comes bounding from the porch to meet me. I ask what he has done so far with Malik, and he tells me about various development projects they have visited. I'm facing the long rectangle of lawn, gazing at it longingly. "Do you have a croquet set?" I ask.

"Not here."

"You've got a good lawn for it."

"But I don't. It's all this weird spongy stuff. Here—come see." He touches my arm and we walk onto the grass. Our feet sink into the springy loam with every step.

"I see what you mean."

"We'll have to do something about it."

We stand there idly talking as the sun slips down over the mountains and the air cools. "I should go," I say. "I have my roommate's farewell dinner."

"And I had better be getting back inside."

But neither of us moves. I suddenly have an overwhelming desire to kiss him. He's almost close enough and sparking away at me like a firefly in the dusk. The thought flusters me, and I tear myself away.

The guards let me out the gate, and I walk down the street in a daze, practically vibrating with joie de vivre. I could gallop the entire way home. But I would be late for Koosje's last night. I turn the corner and keep going, heading to the main street to find a cab. At home, I run all the way up my seven or so staircases and fling myself into the kitchen, where Carolyn is waiting.

"I'm in *love* with the new British ambassador," I say, throwing myself into one of our plastic chairs.

Carolyn looks at me with calm skepticism. "There's a new ambassador?"

"Yes, oh yes. And he's the loveliest man on the planet."

"Isn't he married?"

I sag. "Yes," I say. "I'm not going to run off with him or anything. I just *love* him."

Fortunately for Carolyn, I get too distracted by preparations for Koosje's last supper to keep obsessing about Tim. We're always saying good-bye to someone. Our usual crowd meets at the Arabia Felix hotel, where we have the usual curry and *shisha* blowout bash. Afterward, the whole gang of us escorts Koosje to a taxi and runs waving after her. "*Ma'a salaama!* Safe journeys to the First World!"

Koosje's departure is the beginning of the end of our home. She and Carolyn have become my family, and I miss Koosje like a sister. I'm terribly glad Carolyn has decided to stay.

Later that month, Carolyn and I go to a quiz night at the British Club. Our team does quite well, and I can't help beaming often and inappropriately at Tim, who is also here, standing across the room at the bar. His wife and their visiting daughter, a vivacious seventeen-year-old, are here too, but in another part of the room. It takes me a while to figure out who they are. I don't speak to Tim, but we smile at each other an awful lot.

"Incorrigible flirt," Carolyn says accusingly before heading over to Tim to introduce herself. "He's *my* ambassador, after all," she says. They talk for ages, and when she returns to our table, she looks at me significantly and says, "I see what you mean."

☪

LOCUST SEASON, WEDDING SEASON, and pomegranate season arrive simultaneously; in August, Sana'a is taken over by bugs, brides, and wheelbarrows spilling over with round yellow-green fruit. On my way to work, I see small boys chase fist-sized locusts, catching them with dusty palms and stuffing them into plastic bottles. They carry these bottles home, where the bugs are roasted and eaten.

The locust infestation inspires my hands-down favorite editorial. One Thursday, we finish the paper by four P.M., and I am closing down my computer when Ali pops his head back into my office, looking alarmed.

"Editorial?"

I look up at him. "Oh *no.* I totally forgot!"

"So did I."

I switch my computer back on and open the folder of front-page stories for this issue. Nothing inspires me. Then Jabr's piece catches my eye. He's done a marvelous locust story, including the fact that people in the streets are rejoicing in the bounty and eating them. It sports one of my all-time favorite headlines: LOCUSTS INVADE SANA'A, BECOME SNACKFOOD.

"Ali," I say, "can you get on the Internet and find me locust recipes?"

"Yeah," he says, laughing. "Let's do that."

A few minutes later, he sends me a list of recipes from the UN Food and Agriculture Organization's website, and I write a brief editorial on why we should eat the critters.

HOW TO MAKE THE MOST OF YOUR LOCAL LOCUSTS

Swarms of hopping, soaring locusts have begun encroaching on our territory. These pests are a plague to farmers whose crops they threaten. But in the cities, many of us are rejoicing at the ubiquity of one of our favorite snacks. And why not treat yourself to a handful of locusts? They're cheap, tasty, and readily available. Besides, you'll be doing your bit to help protect crops from their deadly munching. So, with a little bit of help from the Food and Agriculture Organization of the United Nations, here are a few recipes to help you make your locusts even tastier. After all, given that these critters are so intent on eating our food supply, it's only right that we bite back.

Try these at home:

Tinjiya (Tswana recipe)
Remove the wings and hind legs of the locusts, and boil in a little water until soft. Add salt, if desired, and a little fat and fry until brown. Serve with cooked, dried mealies (corn).

Sikonyane (Swazi recipe)
Prepare embers and roast the whole locust on the embers. Remove head, wings, and legs . . . and the rest set on the coals to roast. The roasted locusts are ground on a grinding stone to a fine powder. This powder can be kept for long periods of time and can be taken along on a journey. Dried locusts are also prepared for the winter months. The legs, when dried, are especially relished for their pleasant taste.

Cambodia
Take several dozen locust adults, preferably females, slit the abdomen lengthwise, and stuff a peanut inside. Then lightly grill the locusts in a wok or hot frying pan, adding a little oil and salt to taste. Be careful not to overcook or burn them.

Barbecue (grilled)

Prepare the embers or charcoal. Place about one dozen locusts on a skewer, stabbing each through the centre of the abdomen. If you only want to eat the abdomen, then you may want to take off the legs or wings either before or after cooking. Several skewers of locusts may be required for each person. Place the skewers above the hot embers and grill while turning continuously to avoid burning the locusts until they become golden brown.

Locust Bisque, serves 6

1 gallon locust shells
2 onions, roughly chopped
1 clove garlic, chopped
1 celery stalk
2 carrots
1/2 tsp. powdered mace
1 cup whipping cream
salt and pepper to taste

Put all ingredients except whipping cream into a large stew pot, and fill with water. Bring to the boil, reduce heat, and simmer for three hours. Process in blender or food processor in batches, and strain before returning to clean pot. Add whipping cream, being sure not to allow it to boil. Serve with animal crackers.

My dad writes from Vermont immediately, asking for a recipe for beetles, too. "They're ruining Mom's garden. She wants to bite back."

☾

WHILE I HAVE MINIMAL CURIOSITY about the taste of locust, I've become obsessed with pomegranates (*romaan* in Arabic). I eat at least three a day. Unlike the small, red pomegranates for sale in New York, Yemeni pomegranates are yellowish green and the size of grapefruits. But their seeds are crimson and swollen with sweet, addictive nectar. An inconvenient fruit, they require such intense effort to peel and open that it is impossible to do anything else while dismembering one. I've learned how to run a knife along the rind, weakening it just enough so that I can pry it apart with my fingers, sending ruby-red seeds spraying across my desk. Rarely do I bother anymore to pick the seeds out one by one. Rather, I break the fruit apart and gnaw on the berries inside, red juice dripping down my chin and often onto my shirt. Pomegranates are directly responsible for the slow start to my days my last few months, and for the dire condition of my blouses.

The proliferation of brides also takes a toll on work. Most of my reporters are either preparing for weddings or attending them. Everyone is rushing to get hitched before Ramadan. From nearly every house emanate the yodels of Yemeni women celebrating a bride to be. Several parties precede the actual wedding, parties during which brides are painted with whirly designs, decked in traditional gowns, and feted with sweet tea and biscuits.

Wedding sites in the Old City are marked by strands of bright white bulbs strung along streets and across alleyways. Under the bright glare of these lights, men dance outside to deafening music blared through staticky loudspeakers and climb into a nearby tent to chew *qat*. I grow to dread seeing these lights near my house, as weddings often go on until the following morning, meaning no one nearby can sleep.

Women gather indoors to celebrate, away from the male eyes. It never ceases to feel odd that the bride and groom rarely meet. It's a stark example of the gender segregation that is so integral to Yemeni life. What's the fun of a wedding if you cannot dance with your loved one? What is the fun of a wedding devoid of flirting and champagne? Yet for Yemeni women, it is enough to look pretty for each other, to move their hips on the dance floor with a freedom they don't have in front of men, to drink tea and gossip.

In mid-August, Noor invites me to a pre-wedding party for her sister Rasha. It's a *naqsh* party, at which a local artist paints the assembled women with intricate botanical-looking designs in an inky black dye. These designs, a traditional wedding adornment, stain the skin for weeks. Radia, Jelena of *Arabia Felix*, and I travel together from work to Noor's home, a large modern house in a wealthy part of town. We are seated in the front *mafraj*, where women are unwrapping themselves, drinking tea, and passing plates of date and sesame cookies. Several girls and women dash in and out of other rooms, changing clothing, fixing their hair and makeup, and helping the hidden bride. I hardly recognize Najma when she emerges from another room, after shedding her *abaya* and *hijab*. She is wearing a form-fitting leopard-print top, revealing more than a hint of cleavage, with tight jeans. Her thick hair is tied in a ponytail. I've seen her face many times before, but never her hair. She laughs to see me stare at her and takes my hand to lead me outside, to show me a tent filled with fancy candelabras for the wedding.

Noor rushes around attending to her sister and other family members, also in jeans and a top, her hair pulled back.

A long-haired woman sitting near me asks me what other Yemeni weddings I've attended, and I tell her that I went to the wedding of one of Noor's cousins.

"That was my wedding!" I look closely at her. I would not have recognized her. Like all Yemeni brides, she had been buried in layers of cosmetics, her hair tightly curled and sprayed into rigid obedience. Now she wears a bit of eyeliner but little else on her face, and her hair hangs straight down to her hips.

"Wow!" I say. Then, to cover my surprise, "That was a beautiful wedding."

"Thanks!"

"So how is it going, married life?"

"*Al-hamdulillah.*" She laughs.

What I really want to ask is, How's the sex? But I'm fearful of offending. "I thought you were going to China."

"We *were* going to China, but I have two more years of school so we decided to stay here." I am pleased to hear that she has a husband willing to make concessions for his wife's career. It is the rare Yemeni woman who is granted all the rights we take for granted in the West: the right to work, to choose a career, to decide whether to bear children, to get on a plane by herself, to direct her own life.

Someone hands me a cup of tea, and I am introduced to a dozen more women, who all kiss my cheek several times before moving to kiss the rest of the room.

At last, the *nagsh* is ready, and Jelena and I, as the guests of honor, are shepherded into an adjoining *mafraj* to be painted. Jelena goes first. She wants to get her whole body decorated with the black ink (which I much prefer to the reddish henna that some Yemenis use instead) but settles for both arms and her chest. I sit next to her and watch as an elderly woman still wrapped in her *abaya* paints on the ink with a small brush in short, rapid strokes. She's remarkably fast, and yet each shape looks perfectly formed.

Then it's my turn. "I just want a little," I say, indicating my wrists. The woman protests. Too small a canvas! Why don't I want my whole arms done? But it's my first time, and I am not sure I like the way it looks all the way up the arm. Fading *nagsh* or henna can resemble a skin disease.

Najma and Radia perch on cushions near me, watching closely, as the woman paints bracelets of flowers and leaves around each of my wrists, the designs extending down the tops of my hands to my knuckles. I won't let her do my fingers. "I wash my hands so much!" I say.

"So don't wash them for a few days!" says Najma.

"Impossible!" Some Western habits are just too hard to break.

The ink is cool on my skin, and as it dries, the tattoos tighten around my wrists like ethereal handcuffs.

But the process isn't over when the ink is dry, we discover. We still must be basted with Vaseline and patted with flour before getting wrapped in plastic, to preserve the design. I watch Noor work on Jelena, smearing Vaseline over her *nagsh*. When Jelena is completely greased up, Noor takes out a large blue cloth and drapes it across her lap and the floor. From a pan next to her, she scoops out handfuls of white powder, which she pats onto the Vaseline, sending clouds of it into the air. A woman brings a roll of plastic wrap decorated with green flowers from the back room, and each of Jelena's arms is encased in plastic, another sheet wrapped across her chest. I am very glad that I have just asked to have my wrists done.

Noor works on me next, greasing and powdering each of my wrists and hands before sticking my hands into plastic bags and tying the ends tightly around my wrists.

"How long do I have to keep these on?" Losing the use of my hands and fingers makes me mildly panicky.

"At least an hour."

"An hour!"

"But you really should leave them on all night."

"All night!" I am invited to a dinner party later, and I don't think I'll want to attend with plastic mittens dangling from my arms.

When at last we're finished, we wait for Rasha, the bride, to emerge from one of the back rooms, where she has been suffering body waxing in preparation for her wedding. Yemeni women take everything off—leg hair, arm hair, pubic hair, *everything.*

It's been hours since we got here, and we're growing restless. The girls and women around me began to whoop and clap, prompting Rasha finally to begin her slow progress down the hall to a chair that has been set up for her. She wears a dress of gold lace and a gold tulle veil over a black ski-mask kind of hat. Once again I regret not being able to take a photo. Her eyes are very serious.

I stand around with the other women a while, clapping and attempting the distinctive Yemeni ululation, before pulling on my shirt over my plastic-bag-wrapped arms. I can only ululate for so long before tedium overwhelms me. Najma and I share a taxi. I ask about her family's upcoming trip to Saudi Arabia, and she says that they hope to do *umrah* to Mecca. "I love this place," she says passionately. "I cannot tell you how much I love it." I ask about what she will be doing there, if it will be mostly praying. She said yes, mostly praying. "I pray to my God for things," she says.

"Like?"

"I pray to him for a good husband," she says, laughing.

TWENTY-THREE

she's leaving home

Zuhra hasn't even left yet, and already I miss her. She is suddenly very busy, with all kinds of visa interviews, doctors' checkups, and shopping for her trip to America. We still don't know when she will leave, and I am in a panic at the thought of going even a couple of weeks without her. Whenever I am short of stories on a closing day, Zuhra says, "I will find you one." And she does. Luke said that on the rare occasions I am gone from the office, she takes over control of the copy flow, running around with a chart of stories and bossing people.

Now Zuhra is preoccupied with her own problems. Once the thrill of receiving the fellowship has dimmed, she starts to worry about her family. She will not be able to travel to the United States unless she gets permission from her male relatives. It never occurred to me that she might not be able to go. I feel sick at the thought of anyone keeping her from this opportunity.

Strategically, she first tells Fahmi, her eldest brother who lives in New York. Fahmi is the most westernized and open-minded of her siblings and is utterly devoted to his little sister. He is thrilled and promises to speak on her behalf to her other brother. Aziz, who still lives with Zuhra in Yemen, is initially resistant.

"I am afraid that if they say no I will lose a chance," Zuhra frets, rocking

back and forth on her sneakers. "If I don't go, I might not be given a fellowship again."

Zuhra had thought she'd be sent to Washington, DC, because the administration of the fellowship program is there. Her family fretted about
the safety of the city, but Fahmi worked hard to reassure them. "It's safer
than Yemen," he told them. Then she found she was being sent to Mississippi, and no one knew quite what to think about that.

At last, Aziz relents. "He was only afraid that I would be alone in the
U.S.," Zuhra says. "But Fahmi convinced him after long discussion that I
would be okay and that he would take responsibility for me."

Amazingly, Zuhra, who has never been on an airplane or spent a night
away from home, has no trepidation about the journey. "Not for one single moment," she says. "I am only happy. It is an opportunity, it's great,
and it's not fair to feel nervous."

Privately, she is sad to be traveling away from Kamil al-Samawi, the
human rights lawyer. While it will be some time before I find out, Zuhra
has been falling in love all year. She first realized she was in love with
Kamil last autumn, after fainting while covering a story in a Sana'ani hospital. The chemical smell of the place had made her ill. When she regained
consciousness, Kamil was the first person she rang. He had been so supportive of her, such a close friend, that he was the one she trusted to come
and get her. It was Ramadan, but Kamil gave her juice and food to revive
her and took her safely home. That was before they were in love, she said.
"After this incident I realized I was in huge love with him. I see him and
thought oh my god I want to spend my life with this person. It was deep
down. Lots of changes that happened to me were because of Kamil. He
made me feel confident, he made me love myself, he made me feel I am
beautiful. We knew we were in love after this incident. But it took time.
It's not acceptable to be in love here."

Which is why she stayed silent.

Kamil supports her trip to the United States. They have been discussing
marriage, and she wants to start a life with him, but he promises to wait.
I'll just be gone a little while, she tells herself. I'll be back soon.

☾

In mid-August, I start to panic about my own future. Two weeks left, and I have made no preparations for my departure, other than to try to sort out visas, which as usual has gone wrong. The immigration authorities didn't renew my residency, which will be two months expired by the time I leave. And the exit visa they gave me runs out before I even get to the airport!

I ambush Faris the next day to ask him for help. I also tell him that Jamal Hindi, the owner of al-Mankal restaurant, has offered to host my farewell dinner with my staff. What day would be good for him? He doesn't know. He'll get back to me. He doesn't seem particularly broken up about my imminent departure. Everyone in the office has asked me to extend my contract—everyone, that is, except Faris. I remember sadly the huge banquet he threw for me at the end of my first trip to Yemen and wonder what went wrong. Then he had given speeches lauding me and handed me a pile of Yemeni gifts. Now he can't seem to get me out the door fast enough. He can't bring himself to look at me but fiddles with his pen and stares at his computer.

"Faris? Is everything okay?"

"You've made me a lot of enemies," he says. "Everyone in the government hates the paper. The minister of the interior will not speak to me to this day."

I look at him levelly. "It is not the job of a newspaper to *befriend* the *government*," I say. "We should be the *watchdog* of the government and make sure that it is fulfilling its promises. And frankly, I am not at all convinced that it generally is."

He nods, but not in agreement.

"And everyone I have spoken to, every diplomat, every expat, and even Yemeni officials, has told me how far the paper has come in the past year." I am desperate for just one tiny shred of recognition.

"Yemeni officials? I doubt it."

"Even your friend Jalal." Jalal is now deputy minister of finance.

"Oh, really? What article did Jalal like?"

"Faris, I can't remember a specific article. Look, are you saying you are unhappy with my work?"

"No. I am just telling you the whole picture. Didn't I tell you lately how

I heard everyone is begging you to come back and offering you their houses?"

I stare at Faris. He looks away, at the wall, the desk, anywhere but at me. I linger, hoping vainly for a few kind words about the changes I have wrought in his paper, but Faris is obviously done with me. I get up to leave. If I were to wait around for Faris to pat me on the back, I'd be waiting an awfully long time.

☪

MY STAFF HELP make up for Faris's apathy. Hadi gets more despairing every day. "I will suffer when you leave," he says, likely remembering the pre-Jennifer closes that went on until dawn.

Even my new business reporter Zaki is inconsolable. One day, I am working on the business page with him for one of my last issues, chastising him for forgetting to use quotation marks and to attribute important contentions. He also uses too much incomprehensible business jargon.

"You have to understand that politicians and government officials speak in *bullshit*," I tell him. "It is your job to translate that bullshit into something anyone can understand."

Zaki laughs but says that his story is meant for businesspeople, who are sure to understand this technical jargon. It's his customary argument.

"Any story in a newspaper is a story for all people," I say. "Business can be fascinating even to people not interested in business if you write it engagingly. The more complicated the story, the more important it is that you make it clear to your readers."

Zaki looks at me, his eyes solemn behind his glasses.

"It will be bad when you go," he says. "I learn so much working with you. No one else will help me like this. You have improved me so much."

These conversations always make me feel like a traitor.

"But why do you have to leave?" my reporters ask me. "What are you going to do now?"

I have no answer for them. Perhaps I will find another country that needs a journalist trainer. I've noticed that an NGO in Sierra Leone is hiring, and I've sent in my résumé. How scary could Sierra Leone be after

Yemen? The idea of being a journalist trainer to the world at large, moving from one chaotic country to the next, is rather exciting, too.

My only other prospect is the book proposal I've been putting together about my time here, which I am hoping to show a friend with a brilliant agent in New York. But I can't pin my future to a pipe dream like a book contract.

Faris has finally agreed to give my reporters press IDs, which I've been requesting for eleven months, but this leads to new problems, because now everyone wants one. Hadi walks into my office one day and demands one.

"Why? You aren't a reporter. They are for reporters, so they can get into government events." Hadi's duties don't take him out of the office.

"I *want* one," he says like a child demanding candy.

"But why do you *need* one?" I cannot imagine what use it could be to a designer.

"I just *want one,*" he says, pouting.

"Hadi, I am prepared to give you one if you can tell me why you need it."

"I want one!" he says, stomping out of my office. "*I want one!*"

I sigh. Two more weeks, I think. Just two more weeks.

☾

I INVITE TIM TORLOT to my first farewell party. It's almost all staff, but several of my friends are coming, and I suppose I am looking for an excuse to see him again. He responds immediately. He's terribly sorry, but he has a dinner engagement that night he cannot escape. But he adds how sorry he is that I am leaving and promises to call me before I depart.

I sit at my computer rereading this and finally respond that there's a second farewell for me later that week, at my friend Phil's house. Could he come to that one? He writes immediately that he could! He also says that he will see me even sooner, at his deputy's house the following night, as we're both invited to yet another (nonfarewell) party there.

The next evening, I am nervous as I dress in the black-and-gray sundress I've been wearing to parties for about seven years now. It's a bit shabby around the edges, but I trust the lights will be dim.

At the party, I talk with a friend for a while on the porch, where Tim eventually joins us. My friend fades away and then there is just Tim, standing close to me, his pupils dilating into saucers. I have no idea what we talk about. The newspaper, probably. The vacation to Jordan, Beirut, and Ethiopia I am planning before returning to New York. Things he hopes to do in Yemen. But really, I have no idea. Everything that happens between us has nothing to do with words. I know his wife is somewhere in the room, but I am never introduced to her. I wonder why. Not that it matters. Tim and I are only talking, and what could possibly ever really happen between us? My love for him has no expectations; it just *is*. But why, why must there be a wife?

It's been a funny week. People keep coming into my office just to sit with me. Even Qasim came in the other day as I was closing an issue and just sat watching me.

"What can I do for you?" I inquired, figuring he had come in to try to pressure me into writing about an advertiser.

"Nothing," he said mournfully. "It's just that you are *leaving*." And he continued to sit there, gazing at me.

Luke visits several times, coming downstairs from his new job at *Arabia Felix*. It reminds me how much I miss him. He makes me laugh. As does Ali, who also comes in between editing stories. In my final days, I manage to talk Ali into staying at the *Observer* beyond my departure. He had planned to quit when I did. "I couldn't survive this place without you," he says. But I beg and plead. I tell him I can't bear to see the paper descend immediately into chaos. I tell him that the women need him and that Zaid can't edit. At last, in exchange for a hefty raise, he agrees to step into my shoes. Both Yemeni and a native English speaker, he is the ideal person to be editing the paper. I know he won't last long, but at least I feel better about the paper's next few months. "Write me," I say. "Let me know if you need help with anything."

Ali laughs. "You'll get more e-mails than you could possibly want."

☾

AFTER LUNCH ONE AFTERNOON, Zaid, Ali, and I are chatting in the newsroom about why tattoos will keep you out of heaven, as well as the Arabic words for bellybutton *(seera)* and monkey *(kird)*, when Zaid reaches into his black briefcase.

"I have something for you," he says. He presses play on a small tape recorder, and I hear a familiar voice.

"I have seen quite a lot of progress over the few weeks I have been here . . . but I have a few recommendations as you go forward."

It is the speech I gave to my class a year ago, at the end of my first trip to Yemen. It's the voice of someone with answers, someone who knows a few simple steps to turn the paper around. Someone almost unrecognizable.

". . . and I recommend that you create the position of assigning editor, or editor in chief . . ." It is the voice of someone sentencing herself to a very interesting life.

The day of my first farewell dinner, I look around my office. The windows are tilted open, letting in cats and wind and fluttering curtains. I run my fingers across the dusty gray desk that used to be al-Asaadi's. There is nothing particularly attractive or memorable in this room. Yet I will remember all of it. My wheeled blue chair. The dry-erase board across from my desk. The battered filing cabinet where I lock my wireless keyboard each night. I will remember the sound of men arguing in the hallway. The distant sound of prayer. The not-so distant sound of prayer. Radia and Enass's voices, high-pitched with excitement. Their serious brown eyes peering over their *niqabs.* The Doctor screaming in the hallway.

I sit with myself. I can't do this for long without crying, so I close my computer and pick up my gym bag, and lock my door behind me.

☪

DESPITE MY NERVES, the farewell dinner is lovely. Some fifty people come to bid me good-bye, including Bashir and Hassan, who arrive in suits; Ibrahim; and most of my women. Only Najma and Zuhra are forbidden by their families to come, even though I have arranged for the women to be seated in a separate room. Carolyn comes, as do my friend and fixer Sami, an American filmmaker, Shaima, Phil Boyle, and others. It's a full table.

Most of my reporters come bearing gifts, wrapped in silver paper covered with hearts or red roses. Shaima and her friend Huda give me jewelry. Jabr and Zaki each bring me a spray of flowers tucked into crepe paper. Zaid gives me a pretty bracelet with a handwritten note.

I'll always remember you, no matter what. I wrote this small poem for you last night. It was 3 o'clock in the morning and I hope you'll like it. I wish you all the best and don't worry about the paper.

I will try to hide my tears
I will try to give it a laugh
You might leave Yemen,
But you'll never move a bit
Out of our hearts and minds.

Zaid al-Alaya-a
your successor
Tue 3 A.M.

Al-Asaadi fulfills a promise he made ten months ago and brings me the Yemeni raisins he claims are the best in the country. This perhaps touches me the most.

Faris is late. When he does finally come, he sits in the middle of the table, ignoring me. Despite the odds, I've been hoping that finally Faris will offer me a tidbit of recognition, throw me some crumb of acknowledgment that will somehow validate my year here.

I wait in vain, as I circle the table trying to talk with everyone individually and run in and out of the room where my women are dining without their *niqabs*. Everyone waits. My staff also expects Faris to say something. At least a few parting words. At least good-bye and good luck. That would give me an opening to say a few words of thanks to my staff.

But he does nothing. He sits there, complaining that the main course is too slow to arrive, and then leaves before the end of the night with a hasty "Thanks for the invitation" before practically running for the door.

I stand there in the emptying restaurant, feeling stunned. Just a few of us are left, as some of my male reporters have gone back to work, the women have curfews, and the expats have scampered to have drinks at someone's house. They've invited me, but I've never felt less like a drink.

Shaima and her friend Huda come around the table to comfort me. "He can't even manage a *thank you?*" I say. I am so hurt that I can hardly speak properly. Shaima tries to console me, telling me that everyone else appreciates me, and isn't it my reporters who matter? She is right, of course. My reporters are why I came, and they are why I stayed.

"It isn't Faris's nature to be thankful," says one of the women. "You can't take it personally."

I look at them, so kind and concerned. I try to inhale their patience. They smell of frankincense. They smell of Yemen.

"Thank you," I say, squeezing their hands. "I'm sorry to be so emotional."

They go, and I head home for almost the last time, alone.

☾

THE SECOND FAREWELL PARTY is for people who drink. Phil Boyle from the British Embassy has generously consented to host and does a spectacular job of it. He places little bowls of nuts and chips on the tables and lines up bottles of wine in front of his liquor cabinet. "My farewell gift to you," he says. He's also filled an entire refrigerator with beer and sodas.

I wear a clingy fairy dress in sparkly green, in complete contrast to the modesty I'd demonstrated the night before. My hair is down, and I'm wearing lipstick the color of a stop sign. I'm heading back to the Western world, after all, so I must start to adjust!

Carolyn is the first to arrive, followed shortly by Tim, who comes without his wife. I perch on the arm of the sofa next to him, and we talk about my imminent trip to Jordan, as I have just gotten off the phone with a Jordanian friend who is helping me with arrangements. Tim asks me about my staff, but the second I start to talk about leaving, I am in tears.

"Sorry—we'll change the subject," he says kindly.

My oil worker friends arrive next, followed by a passel of other friends and neighbors, bearing food and drink. Just as the bulk of people begins arriving, Tim tells me he must leave early. He's heading to Aden the next day. I'm sad to see him go. "But I'll be back," I tell him as I walk him to the door, where he kisses me chastely on each cheek. "I know I'll be back."

What happens next depends on whom you believe. I swear that Tim kisses me full on the lips before turning to go, but he is equally convinced that I am the one to kiss him.

"I was stunned all the way back to the house," he says later. "I hadn't thought you liked me like that. Like I liked you."

I find it hard to focus on anything after that. Around eleven thirty, Phil taps on his glass to get everyone's attention and gives a little speech, saying all the things I wished Faris had said, albeit with a wry British spin. He talks about how I have revolutionized the newspaper, turning it from a paper that was "a total rag" into one that is "just a little bit of a rag." But perhaps the nicest thing he says is that I probably have "more Yemeni friends than anyone else here." It's so easy for expats to operate in their own social bubble, but I have striven to integrate myself with Yemenis. They *are* the reason I am here. Phil's speech makes me feel, for a warm minute, that I've gotten something right.

☪

THE NEXT DAY, Thursday, August 30, is my last day of work. Tears stay close to the surface all day; I can barely hold myself together. Noor rings me in the morning to ensure that I am coming in and can edit her interview. I had stayed late at work the night before to edit Najma's last piece before the party. She had sent me an emotional e-mail. "Please Jennifer, edit this yourself and make it a beautiful shape for me, don't give it to anyone else to edit." I honor their last wishes.

As a parting gift, I write recommendations for every single one of my staff members. I rather enjoy doing this, not just to help them, but to remind myself of just how far each one of them has come this year. Farouq now writes in English. Najma, who was unable to keep personal emotions out of her health stories and who had no idea how to incorporate studies into a real story, now is a capable health and science writer. Radia, who was a receptionist when I came, is now a novice reporter.

Noor and Najma come into my office together at the end of the day to say good-bye and to present me with a Yemeni purse woven from goat hair. None of us can speak for the tears. They just hug me, look at me with damp eyes, and hurry away. Even Jabr has to blink back tears as he shakes

my hand good-bye. I am glad Zuhra has already left. I could not have han-
dled all of the good-byes at once.

☪

ZUHRA CAME INTO MY OFFICE the day before and stood uncommonly still
in front of my desk. "I am going to say good-bye now."

I stopped slicing the skin of the pomegranate on my desk and put down
the knife on an old copy of the paper. Pomegranates were taking over my
life. I couldn't go a day without them. I thought about Persephone and
how eating six pomegranate seeds in Hades consigned her to spending six
months of each year in hell. One month per seed. If I were to spend a
month in Yemen for every seed that I have eaten, I could never leave.

I was not ready to say good-bye to Zuhra. Someone is *there* every day of
your life for a year, and then she isn't. There is no transition. Wait, I
wanted to say. I need time.

She came around the side of my desk and I hugged her tightly, my little
bundle of rayon, like holding a Christmas present with all of its wrapping
still on it.

I couldn't say anything. There were no significant last words, no best
wishes, no declarations of love. I could not talk. She didn't say anything
either. We just looked at each other.

Then she was gone.

Feeling numb and slightly queasy, I sat back down at my desk. I picked
up the pomegranate.

When I emerged from my office to throw away the peels, Zuhra was
still standing by Enass's desk, gathering a cluster of plastic bags full of her
possessions.

"If you stay any longer I am putting you back to work," I said.

Zuhra smiled. Or I imagined she did, from the way her eyes glinted for
a moment. "How many times have I said good-bye?" she asked Enass. And
she walked by me to the door. "I'll see you in New York."

I nod.

She hurried across the courtyard, and I turned to follow her. I couldn't
help it. She didn't see me. I walked out of the office to stand at the top of
our three marble steps. She walked quickly, a bustle of black skirts and

plastic bags, with her fringed, brown leather purse banging against her side. I watched her until she stepped out of the gate and was gone. She did not look back.

☪

I WAS AT MY COMPUTER half an hour later when my phone beeped. It was a text from Zuhra, her last before getting on the plane: "I LOVE U."

TWENTY-FOUR
reasons to return

During my worst months in Yemen, when I fantasized only about sleep, broccoli, two-day weekends, and having access to cheese, a friend asked me how my love life was going. "You must be joking," I said. "Even if I had time, everyone in Yemen is married, Muslim, or twenty-three. But knowing my luck, I'll fall in love with someone my very last day and get stuck here."

This, it turns out, is exactly what happens.

During my three-week trip in September to see friends in Jordan, Lebanon, and Ethiopia—my victory lap of the region to celebrate surviving the past year—I find myself horribly homesick, for Yemen. I miss my gingerbread house. I miss the Old City at dusk. I miss my reporters. I miss Carolyn and Koosje. I find myself eager to get back to Sana'a, although I will have only three days there before flying to New York.

I'm obviously not ready to leave. But there's no question of changing my ticket. I now have a meeting with an agent in New York; I have a free apartment and a large orange cat waiting for me to take care of them; and my family would kill me if I didn't return. But I've started to think of the upcoming months in New York as a visit rather than a permanent move.

Going back to *The Week* does not even cross my mind. To return to that office would be to resume being someone I no longer am. What new challenges would there be for me there? The things I want to learn can't be learned doing a comfy job in a comfy First World country. I need new cultures, new people, new languages. I couldn't go back to a predictable work life. Having survived the hardest year of my life, I am suffused with a new sense of confidence. Got a difficult job in a chaotic country? *Bring it on.*

The Sierra Leone job looks good, if they decide to offer it to me. I haven't spent much time in Africa, but I *know* I could handle the work. In fact, despite the myriad challenges of the *Observer,* the idea of training a whole new staff at a whole new newspaper is thrilling. It's particularly alluring because I wouldn't also have to be editor in chief. I could focus *just* on training. It sounds positively *cushy.*

I decide to give up my Manhattan apartment, which I've been subletting. While I have no idea where I'll end up living, I know I am not done traveling. If I sell my book proposal, I'll have to come back to Yemen anyway, at least for a few months to do research. How much fun it would be to live in Yemen while not running a newspaper! I'd get to travel more around the country, spend time with friends, and focus on Arabic. Most important, I'd have time to *write.*

Of course, I don't have to decide just yet. These three weeks I spend traveling are supposed to be pure pleasure, pure respite, before plunging back into New York life and the decisions that await me there. But it's tough to keep my brain from dwelling on these thoughts. It keeps trying to figure out how I could stay in Yemen a bit longer and how I could earn enough money to support myself while writing a book.

And then there's Tim.

☾

DURING MY TRIP, I strike up an unexpected correspondence with Tim. I first write to him from a dingy little Internet café in Amman, to thank him for attending my party and to tell him a bit about my visit to the spectacular ruins of Petra, where I spent three happy days climbing around ancient temples with *bedouins.* He writes back immediately and at length. Thus begins near-daily communication that continues the entire time I am gone.

Every night before I go to sleep in another strange bed, I write him about my day, and just about every night, I dream about him. Vivid, passionate dreams. I don't understand it. I've never dreamed so much and so intensely about someone I hardly know. I dream that I go to his house. I have a piece of paper with notes on it, which I show him. We talk about these notes with great excitement. He is happy to see me. Then his wife comes in. At first she is kind and then sees right through me and realizes that I am in love with her husband. She looks at the notes I have written and she knows. Her face darkens. She begins to yell at me and at Tim, saying cruel things.

I expect Tim to rush to reassure her, but he does not. She leaves, and he turns to me. "I don't love her," he says. "It's terrible to say. But I don't. This won't last much longer, and I adore you. And we can be together. We could marry."

When I wake, my head whirls. It has never occurred to me he could actually leave his wife. I reassess how much I am enamored. Do I really want him on a permanent, long-term basis? I *must* love him that much if he is to sacrifice his marriage for me. To my surprise, I feel simply joyful, without a shred of doubt, at the prospect of a life with him. Of course, in *real* life, this is not exactly on offer.

By the time I arrive in Addis Ababa for Ethiopian New Year, I can hardly think of anything but Tim. What is happening to me? All this from a flurry of e-mails from a married man?

☾

I RETURN TO SANA'A on September 16, 2007, the day before Tim's birthday. As my plane descends into Arabia, the sight of the cookie-colored cubes below brings tears to my eyes. I'm practically soggy with love for this city, this country, these familiar streets. If I didn't have a lunch scheduled with a literary agent in New York, I don't think I would leave at all. As the plane taxies down the runway and the Yemenis begin leaping out of their seats, I switch on my phone. Tim has texted to welcome me home. Sami is waiting for me at the airport and takes me to my beloved house, where I want to hug everything. Carolyn has left for China, but there is too much to do to wallow in lonesomeness. I have to pack up a year of my life in less than three days. The first two I spend stuffing all I can into two suitcases, giving away the rest, and seeing friends.

The third and last day I have saved for Tim, who has asked if I have time to see him before I go.

That morning, I am awakened by a telephone call from one of his body-guards. They'd like to come check out the house, if that would be conven-ient. Still groggy, I agree. Tim texts me, apologizing for the invasion. An hour later, a very polite Yemeni in a crisp white shirt comes to my gate and asks if this is where the ambassador will be coming later. I say it is indeed and promise to keep him safe from all harm.

By the time Tim rings to say the ambassadorial procession is under way from the embassy, I am completely organized. My two overloaded suit-cases sit waiting for their trip to the airport; my house is spotless; Sami has taken the last of my DVDs and books; and my refrigerator is empty except for a bottle of champagne, a Marlborough white wine, and a yo-gurt. Two pomegranates sit in my kitchen waiting for breakfast tomorrow. In my *mafraj,* I light the candles and sit reading until Tim rings me from the gate.

He slips in, smiling like a schoolboy playing hooky, and kisses me on the lips, right in front of the two Yemeni bodyguards who follow him into my courtyard. But the kiss is chaste enough simply to be a friendly greet-ing; I shouldn't read anything into it. Flustered, I start to lock the gate, but Tim reminds me that with two armed men parked at my door, this is hardly necessary. I lead him upstairs, heart hammering, all the way to the roof, shedding my *abaya* on the way. I want to show him my city. Most of the dirt from the roof has been carried away, and the ceiling has finally been repaired, albeit not with the traditional materials UNESCO guide-lines require. Tim has to duck through the low doorway to the roof, and then we are standing under the Sana'ani stars. Leaning our elbows on the dusty parapet around my roof, we admire the glowing *qamaria* and watch children playing under clotheslines before turning to look at each other. A crescent moon plays in his eyes, and I can't stop smiling. In a striped shirt and jeans, Tim looks all of seventeen and profoundly unambassadorial. This is one of the perfect moments of my life. We stand there until a little girl on a nearby roof spots us and begins waving and calling. Having promised to protect him, I hurry Tim back down to the *mafraj* and fetch the bottle of champagne.

Never has my *mafraj* witnessed such an enchanted evening. We talk for so long—about his work in Iraq, Chad, and the Central African Republic, about my uncertain future—that I almost worry that I have misread him. But when we finish the champagne and he opens the wine, I know. We've barely tasted it when he slides a hand under my hair to cup my neck, says, "We probably shouldn't do this," and kisses me.

Something wild takes hold of me, something that immediately eclipses every passion I've ever felt. It is a vertiginous, irresistible fall. How could I have believed I loved anyone before this? How could I ever have been with anyone else when there is a Tim in this world? I can feel, vividly *feel*, my heart leave my body. I'd think this mere romantic fantasy if not for everything that follows.

As we tilt back into the cushions, he stops for a minute and takes my head between his hands.

"Promise me," he says. "Promise me it won't be the last time."

"Promise *me*."

"I promise you. I promise."

"Then I promise," I whisper.

Even after we've made love, he doesn't loosen his grip but wraps me closer in his arms. We stay like that until long past a reasonable hour.

"Why are you leaving?" he says in a pained voice, his arms bruising my rib cage. "Don't go."

"It's a good thing I'm leaving." I'm trying to talk myself into it. "If I stayed, I would be in terrible danger of falling in love with you."

"It's too late," he says, his fingers digging into my shoulders. "Don't you know it's too late?"

☪

I DO LEAVE YEMEN, but not Tim. During my three months in New York, we write every day, unfolding our entire lives. Everything that happened between us in Sana'a happened so fast that I had hardly any time to think about the repercussions. But now, I worry. I worry about feeling so strongly about a man who isn't mine. I worry that he is toying with me and will never leave his wife. I worry about the pain it will cause his family if he does leave his wife.

I share these worries with him. I also tell him about every past lover, every mistake I have ever made. If anything is going to scare him away, I want to know now. But Tim doesn't scare easily. Every revelation only brings a new declaration of love from him. Every time I hit send, I worry I will never hear from him again, but every time I check my in-box, he is there.

Tim tells me about his large, close-knit family; his years living in New Zealand, Chile, Austria, and France; that his daughter has been his greatest joy. He tells me about the women he has loved. And finally, he tells me about his wife. There have been problems for years. They don't share the same values or enjoy doing the same things. He would not have embarked on this relationship had he been happy in his marriage.

Someone once told me that women leave a bad marriage because it is a bad marriage, but that men never leave until they find someone else. Perhaps that's true. I think Tim felt that he couldn't leave unless he had a really good reason—his unhappiness alone wasn't enough to justify hurting someone else.

When I am out with friends in New York, I find myself rushing home as if Tim were actually there waiting for me and writing to him for hours. It scares me how completely I love him. I have made it clear that I cannot continue this, I cannot keep falling in love with him, if there is no chance of a future together. This is what makes him different from other men I've loved—I actually *want* a future with him. I ask to have him all to myself.

"I need to see you," he says. "We need to see each other, to be sure." We worry aloud that maybe we're creating a fantasy relationship and that reality will disillusion us. Tim warns me that he snores. I warn him that I grind my teeth at night. We agree to meet in London.

By then, I have accepted the job training journalists in Sierra Leone. I agonize over the decision, calling my parents, my new agent (the lunch went well!), my friends, and Tim. My parents are not enthusiastic about me heading off somewhere possibly more dangerous than Yemen, but they know better than to try to change my mind. My agent encourages me, reminding me that we haven't yet sold the book I'm writing. It might be

good to have a backup plan. Tim withholds his opinion, telling me to follow my heart. He will wait for me, he says. While I have dreams of staying
in Yemen to be close to him, I am not making any decisions in my life con-
tingent on a married man.

I take the job. After meeting Tim in December, I will fly to Yemen with
him and stay with friends for two months. The Sierra Leone job starts in
February. I figure that even if I do sell my book, I'll have two months to
get cracking on it before I head to Africa.

☪

DECEMBER 7 IS THE BEST DAY of my whole life. It begins before dawn in
New York, when a friend drives me to JFK. I've spent the week meeting
editors but still don't know the fate of my book. The flight to London is
empty. I lie down across empty seats but am unable to sleep. My heartbeat
is too loud. Customs detains me at Heathrow, so I am the last person to
emerge. And there he is, waiting for me. His face is utterly familiar, as if
I've been meeting him at airports all of my life. *"Jenny,"* he says.

He whisks me to a hotel, where I find the room filled with all of my favorite foods. He's memorized them from my e-mails. There are peppered
cashews and blueberry muffins and grilled shrimp. A bottle of champagne
waits on ice. I get teary at the sight of it all. But before I get comfortable,
I have to call my agent. "You have a publisher!" she says without preamble.
I promptly begin to faint and have to lie down on the bed to continue the
conversation. Tim is as ecstatic as I am and uncorks the champagne.

We drink champagne at every meal that week. We go to the theater, the
ballet, and the movies. We ice-skate in front of Somerset House. We wander through art galleries. We walk absolutely everywhere. On our penul-
timate night, we are eating dinner at a dimly lighted French café when
Tim says he wants to talk about us. "I have met the person I want to spend
the rest of my life with," he says. "And it's you. And I need to know how
you feel before I go about disrupting a lot of lives."

Oddly, I don't need time to think about it. In thirty-eight years, I've
never felt this way about anyone. It's funny that I will remember exactly
what he said but not my own words. I am crying with wonder and relief
and love. But somehow, I get my answer across.

Tim had planned to wait until after the holidays to leave his wife, but it doesn't work out that way. By Christmas Eve, he's told her everything, and by January, she is gone. It's messy, complicated, and horrifically painful for his wife and daughter. It's excruciating for me to know I am hurting people I have no desire to harm. But not once has either of us had a nanosecond of doubt that we are doing the right thing. The most inexplicable thing is that we have been so sure, right from the start.

For a few weeks, I hardly see him. I stay with friends while he sorts out his separation and is busy working. The wait is agonizing. I can't bear to be apart from him and keep worrying that he will change his mind. Fortunately, now that I have sold my book, I have plenty of work. I keep distracted with a strict writing schedule and with frequent visits from Zuhra, who returns to Yemen from Mississippi the same time I return from New York.

I've been wrestling with what to do about Sierra Leone. Tim has told me he will wait for me and that he wants me to move in with him as soon as I finish the eight-month assignment. But it has become clear that I will struggle to balance writing my first book with training Sierra Leonean journalists. And every time I think about leaving Yemen, I burst into tears. While I've all but concluded I should turn down the job, I am afraid to tell Tim. I don't want him to feel I am rushing things or putting any pressure on him by staying in Yemen.

Zuhra is dead set against me leaving, worried that she will be replaced in my affections.

"You'll find a new Zuhra there!" she says. "An African Zuhra!"

I tell her about Tim, whom she thinks I would be crazy to desert for eight months. "You would be in huge torture apart from him," she says. "You don't need to go. You deserve to stay with the person you love."

☾

IT IS A SUNNY WINTER DAY when Tim and I take our first Yemen outing together. Thus far, we've only spent time together in private, at his home when the domestic staff is gone for the day. But now that he has announced his separation from his wife and his relationship with me to the embassy, I am no longer a secret. The armored cars drop us off at Bait

Bous, an ancient village on a cliff overlooking Sana'a, and we set off on a long walk. A few of his bodyguards scramble up the mountains ahead of us, and several others follow at a discreet distance.

At the top of a ridge, we stop to catch our breath. We've been talking the whole way up but fall silent as we turn to look down at the city of Sana'a sprawled beneath us. It looks like something I might have made out of sand as a child, with its fanciful minarets and gingerbread houses. No clouds mar the clear blue of the sky. Across from us, distant mountain peaks sharpen in the midday light. Tim takes my hand.

Nervously, I draw a breath. "I've been thinking about Sierra Leone. . . ."

When I finish explaining to him the reasons I shouldn't go, he smiles. "You're absolutely right. Frankly, you'd be mad to try to write a book while working the kind of schedule you were working here. And you really need to be *here* to write this book, don't you?"

"I just didn't want you to feel that me staying means we have to move things any faster. . . . I am sure you need time, and I don't want to interfere with your work—"

"Jenny," he says, cutting me off. "Can I tell you something? I am *so* glad you aren't going to Sierra Leone."

"Are you?"

"I don't think I could actually stand being apart from you that long."

"I can stay with friends for a bit. . . ."

"But I want you to live with me, as soon as it's possible. Will you, Jenny? Will you come and live with me?"

I don't need time to think, but for a minute I can't speak. I look down at the city I love before turning back to the man I love even more. It seems too good to be true that I could have both of them.

"I don't think I could be happy living anywhere else."

 EPILOGUE

Since we both left the **Yemen Observer,** *Zuhra and I have become closer than* ever. She visits me in New York, while on vacation from her fellowship program at Jackson State University in Mississippi, a state that she describes as "just like the Third World! Not so different from Yemen."

It doesn't take her long to adapt to American culture. She revels in her freedom, living on her own in a dormitory, mingling openly with peers, and peeling away her *kheemaar.* She is shocked, she writes, to discover that she is beautiful!

"A handsome man told me that i am so pretty. i was happy. many pple here told me so. and the best thing that i make lots of freinds here. pple here are so freindly, most of them are balcks. They have a good heart. i befreinded with an old police officers. i befreinded the women in the dorms. Aaah, i met the avengilicans, the invited me to the church to teach me English!!!!!i will go to do this."

I get a flurry of excited e-mails during her first month in America. "I bought a jeans and short shirt," she writes. "i look pretty. Jennifer, you won't belive how many men praised me, and there is a handsome and old man said that if i am in 40s, he won't hesitaite to marry me. I don't realise that i am so attractive to this level. Really i mean it, i thought that i am not beatiful and have not attractive personality that people will be hit on."

But for Zuhra there is also a dark side to being found beautiful. When men begin to flatter her, ask her out, and make declarations of love, she feels that she must have done something wrong to attract such attention. *Am I still a good girl?* she asks me in a million ways. Yes, I tell her. The best girl ever.

The first thing I notice when I finally meet her at her brother's home in Brooklyn is that she is wearing purple. "You're in color!" I say. I pick her up in my arms and spin her around. I'm wearing a sleeveless, knee-length dress. I had asked if I should dress modestly, but Zuhra reminded me that we were in *my* country and I should dress however I want. We can't stop talking, sharing one chair in the living room, until her brother Fahmi jokes that he is starting to worry about our relationship.

For Zuhra, returning to Yemen is a much harder adjustment than leaving it. She begins to fret even before she leaves the United States. How can she go back to a life of restriction with the taste of freedom lingering on her tongue? Zuhra knows what awaits her in Yemen, and—Kamil aside—she dreads it.

I arrive back in Yemen a few days before her, and we cling to each other in a time of major upheaval. I am staying with a series of friends and struggling to write while Tim is sorting out his separation. Zuhra is debating a return to the *Yemen Observer* and readjusting to a sheltered life. Ultimately, she decides to take a job with Kamil's human rights organization HOOD, writing and reporting for their website. "I can't go back to the *Observer* without you," she says. "They wouldn't let me report the truth."

It saddens me that so many of my reforms die after I leave. My women, without exception, loathe Zaid, who they say runs the newsroom like a tyrant and is too much a pawn of Faris. Ali, who was keeping things relatively on track, quits in protest when Faris tries to force him to report something he knows is untrue. Noor leaves to work on a newsletter for the German development agency GTZ. "I'm still a journalist!" she reassures me. Radia stops writing entirely, refusing to work for Zaid, and goes back to being a secretary. A few months later, after Qasim quits to start his own business, she is promoted to his position. She's brilliant at the job, says Zuhra, and has received a huge raise.

Farouq, Jabr, Hadi, Ibrahim, al-Matari, and Najma continue to work at the *Yemen Observer,* where they are now among the most senior staff members. Najma's Health and Science page is the best page of the paper. So there's that.

I visit the paper as often as I can and spend time with my reporters, the women in particular. Adhara finishes university in May 2008, and I attend her graduation with Radia, Enass, and Najma. I tell them about Tim, and they are thrilled. No one is more excited than Zuhra, who is the first person Tim and I invite for tea at the residence. The two of them get on so well I don't get a word in edgewise the entire evening. And when I climb into a taxi to escort Zuhra home afterward, she turns to me and says, "I love him at first sight."

"Yes," I said. "I know the feeling."

Adhara stays at the paper for another year, before her frustrations with Zaid drive her to take a job at an organization working on food security. When her new employer asks her to serve as interpreter at their meetings, she shows up on my doorstep in a panic, terrified at the prospect of talking in front of people. I am pleased that she has come to me and help her deal with her anxieties. When I call a week later, she says her job has gotten easier, and she is much happier.

Not long after we are both back in Yemen, Zuhra finally confesses her own secret love. I am pleased that he turns out to be someone I know and respect. "Now I know why you quoted him so much last year!" I tease.

The only drawback is that Kamil already has a wife. I would not have chosen the life of a second wife for Zuhra, and we spend entire afternoons discussing the implications of this decision. Are you sure you want to share your love with another woman? I say. Is it fair that you are giving him all of you, and he is giving you only half of him? Have you thought about how his first wife must feel?

"You are in the same situation!"

"But Tim isn't *keeping* his first wife," I remind her. "And I can't bear to spend one night apart from him."

But Zuhra is a stubborn little thing and will not be dissuaded. No one else will do, she says. You cannot control love. Again, she has to fight for her family's permission and defend her decision to become a second wife. The experience gives her empathy for all minorities, she says. "People say,

'Why you pick a married man?' and I feel like I am a gay person, because people don't understand me." While it's not uncommon in Yemen for a man to take several wives, many families don't desire such a fate for their daughters. But ultimately, Zuhra's family supports her decision and rejoices in her happiness.

I give her my blessing as well, and attend her wedding in August 2008. She is at least choosing her own husband, which is a daring break with tradition. She is also choosing a man who will allow her the freedom to continue her career and to travel whenever she wishes. This is no small benefit. Nothing is as important to Zuhra as her career, and she reassures me she will not give it up. By June, she has sold major stories to both *Stern* magazine in Germany and the Sunday magazine of *El País* in Madrid. She has begun to surpass her teacher.

I'm curious to hear about her married life. "How do you divide Kamil?" I say. "Is there a schedule?" There is. Zuhra gets Kamil every other night. "Do you make him shower when he comes over?" I ask, but she just laughs. Kamil's children visit her often and call her Aunt Zuhra. She loves them but is not ready for her own children. Like me, she worries it will stifle her work. "I have enough to do getting used to a husband," she says.

Zuhra hasn't given up her dream of running a paper of her own someday. She does some freelancing for the *Yemen Times* and hopes that once she has HOOD's website in shape, she will again work as a journalist.

As I write this, Zaid is still the editor of the *Observer.* He calls me every few weeks to ask why I don't visit more often and to tell me he misses me. I'm impressed that he has stuck it out, but I can't bring myself to say how devastated I am by what he's done with the paper. My few remaining staff members are preparing to leave, mostly because they take issue with his management style. Before Adhara quits, she writes me a desperate e-mail telling me how much she and the others are suffering. Faris and Zaid don't respect women, she says. The *Yemen Times* has offered her a job, but she is afraid to take it. "I am afraid Mr. Faris would do something to hurt me," she says. I hope this fear is unfounded.

I hate seeing my women treated poorly. I feel guilty and responsible.

I invite Adhara as well as Zuhra, Radia, Enass, Najma, and Noor to lunch. I now live with Tim in the residence of the British ambassador, surrounded by ten bodyguards and a household staff of five. It's a major adjustment. This morning I get up from my desk in my airy office overlooking our garden and stop short on my way downstairs to the kitchen to discuss the menu with our cook; I cannot believe this is my *life*.

Over shrimp soup, we discuss the paper's dramatic decline and wonder why Faris isn't interested in doing anything about it. "Why does he keep Zaid, when he treats the staff so poorly and publishes such crap?" I ask. In perhaps not those exact words.

"No one else will do it," says Radia.

"No one else is willing to run the paper?" I say.

They all shake their heads.

"But why? It's so easy!"

My women look shocked for a moment and then start to laugh.

"I guess maybe I have to come back."

"If you go back, I will go back too," says Zuhra.

"Really?" I say. I think about it. There are at least two more years left in Tim's posting. And then I remember that Faris will not have changed. He'll still want my staff writing advertorials. He'll still want us to avoid news that reflects poorly on Yemen. He may still want Zaid at the head of the masthead. In practice, he would almost certainly not be willing to re-hire me, a fact that doesn't seem to occur to my reporters. But I also think about my staff and what I could do with them with world enough and time. I've got two more years to kill, after all.

I can't believe I am even thinking about it.

 AFTERWORD

It was the bodyguards racing across our lawn from the pool that first tipped me off. I was pacing from room to room upstairs, trying to lull my five-month-old daughter to sleep, when I looked out of a window to see two of them barreling toward the house.

Curious, I headed downstairs with Theadora Celeste in my arms and walked out to the pool to investigate. Not seeing anything amiss, I stuck my toe in the water to test the temperature. But seconds later, the two bodyguards, now fully armed, appeared at my side.

"Madam! You need to be in the house," they said in Arabic, quickly shepherding us toward the entrance. They continued speaking so rapidly I only understood about half of it. "What is the problem?" I asked in Arabic. "*Mafeesh mushkila,*" they told me reassuringly. *No problem.* "But you need to be in the house."

Obviously, there was a *mushkila*.

When we got inside, our housekeeper Negisti and cook Emebet were hovering near the door. "What's going on?" I asked. They shook their heads. "They told us to shut the doors and stay inside," said Negisti. "I close them, but I did not know you were outside with the baby!"

"They didn't say why?"

They shook their heads again. "Maybe it is protests. The petrol prices are up again. Ten riyals more," said Negisti.

"Not just petrol. All prices," added Emebet.

"No taxis on the street. Girma he said no taxis."

"No *dabaabs* (buses)," said Emebet.

Often we were advised to stay home when there were protests in the street, and it seemed entirely possible that Yemenis were out protesting the increased petrol prices. But I wanted to find out for sure. I rang Tim's work phone but got no answer, so I tried Colin, the head of Tim's bodyguards.

He picked up and handed the phone immediately to Tim. "Hi sweetheart, I was just about to ring you."

"What's going on?"

"My car was attacked on the way to the embassy this morning."

"No!"

"But I'm fine. The guys are fine. We're not sure yet if it was a suicide bomber or a planted IED."

"You're okay?"

"I'm okay. Rather rude start to the morning, but I'm okay."

"Your team? And the car?" I didn't care about the car itself, I wanted to gauge how bad the attack was.

"They're fine. Ali's a bit shook up I think. There was a fair amount of blood on the windscreen. The car is not too bad. The car did its job."

"You're okay?" I couldn't ask this too many times.

"I'm okay. I will ring you later when we know more."

I hung up and immediately realized I'd forgotten to tell him I loved him. How could I have forgotten at a time like this? I'd have rung back, but he'd said his phone was ringing off the hook.

I went downstairs to tell the staff. Negisti's kind, brown face creased with worry and even placid Emebet looked alarmed. It was about eight-thirty A.M. I was expecting Rahel, Theodora's babysitter, to arrive at nine A.M. "Should I tell Rahel not to come?" I asked. If our house was suddenly more of a target than it usually was, I didn't want to put Rahel in danger.

"Yes, have her stay home," they said.

I rang Rahel, who was already on her way. She sounded confused and worried.

My phone continued to ring—Yemeni friends and others from around the world, wanting to know if Tim was okay. An Omani friend was particularly incensed. "How could anyone do this? Tim is *one of us!*" he said. "He's an *Arabist!* He *loves* the Arab world! He is *one* of us!"

Tim rang me again to say it had definitely been a suicide bomber.

"I won't ask when you're coming home, but I hope it's not too long." I never know when Tim will arrive home because he cannot—for security reasons—tell me over the phone.

"I hope so too."

I went numbly about my day, nursing Theadora, reading her books, checking the news online. I was grateful to have Theadora to care for, to force me into some semblance of normalcy. I didn't eat or shower or go to the gym. Guards surrounded our house. There was one on the porch, shouting into his radio. One clattering up the stairs to the roof. One in the garden on his cell phone. We were not to leave the house. Not that we'd left the house much in recent months anyway. Since I'd moved in with Tim and become his official partner, I'd been unable to leave home without a bodyguard.

Negisti came running upstairs to tell me that Tim was on Al Jazeera. "He looked okay, he was smiling." I raced down, Theadora in my arms, and we waited for the bit about Tim to come back on. Theadora had never seen a television screen before and was mesmerized. There was no live shot, just an old photograph of him smiling at the camera. I wondered where it came from. It felt odd to see that photo in the context of the story.

I kept busy. Nothing seemed to settle in me. I read the news stories streaming onto the Internet, trying to make it sink in. BRITISH AMBASSA-DOR SURVIVES SUICIDE ATTACK, said one. *Survives.* The word sent a shudder through me. *Survives.* Meaning, he might not have.

Finally, I heard our gates clatter open at five minutes before five P.M. I slid sock-footed across the marble floor to the door. We waited until he was inside, away from the eyes of his Yemeni guards, before we embraced. "I'm really sorry," he said. "But in five minutes the entire staff of the embassy is going to descend."

We ran upstairs. Tim took Theadora from me and cradled her in his arms. "Hello sweetheart," he said. "Looks like you're stuck with me a while longer." We'd exchanged only a few words before the doorbell rang. When Joanna, the head of the UK Department for International Development, arrived, she apologized. "I got here early but was waiting outside, so you and Tim could have some time together, but then I saw everyone else coming in. . . . *Did* you get any time with him?"

"About a minute and a half?"

The rest of the evening was a blur. There was the meeting, at which Tim told the staff what had happened and announced some changes in security. There were drinks afterward, people lingering over beers and Tim's famously strong gin and tonics. There were concerned hands patting my bare arms and a whirl of voices. At 6:30 I went upstairs, fed Theadora, and put her to bed. For the first time in two months, she went to sleep without a murmur.

Only hours later, when the last guests had left and the staff had gone home, were Tim and I at last alone together.

☪

THE NEXT MORNING I was about to get into the shower when I looked out our bedroom window to see one of our bodyguards and his AK-47 sitting on a bench right next to Rahel and the baby. Rahel was reading a story to Theadora, who lay kicking on her playmat. The sight of my tiny daughter waving her green rattle at the foot of a man so heavily armed shook me. Dear god, in what kind of place am I raising my daughter? I ran downstairs.

When I got to the playmat I was suddenly unsure of what to say. "Please," I said to Mohammed. "You are careful with the gun? I mean, I *know* you are. But I just want to make sure it wouldn't go off accidentally? With the baby here? And Rahel?"

"*Aiwa* (yes)," he reassured me, smiling and moving the gun to the side of the bench. "Careful."

"Okay." I paused, feeling confused. I didn't want to leave Theadora outside surrounded by men with guns. And I didn't want to deprive her of fresh air and sunshine. And what if the house were attacked? I was trembling and nauseated. "Rahel? If the guards tell you to go inside, go inside, okay?"

"Don't worry," she said. "I will take care of her."

A few minutes later, the rains began, and Rahel gathered the baby up to rush her inside. Only then could I relax enough to finally get into the shower.

Things had been getting worse for the last couple of years. Attacks on Westerners had escalated, and our movements around the country had become increasingly restricted. I was grateful I had done so much traveling on my own before I moved in with Tim and became subject to embassy regulations. Then in August 2009, when I was six-and-a-half months pregnant, I was held at gunpoint by eight Yemenis tribesmen while hiking with four other women. There's nothing like having an AK-47 pointed at your head—a *cocked* AK-47—to make you re-evaluate your decision-making. I had been hiking all over Yemen for three years without incident. You don't really think it can happen to you—until it does. We were fortunate to escape an extremely tense situation unharmed after swift intervention by the British Embassy and the minister of the interior.

All of this had made the decision to return to Yemen with Theadora after giving birth to her in London a difficult one. I kept her in England for three months so that she could grow strong enough to travel and receive her first vaccinations.

We hated being away from Tim, who hated being away from us. But trepidations about returning to Yemen remained. I was afraid of bathing Theadora in nondrinkable water. I was afraid of the diseases she could catch there. I was afraid of not getting her on a plane fast enough in an emergency.

One night in London I dreamed I had plucked a bunch of pale green grapes from a grove hidden in a snowy winter forest of shivering pines. Cupping the icy fruit in my fingers, I painstakingly peeled away the skin, exposing a miniature of my daughter, about the size of my thumb. She was perfectly formed, pink and blue-eyed. I showed her to friends who had gathered around. I wanted them to say how beautiful she was, but they only gazed at her in horror, appalled that I had exposed her to the elements so tiny and vulnerable. I woke thinking, if I take my baby to Yemen, isn't that how people will react?

We debated whether Theadora and I should go instead to Vermont to stay with my parents. But after some reassuring conversations with our doctor and others in Yemen, we decided to stay together as a family. We had wanted Theadora because we loved each other and wished to raise her together. Not 7,000 miles apart. So, with a suitcase full of just-in-case, Western pharmaceuticals, I carried her back to Yemen.

Theadora had been happy in Sana'a, playing outdoors every day in the garden, surrounded by people who doted on her. She had her own room and plenty of other rooms to explore. I took walks with her in the Old City, where I showed her my first Yemeni house and where passing women touched her round cheeks and fair hair and asked me if she were a doll.

But since the attack on Tim, the decision whether to stay in Yemen was no longer ours—it was the Foreign Office's.

A couple of days and many security meetings later, it became clear that Theadora and I, along with the rest of the spouses and partners of the embassy staff, were going to have to be evacuated. Many would return to homes Britain, but we had nowhere to go. We had no other home.

Tim hadn't stopped working since the attack, maintaining energy and buoyancy I wouldn't necessarily expect from someone who had just narrowly escaped an attempt on his life. But when he told me Theadora and I were to be sent away, he finally broke down. "Suicide bombers I can cope with," he said, "But not losing you."

"You're not losing me. You aren't losing us. It's only for a short while. . . ." But it was hard to be consoling when I was crying too.

"I thought Theadora was going to learn to walk in Yemen. I wanted her to see Soqotra. I wanted us to go camping together, to have pictures of her here. There is so much I wanted to do here with you."

"I wanted to take her to Shahara with us and walk over the bridge. I wanted her to meet Zuhra's baby. I'll never see Zuhra again," I said. I hadn't been able to see Zuhra since Theadora was born because she had typhoid. She was also pregnant, due in less than a month. Now she would never meet Theadora, and I would never meet her little boy.

We also worried about our staff. Every morning when I carried Theadora downstairs, Negisti hurried to take her from me. Emebet, Rahel, and the rest of the household staff also adored cheery little

Theadora. The enormous, echoing residence felt cozier and more of a home with her in it.

When Tim and I sat down with the residence staff to explain about the evacuation, Negisti pulled her apron over her face and wept. Emebet and Salaam were also in tears. We couldn't think of anything to say to comfort them.

On our last morning in our house, I gave photos of Theadora to each of the staff and taped more pictures to the refrigerator. We took only two suitcases. Everything else we had to leave behind: all of Theadora's books and toys, her bed, her changing table, her room. I didn't mind leaving my own things behind, but I hated leaving behind everything Theadora knew as home.

When Tim came to take us to the car, the staff wouldn't let go of us. I had to actually pry Theadora out of Rahel's arms. Crying, I hurried to the armored car. And we were off, leaving behind the house that had been our home for three years, the only real home Theadora had ever known, and the country that had been my home for four.

This wasn't how I planned to go. I wasn't ready. There was so much of the country still left to explore. We had so many friends. And I was finally making progress in my Arabic lessons.

But I can't say we didn't make the most of our time. The years I spent living with Tim in Yemen were the happiest of my life. I moved in with him in the spring of 2008, though we had been spending every possible spare minute together for months before that. We were both working insanely hard at our respective careers, but we were both engaged in work we loved. I was writing this book and doing some freelance reporting, and Tim was working approximately eighteen hours a day as the British Ambassador to Yemen.

Nearly every day, Tim rose at six A.M., and I got up with him so we could have breakfast together before he left for the office at seven-fifteen. Then I was free to swim, do yoga, and work for several hours before he reappeared in the evenings. As soon as I moved in, Tim created an office for me in the top floor of our house. I had a room of my own, a massive desk overlooking our garden and pool, and a mini-kitchen next door where I could make coffee and tea. Our upstairs refrigerator was full of dried fruit, nuts, dark chocolate, champagne, and soy milk. It was paradise.

If there was time in between our workdays and dinner, we'd have a sherry or gin and tonic and sit on a kitchen counter swinging our legs and talking. Late at night we read plays or short stories out loud to each other. On weekends, we went for long hikes in nearby wadis or in the Haraz mountains.

Many of my reporters visited me, but Zuhra came most often. We'd have tea and sit talking in the parlor or my office. She wasn't in the least bit awed by the grand house and made herself at home, even letting me know in advance what she'd like Emebet to make her for lunch.

I found I missed working with Yemeni reporters. So I was happy when Nadia al-Sakkaf asked me to come train some of her reporters at the *Yemen Times,* my former rival. It was almost exactly like my first training course at the *Yemen Observer*—the reporters had the same challenges and the same questions. But this time, I was much more relaxed and had a few more answers.

Adding to the luxury of my daily existence was the household staff. A household staff! I had never even hired a cleaning person before I moved to Yemen, and suddenly I lived in a house with a housekeeper, cook, cleaner, and gardener. I had no idea what to do with them. When Tim and I came down to breakfast in the morning, Negisti had already laid the table with fresh-squeezed orange juice, fresh fruit, muesli, and yogurt. As soon as we were seated she poured us fresh coffee. It was overwhelming and it made me shy.

For weeks I couldn't bring myself to ask the staff to do anything. Emebet would ask what I wanted for lunch, and I would say, oh, I'll make myself a sandwich, don't worry. At night I'd sneak down to do my own laundry instead of putting it in my assigned hamper. But slowly it dawned on me that I was depriving our staff of the opportunity to do their jobs. This was the work they were paid to do. So I began to timidly suggest that if Emebet were not terribly busy, would she perhaps be able to make me a Thai salad with tofu?

Negisti, Emebet, and Alem quickly became family. I spent hours pouring over recipe books with Emebet, planning menus for diplomatic dinners, and asking her to experiment with vegetarian, whole-grain foods. I attended the wedding of my driver's daughter with all three women. I spent more time talking with our staff than with almost anyone else in my life other than Tim. The birth of our daughter, Theadora, brought us all closer. "She has many mothers," Negisti would say. And it was true. If I ever needed anyone to hold Theadora, settle her for a nap, or make her laugh, I had plenty of volunteers.

For years, I tried in vain to get the staff to call me Jennifer or Jenny instead of madam. They would smile in agreement, say "like family?," and then keep calling me madam. Not until Theadora and I were evacuated, and Emebet began sending parcels of our favorite foods to me in Jordan (where we stayed until the end of Tim's posting), did she write on the note taped to a box of muffins that they were for "Jeny and Teodora."

Having a staff was only the beginning of how surreal my life became. Suddenly I was hosting dinner parties several times a week for Yemeni politicians, business people, hostage negotiators, other ambassadors, development workers, or visiting British ministers. Every official I met—and I met many!—treated me with respect and kindness and as though I were Tim's wife. Divorce is common in Yemen and Yemenis (many of whom have more than one wife) were warm and understanding about our relationship.

There was hardly a night when we didn't have official cocktails or dinner at the house or a National Day to attend elsewhere. Mostly, I loved this. I am a social person, and it was great fun to meet and talk with such a wide range of people—and to practice my Arabic. But I did occasionally worry I would get myself in trouble by talking too much or too freely. I once got into a debate with the foreign minister about the freedom of the Yemeni press. He had claimed, over the soup course, that the Yemeni media was unfettered. Having run a Yemeni newspaper, I knew differently and said so. No, the Yemeni press is free! He insisted. What was it that I couldn't write about?

Well, for starters we couldn't criticize the president by name, I said. And we couldn't write that there was an argument against capital punishment. And we couldn't write freely about religion. I went on.

Yes, yes, said the minister. But there are good reasons for those things!

I guess I just have a different definition of "free," I said.

We both laughed.

☪

THE MOST ASTONISHING THING happened at a holiday party during my last year in Yemen. Faris, my former boss whose approval I had fruitlessly sought for the length of my tenure at the *Observer*, told Tim that the newspaper had never been better than it was under my leadership. Which was bittersweet news, as it made me wish I were still at the paper at the same time that it filled me with a warm sense of closure. It wasn't long after this that Faris approached me at a party to ask if I would come by the office to talk with the new American woman running it. "If you could just give her some advice," he said. "Just tell her what you did with the paper to get it the way it was."

But the attack on Tim brought all of this to a premature end. We had to leave. After a family vacation in the United States, Theadora and I moved to Amman, to be as close to Yemen as possible. I rang the only person I knew in Jordan, my friend Saleh whom I'd met when he worked in Yemen. A week later, he had found me both a comfortable apartment and a babysitter. Tim visited us whenever he could, but he was extremely busy in the final few months of his posting. It was a hard, hot summer alone with a baby in an unfamiliar city.

Amman was a world apart from Sana'a. At the gym near my house, most women didn't wear hijabs, and they all showed up in full makeup, carrying designer bags. Teens socialized at massive shopping malls. Alcohol was available everywhere. I found the conspicuous consumption overwhelming. I pined for Yemen.

Eventually, I settled into a social life with a few Jordanian friends and with other parents I met at the British Club and an American playgroup. By the time I discovered people with whom I really enjoyed spending time, it was time to move again. We left Jordan in October 2010, again taking a quick trip to the United States to see family before landing in the UK in November.

Tim, Theadora, and I are now happily ensconced in a (much smaller) new home in London. Though as I write, almost all of our belongings are still in Yemen. Since the parcel bombs mailed from Yemen were intercepted, the UK has refused to accept air freight from Yemen. Including all of our worldly goods.

I miss Yemen every day. I miss its beauty, I miss the openness of the people, and I miss my former reporters, who write to me regularly on Facebook. Zuhra and I send each other long letters and photographs of our children. I still hope that someday it will be safe enough to take Theadora back there. I want her to see the country where her parents met and where she was first imagined.

Only occasionally do I read newspaper articles on Yemen. It's pointless, as no one ever gets it right. No major newspaper has a full-time correspondent actually based in the country, so most stories are written by reporters parachuted into Sana'a for just a few days.

After running a newspaper in Yemen for a year, I was only just getting to grips with where to find information and which sources to trust. It's not a country a reporter can figure out in a flying visit. So I don't trust anything I read. The only way to stand a chance of knowing what is really going on in Yemen is to *be* there.

And even then the truth is elusive.

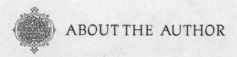 ABOUT THE AUTHOR

JENNIFER F. STEIL spent a year as editor of the *Yemen Observer,* a twice-weekly English-language newspaper published in Sana'a, Yemen. Before moving to Yemen in 2006, Steil was a senior editor at *The Week,* which she helped to launch in 2001. She has also worked as an editor at *Playgirl* and *Folio* and as a reporter at several newspapers. Her work has appeared in *Time, Life, Good Housekeeping,* and *Woman's Day.* Steil has an MS in journalism from the Columbia University Graduate School of Journalism and an MFA in creative writing from Sarah Lawrence College. She lives in London with her fiancé, Tim Torlot, and their daughter.